Suzy Gershman's

BORN TO SHOP

HONG KONG, SHANGHAI & BEIJING

*The Ultimate Guide for
People Who Love to Shop*

4th Edition

Wiley Publishing, Inc.

For the Hong Kong Home Team: Peter and Louisa, Glenn and Lucille, and Les Girls: Carole, Lynn, Sian, Susan, etc.

With thanks and love and double wishes for double happiness.

Published by:

Wiley Publishing, Inc.
111 River St.
Hoboken, NJ 07030-5774

ISBN: 978-0-470-14435-0
Editor: Alexia Travaglini
Production Editor: Eric T. Schroeder
Photo Editor: Richard Fox
Cartographer: Roberta Stockwell
Born to Shop Editorial Director: Sarah Lahey
This edition revised by: Suzy Gershman & Sarah Lahey
Production by Wiley Indianapolis Composition Services

For information on our other products and services or to obtain technical support, please contact our Customer Care Department within the U.S. at 800/762-2974, outside the U.S. at 317/572-3993 or fax 317/572-4002.

Wiley also publishes its books in a variety of electronic formats. Some content that appears in print may not be available in electronic formats.

Manufactured in the United States of America

5 4 3 2 1

CONTENTS

MAP LIST

ABOUT THE AUTHORS

Suzy Gershman is a journalist, author, and global-shopping goddess who has worked in the fashion and fiber industry for more than 25 years. Her essays on retailing have been used by the Harvard School of Business; her reportage on travel and retail has appeared in *Travel & Leisure, Travel Holiday, Travel Weekly,* and most of the major women's magazines. She is translated into French for Condé Nast's *Air France Madame* magazine. The *Born to Shop* series, now over 20 years old, is translated into eight languages. Gershman is also the author of *C'est La Vie* (Viking and Penguin Paperback), the story of her first year as a widow living in Paris. She divides her time between her home in San Diego, a small house in Provence, and the airport.

Sarah Lahey retired from her career in home style to raise a family and recently rejoined the work force as Editorial Director for the *Born to Shop* series. Sarah also shows and sells English smalls at several Northern California antiques fairs. She lives with her husband and dog, Bentley, outside of San Francisco and wears the same size as Suzy (so they can share clothes).

Aaron Gershman is a singer-songwriter living in Los Angeles, as well as contributing editor to *Born to Shop*. He writes on guys' fashions, boy toys, and electronics.

Jenny McCormick has advanced degrees in sociology and psychology and will soon be going to law school. She is currently a paralegal, a guidebook blogger and part-time *Born to Shop* editorial assistant. She writes on fashion and trends for young women.

TO START WITH

Hong Kong has long been the door to the Orient. It's an important destination for those who will be visiting mainland China as well. Many go on to Bangkok; trendy travelers are keen on Cambodia and Laos. Truth be told, I am dying to write *Born to Shop Asia* because so much is going on in the Pacific Rim, and Hong Kong is such a great starting point. I'm getting there slowly, so this edition includes information about Hanoi, Saigon (HCMC), and Taipei as well as a chapter on the Pearl River Delta. I have also expanded the Shenzhen coverage and added lodging information.

This edition still has a whole lotta Hong Kong. Despite threats from the mainland to outpace it, I find that Honkers is still the brightest star in the sky and the one where the most people speak English. Hong Kong continues to amaze me with its ingenuity and determination to be recognized and to give visitors the most for their money. Here's hoping you have as much shopping fun as we did, enjoy as many great family travels, and do not pay as many overweight charges.

Suzy Gershman
Hong Kong, December 2007

ACKNOWLEDGMENTS

Although by now I consider myself an old China hand, I am extremely indebted to Sarah Lahey, who schlepped all over Asia with me for this revision, and to the team in Asia that continues to help me, guide me, and translate for me. Carole Klein at InterContinental Hotels is my constant source and is the creator of the *Born to Shop* & Spa Tours done each year in conjunction with InterConti. Everyone at InterContinental Hong Kong helps me invaluably—I thank you all.

At the Pen, I am also grateful for a full team of support from front desk to behind the stoves/ovens to upstairs with the careful touch of Lamey and Sian.

In the twenty-some odd years I have been a regular in town, I have come to depend on the Vessas, the Peter Chans, and a handful of woman friends who keep me up-to-date. I thank all of you from the bottom of my cheongsam and say *Shishi* to one and all.

Chapter One

....

THE BEST OF HONG KONG, BEIJING, SHANGHAI & TAIPEI

There is an old Chinese curse that goes something like this: May you live in interesting times.

Perhaps all times are interesting, none more so than those related to the New China . . . of 2008 and the Olympic Games and the World's Fair in Shanghai in 2010. China Onstage.

So I'd like to twist the ancient curse into a prayer for you and yours: May you shop in somewhat dirty street markets but contract no disease. May you never pay more than 100 of anything (yuan, Hong Kong dollars, euros—whatever). May you gaze at the New China and understand that you see the future—and it is powerful.

Hey, I know there's a real China out there, that miners are dying in horrific accidents, and that many couples still are permitted only one child. But as a visitor to glam parts of Shanghai and Beijing, you will be hard-pressed to find it.

With the Olympics considered a turning point for the government, everything has become cleaner and more generic, brighter, and even garish. Hong Kong still shimmers as an oasis, although prices are higher on most items (except designer goods, which cost 20% less than in mainland China). This is the new China, and it has been built by the world's finest architects. You can't help but be impressed.

1

If you're antsy about the rate of exchange on the dollar against the euro, Asia is your new best friend. The rush is on, so get going now. This chapter will help guide you to the best, the brightest, and the most brilliant according to budget.

Please remember that coming up with a single best of anything is pretty difficult. "Best" is a subjective thing. Each choice here is based on a combination of location, value, and convenience.

Believe it or not, there is little crossover in merchandise in the cities this book covers; once you have left a destination, you may not have the luxury of another crack at a particular item, often resulting in the "Why didn't I buy more?" syndrome.

THE 10 BEST STORES

Along with my alphabetical list comes the usual disclaimer—these choices are based on my personal visits. China is changing fast. As soon as we go to press, a bigger or better resource might pop up.

ASHNEIL
Far East Mansions, 5-6 Middle Rd., Shop 114 (up the stairs), Tsim Sha Tsui, Kowloon, Hong Kong (MTR: TST).

Calling this a store may lead you to believe it is bigger than a postage stamp, which it is not. More than two shoppers make it feel crowded. But that's only because it's piled high and deep with handbags of all sorts. These babies are no fakes either. They're excellent-quality items that look like styles you know and love—but, with no phony parts, they're totally legal. Prices begin at around $150 and go up (sometimes way up), but you often can't tell the bags from the $1,000 versions. You can have your purchases delivered to the U.S. (saving on the Customs allowance), order something made in a custom color, or buy small leather goods such as belts and wallets. Credit cards accepted.

BLANC DE CHINE
Pedder Building, 12 Pedder St., Room 201, Central, Hong Kong (MTR: Central).

Armani meets Shanghai Tang (see below). Expect to pay $500 or more for a jacket, but the quality and appearance will melt you. Mens, womens, and home styles.

CITY SUPER
Times Square Mall (MTR: Causeway Bay); Ocean Terminal, Harbour City, Kowloon (MTR: TST); IFC2 mall (MTR: Central); all Hong Kong.

As the name implies, this is a supermarket. The branches are not all equal—the one at Times Square is the best—but all are good enough to qualify for this list. You can buy Asian products (which make great gifts) as well as bath and beauty items and housewares.

HU & HU ANTIQUES
1685 Wuzhong Lu, Shanghai (no nearby Metro).

If you aren't interested in furniture, then you can skip this establishment. If you love to look at pretty things and adore high style with ultra-panache, this is the most chic furniture store in all of China. The woman who runs it is American-Chinese and speaks English like few others in Shanghai. In addition to two warehouses filled with furniture, you'll also find smaller tabletop and gift items. I bought an ancestor scroll once. Have your taxi wait . . . even if it's for a few days.

LOTUS CENTRE/TESCO
Super Brand Mall, Pudong, Shanghai (Metro: Lu Jia Zhui).

Lotus Centre is a chain, and I recommend any branch you can get to—this one is just easy for tourists. It is Target with a fancy supermarket: two floors of clothes, food, lifestyle goods, and everything you want. Did I mention great prices?

MAYLIN
Peninsula Hotel Shopping Arcade, Salisbury Rd., Kowloon (MTR: TST), Hong Kong.

The Birkin bags are all gone but the store has expanded and is now heavy into woven leathers that look surprisingly like, hmmmm, what was that Italian brand? Prices hover around $250 for a nice sac. They take credit cards but are not big on charm.

SHANGHAI TANG
Pedder Building, 12 Pedder St., Central, Hong Kong (MTR: Central).

This is undoubtedly one of the must-see, must-dos of Hong Kong, even if you don't buy anything. In fact, there is a good chance you *won't* buy anything. Still, the store is gorgeous to look at and inspirational in its creativity.

Shanghai Tang stocks souvenirs and fashions, Mao-mania, and original artwork by contemporary artists—all imported from China. Get a load of the gift wrap! Wander, drool, buy, have a cigar, sit down for tea, or shop 'til you're late for your next appointment.

SHIATZY CHEN
7 The Bund, Shanghai.

Religious encounter of the fourth dimension. Okay, so that's a little glib, but I am sincere. The first few times I walked into this store it was truly a religious experience; the earth moved. The Taiwanese designer makes men's and women's clothes as well as accessories; they have stores all over Asia. The look is "Armani meets Blanc de Chine" kicked up many notches into couture. In short, gorgeous clothing, usually beginning at $1,000.

Airports & You

Many businesspeople are in such a great hurry getting from meeting to meeting that they wait to shop at the airport duty-free shops as they're leaving town. Depending on your point of departure, this may or may not be such a hot idea.

The **Hong Kong** airport may be a virtual shopping mall, but note that prices are not the same as in town. Even duty-free prices are high. I suggest hitting the gift shop at your hotel in Hong Kong if you're willing to pay top dollar anyway. Gift shops will have slightly more budget-friendly prices and less pressure of the "Oh my, I'd better grab it" variety.

The **Beijing** airport's duty-free shop is excellent for last-minute shopping. I can't tell you that the prices are the lowest in town, but the selection is wide enough for all of you last-minute shoppers to at least accomplish all of your shopping goals.

Shanghai's Pudong Airport gift shops are even more sophisticated in the TT (tourist-trap) department. I've stocked up on chocolate-covered litchis and the most extraordinary embroidered satin bedroom slippers. Shanghai's Hong Giao Airport is neither new nor spiffy but has some basics for giftables.

Taipei's airport is the biggest surprise—the old-fashioned CSK airport is gone and this new beauty has tons of shopping and eats. Yep, even a Starbucks. Note that this airport may have better shopping than in town and is a far better hub to Asia than Narita (Tokyo), so worship for awhile if you can.

SUZHOU COBBLER
3 Fuchow Rd., Shanghai.

Don't sneeze or you will miss this tiny shop that specializes in a sophisticated twist on an old Chinese art: the embroidered slipper. About $50 a pair, but they look like a million.

SPACE 798
Dashanzi Art District (no nearby Metro).

Yes, I know it's off the beaten path; but this trendsetting reclaimed factory is well worth it, with all sorts of shopper's delights in store for you: photography, art, and a little bit of clothing. Look, touch, and splurge. You can even grab a drink or a light meal to reward yourself for making it out there. (See p. 295, in chapter 9 for tips on how to get there and make the most of your excursion.)

GREAT INEXPENSIVE GIFTS

- **Tea mugs.** Chinese tea mugs (complete with lid) cost about $3 each in any Chinese department store. You'll have to wrap them yourself (pack with care), but they make marvelous gifts and are especially unique for giftees who don't have the privilege of having a Chinatown in or nearby their hometowns.

- **Chinese tea.** From high-end brands and makers (such as Fook Ming Tong, in Hong Kong) to any old brand in a great-looking package sold on the street or at a Chinese department store, tea makes a very traditional gift, and it doesn't break. Prices vary with brand and venue. If tea strikes you as old hat, look for the flower teas that are the size of a ping-pong ball and open into a beautiful blossom inside the cup as you make the tea. Excellent party trick. Buy flowering tea (of the jasmine variety, for example) in a gift bag for about $10 to $12.

- **"Jade."** I buy "jade" doughnuts by the dozen at the Jade Market in Hong Kong and then string each one individually as a gift. They cost about $1 each and are not real jade. If you're willing to pay $10 to $15 per gift, you can purchase animal figurines.

- **Chops.** You can be sure that no one else has one of these. A chop, or Chinese signature stamp, costs about $25 and can usually be carved while you wait.

- **Chopsticks.** OK, so more people in your social circle are likely to have a few sets of these. But I found some really chic ones—pearl inlay and all that—in Hanoi (not in China, incidentally). They are indeed a bargain at about $2 per pair.
- **Perfume bottles.** Many people like perfume bottles painted on the inside, but I prefer the fake antiques that look like smoked glass from the 1920s for $10 to $20. I have a collection of tiny cinnabar bottles for which I paid about $15 each. They are fake antiques, true, but good-looking nonetheless.

THE BEST SHOPPING EXPERIENCES

- Trolling for bargains on Fa Yuen Street, Hong Kong
- Having a garment made to measure in Hong Kong
- Any flea market in China
- Shenzhen
- Museum-store shopping in Taipei (and I don't mean the National Palace Museum)

BEST NEW SHOPPING CONCEPTS

The big-name luxury hotels are fighting it out and opening in Hong Kong shopping malls that specialize in the combination of luxury sleep, happy eats, and shopping ops right out the front door—or at the end of the concierge's magic wand. Two of the biggest names in town will knock your socks off with shopping deals, packages, and perks: the **Mandarin Landmark** in the Landmark and the **Four Seasons Hotel Hong Kong** in the IFC Tower.

In **Beijing,** shopping for Olympic souvenirs isn't new, but the officialness of doing business is. The crackdown on fake Olympic merchandise—as well as designer fakes and DVDs—is impressive.

In fact, the crackdown on fakes all over Asia is staggering. If you are caught crossing from the PRC into HKG with pirated DVDs, you will be fined $HK1,000 (about US$130) *per* disc. Since no one buys just one DVD, you are looking at confiscation plus a nasty fine.

OTHER CONCEPTS

INSIDER CONCIERGE
InterContinental Hotel, Salisbury Rd., Tsim Sha Tsui, Hong Kong (MTR: TST).

Insider Concierge is an InterContinental trademark for a program in which the chain's super-duper concierges locate whatever you need. Actually, any good hotel concierge can provide this service, but InterConti backs this up with a fabulous team. The concierge can even arrange for potential purchases to be brought to your hotel room for you to look at, or for fittings to be done in your room.

XINTIANDI
Huai Hai Rd. E., Shanghai (Metro: Huang Pi Nan Rd.).

Maybe it's not fair to call this an urban-renewal effort—it's an entire city of stone houses that have been renovated into bars, restaurants, and shops with walkways in between and the most chic customers in all of China. You don't come here so much for the shopping as for the whole package, usually at night, when the stores stay open late and you drink and stroll and then have dinner.

BEST WINDOW-SHOPPING CONCEPT

THREE ON THE BUND
No. 3 The Bund, 3 Zhong Shan Dong Yi Rd., at Guang-dong Rd. (Metro: Renmin Guangchang), Shanghai.

I didn't come to Shanghai to buy $400 Armani jeans, but this experience is still a thrill. Check out several floors of retail, eat at one of the restaurants, and plop down in the Evian spa. The whole shebang is so beautiful that you don't want to miss out.

THE BEST SOURCES FOR ANTIQUES

Antiques in China are tricky—you simply don't know what's real and what isn't. Hong Kong's Hollywood Road is an excellent stroll for antiques shopping, getting an overview of what is available, and learning about the prices. Don't buy anything serious from a dealer who is not known in the trade.

Macau is an excellent source for antiques—that is, if they weren't just made right there!

Both Shanghai and Beijing abound with shopping ops for small decorative items and antiques, real and fake. Prices can be half those in Hong Kong. But then, reliability can be, too.

THE BEST MARKETS

JADE MARKET
Kansu and Battery sts., Yau Ma Tei, Kowloon, Hong Kong (MTR: Jordan Rd.).

Two tents' worth of dealers with beads, jade, more jade, and a few antiques. Do-it-yourselfers will go wild. Check out Jenny Gems. To reach the market from the Metro, walk or take a taxi.

PANJIAYUAN ANTIQUE AND CURIO MARKET/DIRT MARKET
Huaweiqiaxi Nan Dajie, Beijing (no nearby Metro).

If you are a flea-market person, you owe it to yourself to arrange your trip so that you have a few hours here. Also known as the Dirt Market (it once had a dirt yard), the market includes some aisles of dealers under tin rooftops, and masses of real people with their goods laid out on the ground. Beware of fakes. The best time to shop is before 10am, when it gets very crowded. Open Saturday and Sunday only.

PEARL MARKET (HONG QIAO MARKET)
Near the Temple of Heaven, Beijing (no nearby Metro).

This indoor mall sounds a lot more romantic than it looks, but if you can adjust your expectations, you'll be on your way to heaven. . . and the Temple of Heaven is conveniently across the street.

The first floor has watches and small electronics (including Mao lighters), along with leather goods and fakes. Also on this floor is luggage, which comes in handy when you run out of packing space and are desperate for cheap new bags. At the far end of this floor is a series of stalls selling Chinese arts and crafts and souvenir items. Next up is a floor of pearls and pearl wannabes, beads, gemstones, clasps, and more beads. The rear of this floor holds a small mall of antiques shops.

SHANGHAI SOUTH BUND SOFT SPINNING MATERIAL MARKET
399 Lujiabang Lu (no nearby Metro).

This enclosed market is filled with stalls staggering under the weight of bolts of fabric. It also holds some tailor shops, and a few of the fabric shops sell ready-made garments or gift items. Fabric I saw for 86€ per meter ($135) at the fabric market in Paris was $15 here.

THE BEST TAILORS

Prices in China for custom-made clothing may be less than in Hong Kong, but don't be tempted. If you want top-of-the-line quality that competes with the best of Savile Row, you want a Hong Kong tailor (whose family probably came from Shanghai anyway).

Hong Kong has no best tailor—it has two. They stand head and shoulders above the others for one simple reason: They have their own workrooms and do not send their piecework to China. Only W. W. Chan & Sons has expanded to mainland China—it has a shop in Shanghai. Prices in Shanghai are approximately 20% less than in Hong Kong; the quality is the same.

A-MAN HING CHEONG CO. LTD.
Mandarin Oriental Hotel, 5 Connaught Rd., Hong Kong (MTR: Central).

W. W. CHAN & SONS LTD.
Burlington House, 92-94 Nathan Rd., Second floor, Kowloon, Hong Kong (MTR: TST); 129A–2 Mao Ming Rd., Shanghai (Metro: Shi Men Rd.).

BEST SHIRT MAKERS

All good tailors also make shirts, but two incredibly famous names in shirt making specialize in men's shirts, shorts, and pajamas only.

ASCOT CHANG CO. LTD.
The Peninsula Hotel, Salisbury Rd., Kowloon (MTR: TST); InterContinental Hotel, 18 Salisbury Rd., Kowloon (MTR: TST); Prince's Building, Chater Rd. (MTR: Central); all Hong Kong.

DAVID'S SHIRTS
Victoria Hotel, Unit 201, Shun Tak Centre (MTR: Sheung Wan); Mandarin Oriental Hotel, 5 Connaught Rd. (MTR: Central); 33 Kimberley Rd., Kowloon (MTR: TST); all Hong Kong.

My Best Finds

by Suzy Gershman

- **Shinco DVD Player:** I thought Shinco was a no-name Chinese brand, but the Sony store near me in Paris also sells it. So do Fortress and Broadway, two reliable electronics chains in Hong Kong. My latest score is a portable DVD player the size of a CD player for $135. It's dual voltage (110–220), so I can use it anywhere in the world.
- **Bubble Tea:** Once you've tried this dessert-like drink (see p. 48), you'll never be the same. Buy the supplies in Taipei or online. I serve it often and give my guests a unique experience.
- **Face Cream:** I can't tell you that wrinkle creams and moisturizers really work, but I'm not taking any chances. I like the big-name brands, the ones that cost about $100 a jar (sorry, I can't afford the ones that cost $1,000). I used to buy them at duty-free stores. Now I buy from the stands at the Pearl Market in Beijing.
- **Eyeglasses:** I have bought eyeglasses and had the prescription filled at the Eye Mart in Beijing and been pleased with the adventure and the quality. But my best trick is to go to **New Fei Optical** in Kowloon (Hong Kong), where I can get designer frames plus my prescription for about $100 per pair.
- **Chinese Shirts:** From Kenki, a small chain of arts-and-crafts clothing stores in Hong Kong, I bought reversible velvet-silk Chinese big shirts for $40.
- **Custom-Made Jewelry:** I brought a set of aquamarines that I bought in Brazil to Hong Kong and had a pair of David Yurman–like earrings made in sterling. It took 1 week and cost $250, not counting the price of the stones.

- **Designer Fashion:** Not just any designer mind you, but Taiwanese legend **Shiatzy Chen.** I fell into a sale with prices marked down 20%, and I got a men's tailored black silk Chinese-style jacket that would make the door gods weep (for a total of $455).

My Best Finds

by Sarah Lahey

- **Silk Clothing:** In Saigon, Suzy and I found several shops on **Le Loi Street** selling good-quality silk clothing in sizes large enough to fit us. I bought a dressy cinnamon silk velvet jacket with ruched collar and placket for about $50. Suzy bought one in moss green and we almost fought over a little black number. Ultimately, a truce was called when the black sleeves proved to be too short for our long arms.
- **Chinese Jacket:** From the Shanghai/Pudong branch of **Lotus Centre,** I bought a men's navy embossed corduroy blazer with a tab collar, lined in silk, for about $25. I had to replace the cheap buttons, but it now looks like a $500 jacket. Similar styles were available for (small) women.
- **Armani Sweater:** I found a Giorgio Armani Collezione pale sage double-breasted cotton tunic at the **Joyce Warehouse** in Aberdeen, Hong Kong, for $40.
- **Embroidered silk tote:** Lots of vendors at the **South Bund Soft Spinning Material Market** sell accessories along with yard goods; here, I bought several stunning tote/carry-on bags for $10 each. Large enough to hold my computer, travel pillow, and other necessities, the bags are made of jewel-toned heavy-duty embroidered silk.
- **Eyeglasses:** I brought my prescription (and my husband Tom's, too) from home and had several pairs of eyeglasses made. The best selection of frames and best prices (under $75/pair) were at **New Fei Supply** in Hong Kong, but I also had a pair ($90) made for my husband Tom at **Ming Jin Yuan,** at the Beijing Eye Mart.

My Best Finds

by Aaron Jame

- **CDs:** In Shanghai you can find cheap and legal CDs in local stores—just weed through racks of Backstreet Boys and eventually you may find something decent.
- **Video Games:** I found Game Boy and other game system cartridges and cassettes in the Shanghai street market. Video-game cassettes are cheap and contain several games in one. Of course, they may not be legal, and they may repeat the same game over and over.
- **Mao Bags:** Street vendors, especially in Shanghai, sell these. An over-the-shoulder Mao bag is a must for any young revolutionary.
- **Custom-Tailored Shirts:** In Shanghai I visited the show-room of W. W. Chan & Sons Ltd. (my father's tailor from Hong Kong) and was fitted for my first custom shirts. The quality of the shirts is unmatched. I work in the music business in L.A., so I like to wear a good shirt, with a simple, almost invisible monogram on the cuff, with a pair of jeans. If I'm really going to dress up, I can throw on a blazer.

My Best Finds

by Jenny McCormick

- **Hair Sticks:** Plastic chopstick-style fashion statements that you poke into your hair—everything from faux tortoise shell to Burberry plaid. Talk 'em down to $1 each. Best selection: ground floor of the Pearl Market, Beijing.
- **Fake Jade "Doughnuts":** The Pearl Market and elsewhere, about $1. These babies are great for stringing individually onto a cord or chain of your choosing to make a striking pendant.
- **Bamboo Handbag:** About $10 at the Dong Tai Market in Shanghai.
- **Mao Watch:** About $2. Available at most street markets but sold by the dozens at Hong Qiao and in the booths along Wangfujing, both in Beijing. Extra points awarded for their excellent kitsch value.

Chapter Two

························

ORIENTATION

THE YEAR OF CHINESE MAGIC

··

Whether it's the year of the rat (2008) or the ox (2009), it is always the year for China and its neighbors, from Hong Kong to Macau to Taipei and beyond. Open the newspaper or look online, and the hits just keep coming:

- Yao Ming (China's Michael Jordan) will actually be allowed to market for Nike within China itself.
- Delta has been awarded new routes from the U.S. to China.
- Sofitel decides to open five-star luxury hotels and kicks off the inauguration not in France, the HQ country, but in Beijing.
- Beijing opens Terminal 3 at the Capitol Airport as the cherry on top of the cake of all the new architecture, innovative buildings, and jaw-dropping changes that have spiffed up the city.
- Not to be out-done by Beijing, Hong Kong is on a building spree that wreaks devastation everywhere. As prime real-estate in Kowloon has gone under the bulldozer, new buildings and even new neighborhoods are as populous as dim-sum.

Everything is up-to-date in China and getting hotter, and cooler, every day. Make that wei-cool.

THE MAGIC OF HONG KONG

Much talk has been made of Shanghai being the new Hong Kong, and speculation abounds that Beijing will be on top of the world after the 2008 Olympics. The way I see it, despite all Shanghai's news, glitz, and energy, Hong Kong has not lost out. Hong Kong is, in fact, going gang-busters with new stuff.

In fact, to me, Honkers will always be a little bit of heaven. It will remain the diamond in the crown for years to come simply because the locals speak English better than most residents of mainland China (as well as the offshore islands). They also understand customer service better, do luxury as it's never been done before, and offer shopping options in both European fit and Asian fit.

Sure, China's big cities offer plenty of European designer goods, but they cost 20% more than in Hong Kong, and they probably won't fit you. And the linen sheets at the Mandarin Oriental? The bar at the InterConti? The E-Spa system at all Peninsula Hotels and anchored in Hong Kong? Oh, my dear.

Hong Kong is still the gateway to China, and the best place to begin and end any trip to the area.

THE NEW CHINA

This book covers the most obvious cities a tourist will visit, but I don't want you to think that Shanghai and Beijing are the only chic cities in China, that the new China is only along the east coast, or that there ain't a whole lot of shakin' goin' on.

To make this clear, I'll list the cities where the Italian brand Max Mara has stores: Beijing, Changchun, Chandu, Chongqing, Dalian, Guangzhou (Canton), Hangzhou, Harbin, Kunming, Qingdao, Shanghai, Shenyang, Shenzhen, Urümqi, Wuhan, and Xi'an.

Welcome to the new China. Get out there and shop. Study a map, learn these cities, and book another ticket to come back.

This book also offers, for the first time, a look into Taipei, the capital of Taiwan. I am not about to tell you that Taipei is a shopping mecca. You go for the museums, the tea plantations, the hot springs, the bubble tea . . . and the surprises you'll find along the way. Academics will enjoy Taipei as it works to find its place between Hong Kong and the Mainland.

WELCOME TO CHINA

I try to put politics aside when I write about China; after all, my mission is to shop. I can't help but note, however, that the Chinese are the most capitalist communists I've ever seen. They grasp the big picture and, my God, it's impressive.

Beijing and Shanghai are masterworks of marketing, in all senses and subtexts of the word. To market, to market, to score some fine buys. To market, to market, to influence the world. Napoleon was right: When China awakes, the world will indeed tremble. China is the future.

Getting a Visa

U.S. citizens do not need a visa to enter Hong Kong or Taiwan. They do need a visa to enter the People's Republic of China (PRC), even on a day trip from Hong Kong. It is virtually impossible for a U.S. citizen to get a visa to enter China outside of the U.S. except through London, or in Hong Kong after you arrive. *Note:* Visa prices and systems have recently changed.

American and British passport holders living in Hong Kong will pay a dear price for their visas. The most expensive is the 1-year, multiple-entry visa, which a tourist probably will not need. Tourists, however, can now get a single or multiple-entry visa for a flat fee of $100 from a Chinese embassy or consulate. A visa service will charge you more. If you allow yourself 48 hours in Hong Kong, you can possibly get the visa there for a little less.

You can get a visa in a number of ways:

China

- Apply for a visa through the Chinese consulate in your city; you must pay with cash or a cashier's check.
- If you carry a secondary passport from a country other than the U.S. or U.K., present it at the Chinese Embassy (or consulate) to secure your Chinese visa. It can be much less expensive.
- If you are willing to pay the money or you live in a city that does not have a Chinese consulate, contact a visa service. Download the necessary papers, fill them in, then send off your passport, one passport-size photo, and a big fat check via FedEx or another provider that offers package tracking. I use **Zierer Visa Service** (© **866/788-1100** or 212/265-7887; www.zvs.com). It charges about $50 in service fees (the price of the visa is additional), but you are paying for convenience and will get your passport back, with hologram visa, in about a week. Zierer also has a **London branch** (© **44/207-833-2700**; www.visaservice.co.uk).
- Get your visa in Hong Kong. This can be pricey, especially if you need fast service. Visa services are offered in the airport and throughout town. It's a cinch at the airport and costs about $150, but it takes about 4 hours, which means hanging out at the airport or schlepping back and forth.
- But wait, there are other ways. For me, it was far easier to have my hotel concierge do all the work, though that's more expensive. When the concierge obtains your visa, your total bill is usually divided in two: the cost of the actual visa (about $150) and the service charge (about $50). *Note:* You do not have to add a tip to a service charge. My friend Toby just got a visa in Hong Kong from her hotel concierge for $50. Go figure.

Chinese Arrival Details

1. The amount of foreign cash you can legally bring into the PRC is unlimited. However, if you have more than US$5,000, you must declare it.
2. No pornographic materials, guns, or bombs. Duh.

3. No live animals. Regulations on pets are being eased, however. (The new Chinese chic is to walk your dog—but dogs are prohibited from most public spaces.)

FLYING CONCEPTS

With the PRC opening up, demand has created more plane routes into China. More and more airlines are fighting for hubs and for the loyalty of business and leisure travelers. The number of flights into China has doubled in the last 2 years. The number of airline alliance relationships is also increasing. Code shares are on the take-off.

The type of craft flying long-haul routes is also changing. In fact, after my most recent trips, I can't tell you how important it is to check the kinds of craft making the haul and adjust your plans accordingly. The difference of a 12-hour flight in a new 777 versus an old 747 is enormous. Airlines are working to make the trip more comfortable with the addition of a new class of service: executive economy, extended economy, economy plus—whatever they want to call it.

Note also that technology has now made it possible for a plane to fly for about 18 hours on a nonstop basis. (A direct from New York to Hong Kong in slightly over 17 hr.) You may not want to sit that long, but at least it's your choice.

Finally, if you are doing a Pacific Rim or multidestinational visit, choose your hub city carefully. Both Hong Kong and Taipei are good choices, but avoid Narita if you can. Depending on the routing and the carrier, it may pay to fly nonstop to Shanghai and use that as a hub for southern Asia.

The destination chapters that follow include specific tips on carriers, flights, and savings. Below are some concepts that will help you organize your trip.

If you are planning on exploring China or are looking for promotional deals, don't forget to check out the international airports of the Pearl River Delta, which include the almost new

Petty Pekin Announcement

For those of you who will book all or part of your trip through Beijing, be aware that most airlines refer to Beijing as Pekin. When checking flights listed in alphabetical order, look under *P* for Pekin. I even had trouble getting tickets to Beijing when the agent told me that the carrier served only Shanghai and Pekin in China, and I had to choose one.

Baiyun International Airport in Guangzhou. Shenzhen also has an international airport (as does Macau).

Transpacific Flying

Many flights from the major West Coast cities (Los Angeles, San Francisco, Seattle, Vancouver) connect through Narita, Taipei, or even Seoul. You may not enjoy the layovers.

Travelers increasingly prefer transpacific nonstops, most with flying times of 13 to 16 hours. The longest flight these days is New York to Singapore on a transpacific route, some 18 hours of flying time, with **Singapore Airlines** (www.singaporeair.com).

Continental Airlines (www.continental.com) flies nonstop from Newark Liberty International Airport. Its BusinessFirst class offers a first-class experience at a business-class price.

Cathay Pacific (www.cathaypacific.com) also flies a transpacific route from New York. They have two flights a day from both Los Angeles and San Francisco.

From the South or Midwest, you may want to travel through the major West Coast gateway cities listed above.

I like **Northwest** (www.nwa.com) for several reasons, including the possibility of a layover in Minneapolis, not far from the Mall of America. Northwest also uses its Detroit hub for flights to China—it's less crowded than other U.S. international airports, and a secret worth remembering.

Smart shoppers and travelers know about **EVA Air** (www.evaair.com), which flies the Taiwanese flag. It offers service from major cities around the world including several U.S. West Coast cities (even Seattle) and is known for the excellent luxury-coach section of the plane. Trust me on this: Taipei is a great city for making connections, and EVA has the best value in the skies. For my money, if you are not on a nonstop to HKG, Taipei is the best hub city in Asia.

Finally, see specifics of travel to each destination in this book in subsequent chapters.

Transatlantic Routes

You can get to Hong Kong or the PRC from a variety of European hubs that offer ongoing flights to Asia. The transatlantic approach from the U.S. makes sense only if you take the time to layover for at least 1 night; the next 6 hours of jet lag will be a lot easier to handle.

Lufthansa (www.lufthansa.com) operates 60 flights a week to Asia, so check their options on a transatlantic route. **KLM** (www.klm.com), which code-shares with Delta and Air France, has flights from Amsterdam for about $750 in class H.

Competition on U.K.-to-China routes is fierce, so deals abound. **Virgin Atlantic** (www.virgin-atlantic.com) flies to Hong Kong and Shanghai, with four classes of service, plus double beds on long-haul flights. **British Air** (www.british airways.com) and **Cathay Pacific** (www.cathaypacific.com) also fly from London. Each airline will match the others' promotional deals. I've heard of round-trips from London for $300. But note that if you have an economy ticket (poor you), you can only check one valise.

Note: When you are departing China, be sure to show your U.S. through-ticket even if you are laying over in a European destination. If you have a ticket to the U.S., the less rigid U.S. luggage allowance will apply.

Unusual Connections

- **Hawaii:** Service from Hawaii to Hong Kong is available, as is service to China. This means that those who want to break up the flight and avoid Narita can stop over in Hawaii.

- **Tel Aviv:** This route is unusual, but it works. El Al uses Tel Aviv as its hub city and has ongoing service to Beijing and Hong Kong as well as other major cities in the Far East. It's not as strange as it sounds—the flying time from New York to Tel Aviv is about the same as New York to Tokyo. A layover in Israel goes a long way toward eliminating jet lag once you get to China. Furthermore, El Al has a code share with American Airlines, so you can use frequent-flier miles, book through American, or perhaps connect an around-the-world deal with American, El Al, and Cathay Pacific, also a partner.
- **Detroit:** This U.S. hub is not as well known as Chicago, so you have a better chance of using frequent-flier miles. Northwest Airlines flies from Detroit to Guangzhou. But, speaking of Chicago, it has nonstops to the mainland.
- **Seattle:** Count on EVA Air to make this one easy.

Flying on Miles

While you may indeed be able to use frequent-flier miles for your ticket to Asia, do check if the routing is worth it. My friend Mary had to fly West Palm Beach to Atlanta, Atlanta to L.A., L.A. to Seoul, and Seoul to Hong Kong. On one of her other trips, she had a 6-hour layover in Tokyo before the 5-hour flight to Hong Kong. In booking the trip, she was able to get only certain legs in business or first class and had to endure portions of her 30-hour journey in an economy seat.

Ticket Deals

Because they buy in bulk, wholesalers often get a better price. Enter **Lilian Fong,** Pacific Place, 288 W. Valley Blvd., Suite 206B, Alhambra, CA 91801 (© **626/943-1212;** pacplace@att.net.com), my personal secret weapon in the U.S., and **Chen Voyages,** 137 Rue de Tolbiac, 75013 Paris, France (© **011-33-1-45-70-76-08;** www.chenvoyages.com), my French connection. It was Lilian who first introduced me to EVA Air, by the way. I have, in fact, been using Lilian for over 20 years; I swear by her and the deals she can find.

If you want to travel through Paris (or any other European city) or want to pay your fare in euros, try Chen Voyages. The staff speaks English fluently, and they offer excellent deals.

Other thoughts:

- Talk to your travel agent about coupons or deals that can upgrade you to first class. Lilian once offered me first-class upgrade tickets if I paid the full fare for business class; that's a pretty good deal. The deals come and go with the seasons and the world news. Note that travel to Asia is up, so deals are not as easy to come by as they once were.
- Airlines have so many code-share partners these days that you can have seamless ticketing; however, you may want to know which carriers are taking you on which legs.
- Do look for new carriers, new routes, and new connections that might offer promotional deals. EVA Air, a Taiwanese airline, is only a few years old but has gotten a lot of attention for its price, comfort, and snazzy lounges.
- Airlines often wage "mile wars"; recently you could fly coach to Hong Kong for 40,000 miles on a promo deal.
- As the PRC loosens up and technology allows airliners to fly farther, possibilities multiply. Watch for flights like Detroit–Shanghai, Minneapolis–Beijing, Houston–Taipei, and so on.
- Look for flights into unfamiliar Chinese cities, such as Shenzhen or Guangzhou (Canton), both of which are near Hong Kong but in the PRC.
- Hunt down little-known promos. For example, if you hold an American Express platinum card, you qualify for a free ticket to any destination when you buy a full-fare business-class ticket for yourself.
- Online fares may offer deals. Cathay Pacific's newsletter provides e-mail updates about contests, deals, and even auctions.
- Check if the airline will let you buy a coach seat and a confirmed upgrade at the same time. To get a deal on these, you

All About EVA

EVA Airways (www.evaair.com) is a Taiwanese carrier that flies to Hong Kong, Taipei, and various Southeast Asian/Australian destinations. I ♥ EVA. They have a fleet of various planes (the 747s seem a bit tatty these days), including brand-new 777s and Airbuses. This airline offers "extended coach"—as good as business class at half the price—plus Taipei as their hub city, a much better choice than Narita (Tokyo).

Fares are excellent. If you buy a promotional business-class ticket (the best deals are available online), it's less than $4,000 round-trip. Executive coach goes for about $2,000. U.S. cities served include Los Angeles, San Francisco, Seattle, and Newark. EVA also flies from Paris.

have to fly on certain days of the week and may not get the upgrade in both directions.

- Use your miles to upgrade, but only if the upgrade can be confirmed.
- Around-the-world fares may offer you the best price, especially in business and first class. They are allegedly more forgiving on jet lag because you continue going in the same direction. Fares vary with the airline and the point of departure.
- A multiple-city trip around the Far East can be a great deal. Cathay Pacific's All Asia Pass costs less if you buy it through their website. *Note:* A pass may not earn mileage points.
- Check out age-related discounts. Cathay Pacific considers you a senior at age 55, and you get a $100 discount. Also inquire about price breaks for students and children.

Chinese Carriers

AirChina (www.airchina.com.cn) is the best-known Chinese airline; it has code shares with a variety of well-known airlines and flies some 260 routes within China and over 50 international routes. Other brands to know about—especially for domestic flights in China—include **China Eastern** (www.ce-air.com) and **China Southern** (www.cs-air.com). China Southern also serves international routes.

Cathay Pacific flies the Hong Kong flag and is part owner of **Dragonair** (www.dragonair.com), the best and most trusted of the short-haul carriers from Hong Kong into China. It is also my main choice for a long haul if I am coming from Paris or San Francisco. Dragonair has recently won rights to fly within China, so count on them as needed. I also like EVA and fly them often, especially when money is tight (see below).

SLEEPING MATTERS

Each city chapter of this book includes specifics on hotels in the area. As China becomes increasingly accessible, more hotels want part of the action. Where there are openings, there are promotional deals. **W Hotels,** a division of Starwood, has sprouted up across the country, along with W Retail, the store that sells objects modeled in the rooms themselves. Starwood is branding the Paris icon, The Crillon, into a hotel group to outdo their St. Regis brand; it is soon to hit China.

Sofitel is bringing French charm to China. Peninsula has several new hotels in Asia and opens in Shanghai in 2009. As always, the Pen's hotels offer luxuries, amenities, cooking and crafts lessons, and (usually) one of the best locations in town.

Note also the trend for big hotel chains to open two locations in the same city. When you book any hotel, be sure you know which is where. **InterContinental** has opened two hotels in Beijing, on opposite sides of the city. InterConti's new hotel in Shenzhen is totally amazing—it's alongside a theme park and has a theme of its own.

Hilton is expanding like mad, especially in China. **Hyatt** has one of the most dependable businesses in terms of consistent product, achieved elegance, good spas, and solid business amenities.

If you are interested in discounts, check out **www.asia-hotels.com**. (Hey, you never know.)

Websites for the major hotel chains represented in Hong Kong and the main cities in China are as follows:

- www.accorhotels-asia.com
- www.fourseasons.com
- www.hilton.com
- www.hyatt.com
- www.interconti.com (includes InterContinental and Holiday Inn)
- www.landishotelsresorts.com
- www.mandarinoriental.com
- www.peninsula.com
- www.starwood.com (includes Sheraton, St. Regis, Westin, and W Hotels)

MONEY MATTERS

The major currencies in this part of the world are:

- Hong Kong dollars, represented by HK$ preceding the amount.
- Chinese yuan, often represented by a ¥ symbol following the amount. Yuan are also called RMB.
- New Taiwan dollars are written $NT.
- Patacas, used in Macau and written MP$.

Money Tips

Having watched the fall of the dollar over the past few years, I can't begin to stress how important it is to shop in foreign destinations that are not affected by the rise of the euro. Well, it's important if you care about price.

So just being in Asia and shopping smart is **Tip #1.**

Tip #2: Hong Kong dollars are no longer accepted in eastern China. If you can get someone to take them, they will charge you 6% more.

Tip #3: If you visit Hong Kong before heading into the PRC, some banks will allow you to withdraw Chinese yuan, which appear on the screen as RMB. That means you won't have a money crisis as soon as you land or cross the border. But there's no need for a money crisis; ATMs are located at most border stations.

Tip #4: The yuan is being artificially suppressed by the Chinese government and will probably increase after the Olympic Games. Expect the yuan to go up to 8 (or more) to the $1.

Currency Rates

One **U.S. dollar** is approximately equal to 7.7 Hong Kong dollars or 7.4 Chinese yuan. The $NT trades at 30 New Taiwanese dollars to one USD.

Note that the exchange rate varies widely depending on where you exchange your money; hotels and currency-exchange offices often have the worst rates.

Charge It, Please

Credit cards are more widely accepted in China than in the past. That doesn't mean you can use your card with wild abandon in the PRC, however. You will actually find it easier to bargain and to pay in cash. ATMs are readily available.

In fact, ATMs are all over China, Hong Kong, and Taipei, so you can get cash relatively easily. Be aware, however, that your bank may charge a high fee for international withdrawals.

About Those Tips

In mainland China, a communist country, tipping is frowned upon. Yet in western style hotels and service businesses, everyone seems to want or expect a tip. Therefore, I have noted specific tips in sections of this book in local currency.

For my part, I think tipping helps to teach capitalism. You can tip in U.S. dollars in any of these countries. If I were you, I'd sit on the euros—they're more expensive for you and less convenient for the recipient.

Cheat Sheets

If you are mathematically challenged, go to www.oanda.com and make yourself a currency cheat sheet.

Final Money Note

Prices given in this book are in U.S. dollars unless otherwise specified.

PHONING HOME

The least expensive way to phone home from Asia is with a phone card. You have to dial a lot of numbers, but you can talk for an hour at a cost of about $10.

You can usually buy a phone card from your hotel concierge or business center, as well as any convenience store (such as 7-Eleven) in Hong Kong or China.

My international travel phone accepts a SIM card, so I buy a new one for most destinations. You will pay about $20 for activation and can then buy blocks of time as needed. In Hong Kong you can buy a single SIM card that will also ring in China with a different number—this is easier than changing cards and handing out multiple numbers.

If you prefer the old-fashioned way of dialing through a U.S. phone carrier, here are access numbers for **AT&T:**

Hong Kong: 800-96-1111 or 800-93-2266
Beijing: 108-888
Shanghai: 108-11

COMPARISON SHOPPING

People often ask me what city has the best deals or what to buy where in order to save money. Unfortunately, there is no clear answer to that question. To confuse you more, a chart I found in the *Wall Street Journal Asia* compared prices for a 700-milliliter (1½-pint) bottle of Chivas Regal: It cost $25 in Shanghai and $42 in Hong Kong. Who would have thunk it?

In terms of goods, I find different things in each city, without much crossover. In fact, I could find very few items I wanted from Hong Kong that were even for sale in Taipei.

As a rule of thumb, China is less expensive than Hong Kong on basics and more expensive on designer goods and imports. Prices for Hong Kong designer goods are competitive with prices in Europe, but the same goods in the U.S. may still be less expensive.

THE WHOLE SHEBANG

As you organize your tour of Hong Kong, the PRC, and the Pacific Rim, perhaps you'll be interested in a recent survey from the Pacific Area Travel Association. Of the 39 official destinations in the area, the top 15 destinations in order of tourist entries are: Cambodia, Macau, Mongolia, Taiwan, Laos, Malaysia, Myanmar, Singapore, Maldives, Thailand, Guam, China, Hong Kong, Vietnam, and the Cook Islands. You can get to all of these places from Hong Kong and/or Taipei.

Chapter Three

....

A DICTIONARY OF CHINESE ARTS, CRAFTS, STYLES & CUSTOMS

AN ALPHABETICAL GUIDE

Ancestor Paintings

Available on paper scroll or canvas scroll, these large paintings, most often family portraits, are called "ancestor paintings" in English and represent a very specific art form. They are widely copied and reproduced, so fakes abound. The best one I ever saw was of two female twins. My guide that day translated the inscription—about what venerable old ladies they were in that, their 42nd year on earth.

Genuine antique paintings on canvas cost $500 to $3,000 each in China, depending on size and condition. Fake ancestors abound. I recently bought two beauties; the canvas was original but had been painted over. Although this totally ruins the investment or resale value, it made for two glorious wall hangings.

Antiques

Ha! I've seen antiques being made right in front of my eyes, and if I can't tell the difference, you can't, either. Be an expert, use an expert, or go to a trusted gallery.

The U.S. government defines an antique as any item of art, furniture, or craft work over 100 years old. If you return to the States with a genuine antique, you pay no duty on the piece.

True antiques are a hot commodity, and unscrupulous dealers take advantage of the demand by issuing authenticity papers for goods that are not old. To make matters worse, Hong Kong does not require its dealers to put prices on their merchandise. Depending on the dealer's mood or assessment of your pocketbook, he might quote you a price of HK$100 ($13) or HK$1,155 ($150) for the ginger jar you love. He also might tell you it's 10 years old or 10,000. If 1,000-year-old eggs, sold in all markets, aren't even born yet, imagine how that translates to antiques.

Pick a reputable dealer, and ask a lot of questions about the piece and its period. If the dealer doesn't know and doesn't offer to find out, he probably is not a true antiques expert. Get as much in writing as possible. Even if it means nothing, it is proof that you have been defrauded if you find out later that your Ming vase was made in Kowloon around 1995.

Your invoice should state what you are buying, the estimated age of the item (including dynasty and year), where it was made, and any flaws in or repairs made to the piece.

In good shops, the dealers want to tell you everything they know about a piece or a style you have expressed interest in; they're dying to talk about the items and to educate you. They take pleasure in talking about and explaining the ins and outs of entire categories of goods. If a dealer does not readily offer these free lessons, walk out.

Expect most, or many, of the antiques in markets in Hong Kong, Macau, and mainland China to be fakes.

Blue-and-White

Blue-and-white is the common term for Chinese export-style porcelain, which reached its heyday in the late 17th century, when the black ships were running "china" to Europe as if it were gold. After 1750, craftspeople in both England and continental Europe had the secret of bone china and were well on their way to creating their own chinoiserie styles and manufacturing transfer patterns for mass distribution and consumption.

The untrained eye needs to look for the following: pits and holes that indicate firing methods, the nonuniform look of hand drawing versus stencils, the truer shades of blues of the best dyes, and the right shades of weathered gray-white as opposed to the bright white backgrounds of new wares (not to mention new replications of the former color). Marks on the bottom are usually meaningless. Designs may have European inspiration (look for flowers and arabesques), which will help you determine if you are looking at a Chinese or a European good.

Bound Feet

Because a woman's place in ancient China was unquestionably in the home and because women were to be kept barefoot (figuratively) and pregnant (literally), the feet of aristocratic women were bound during infancy. The women could not walk—meaning they had to be carried, were most comfortable prone, and certainly couldn't work.

The binding process brought the toes underneath the foot toward the heel and resulted in a permanently deformed foot. As a result torturous, special shoes were needed to maintain the foot's misshapen pose, and these "lotus" shoes—still available in flea markets today—are highly collectible. Watch out for cheap reproductions, however.

Bronzes

Several Hong Kong museums, such as the **Hong Kong Heritage Museum**, 1 Man Lam Road, Sha Tin (©852/2180-8188; www.heritagemuseum.gov.hk; Metro to Sha Tin or Che Kung Temple stations) for one, feature antique Chinese bronzes, making the art form an easy one with which to commence your education in Chinese art. Visit several local museums to sharpen your eye; you'll want to completely understand the difference between what will cost you thousands of dollars and what you can buy for a few hundred. The lesser price indicates a fake. As with all Chinese art, you must be able to recognize subtle changes in style and form that indicate time periods and dynasties in order to properly date your fake.

Carpets

Carpets come in traditional designs or can be special-ordered to your specification directly from factories. The price depends on knots per square inch, fiber content, complexity of design, the number of colors used, and the city or region of origin. Any of the **Chinese Arts & Crafts** stores is a good place to look at carpets and get familiar with different styles and price ranges.

When considering the material of the rug, think about its intended use. Silk rugs are magnificent and impractical. If you're going to use the carpet in a low-traffic area or as a wall hanging, great. Silk threads are usually woven as the warp (vertical) threads, with either silk or cotton as the weft (horizontal). The pile in either case will be pure silk. Wool rugs are more durable.

Ceramics & Porcelain

Ceramic and porcelain wares available in Hong Kong and China fall into three categories: British imports, new Chinese, and old Chinese. For a short lesson in buying blue-and-white, see above.

New Chinese craft pottery and porcelain is in high demand. Although much of the base material is being imported from Japan and finished in Hong Kong, it is still considered Chinese. In fact, the better wares are coming out of Hong Kong, and the mass-market stuff is more likely to come from China. Most factories will take orders directly. Numerous factories in Hong Kong will allow you to watch porcelain wares being created and to place a personal order.

Porcelain is distinguished from pottery in that it uses china clay to form the paste. Modern designs are less elaborate than those used during the height of porcelain design in the Ming

Chinese New Year

During the Chinese, or lunar, new year, most stores close. For a few days preceding the festivities, it is not unusual for local retailers to raise prices: Shopkeepers take advantage of the fact that the Chinese like to buy new things for the new year.

dynasty (A.D. 1368–1644), but the old techniques are slowly being revived. Blue-and-white ware is still the most popular. New wares (made to look old) can be found at various Chinese government stores, including **Chinese Arts & Crafts,** in zillions of little shops on and off Hollywood Road in Hong Kong, in Hong Kong's **Stanley Market,** in Macau, and just about everywhere else. Fakes abound, so buy with care. When you order ceramics or ceramic lamps, you may even be asked whether you want "antique finish."

Cheongsam

You already know what a cheongsam is, you just don't know the word, so you're temporarily thrown. Close your eyes and picture Suzie Wong. She's wearing a Chinese dress with Mandarin collar and silk knot buttons that run from the neck across the shoulder and then down the side, right? Possibly in red satin with a dragon print, but that's an extra. The dress style is called a cheongsam. Really touristy ones come in those silk or satin looks, but you can buy a chic one or you can have one custom-made. In Shanghai a cheongsam may be called a *quipo*.

Chinese Scrolls

Part art and part communication, Chinese scrolls are decorative pieces of parchment paper rolled around pieces of wood at each end. They contain calligraphy and art relating to history, a story, a poem, a lesson, or a message. Some scrolls are mostly art, with little calligraphy; others are just the opposite.

It is usually not possible to identify the author or artist, but doing so makes the scroll more valuable. Chinese scrolls make beautiful wall hangings and are popular collector's pieces.

Chinoiserie

Exports from Asia were so fashionable in Europe in the late 18th century, and again in the Victorian era, that they started their own trend. Western designers and craftspeople began to make items in Asian styles. Much was created from fantasy and whimsy; the influence of Indian and other styles mixed with the purely Chinese. Decorative arts and furniture in Asian style, made in Europe, are considered chinoiserie. Chinoiserie is not actually made in China.

Chops

A chop is a form of signature stamp on which the symbol for a person's name is carved. The chop is then dipped in dry dye and placed on paper, much like a rubber stamp. The main difference between rubber stamps and chops is that rubber stamps became trendy only in the 20th Century, whereas chops were in vogue about 2,200 years ago. Because chops go so far back, you can choose from an antique or a newly created version.

Cloisonné

The art of cloisonné involves fitting decorative enamel between thin metal strips on a metal surface. The surface is then fired at just the right temperature, and the finish is glazed to a sheen. It sounds simple, but the work involved in laying the metal strips to form a complicated design and then laying in the paint so that it does not run is time-consuming and delicate. It is an art requiring training and patience.

Antique works by the finest artists bring in large sums of money. Most of what you'll see for sale in Hong Kong (outside of the finest galleries) is mass-produced cloisonné that is inexpensive—a small vase sells for about $20; bangle bracelets are $3. You can also find rings, mirrors, and earrings for good prices at most markets. These make good souvenir gifts. Frankly, I prefer the Hermès version.

Embroidery

The art of stitching decorations onto fabric is known as embroidery. Stitches can be combined to make abstract or realistic shapes, sometimes of enormous complexity. Embroidered goods sold in Hong Kong include bed linens, chair cushions, tablecloths, napkins, runners, place mats, coasters, blouses, children's clothing, and robes. All of those items are new. Another market deals in antique embroidered fabrics (and slippers), which, of course, can be very expensive.

Traditionally, embroidery was hand-sewn. Today machines do most of the work. Embroidery threads range from the finest silk to the heaviest yarn. Judge the value of a piece by whether it is hand-stitched or machine-stitched and by the fineness of the thread or yarn.

Fakes

China has seriously cracked down on makers of fake name-brand goods. Officials mostly go after the factories that produce the goods, so vendors still have the items, which they sell when conditions appear to be safe. Often the branded fakes are put away and you must ask to see them.

Buying a fake doesn't make you safe, however—many are confiscated when you leave the area or when you enter the U.S. and E.U. countries. If you are caught coming from Shenzhen into HKG with fake DVDs, they will be taken away and you will incur a $150 (US!) fine per unit. If you are caught bringing fakes into the U.S., you will be fined and entered onto the master computer list, which means your luggage will be ripped apart every time you reenter the U.S.

Not all of the fakes for sale are handbags or DVDs. I swear that the Ambien I bought with a legal French prescription from a pharmacy in Kowloon is totally fake. And I paid a lot of money for those little pills.

Furniture

Chinese styles in furniture once caused a major sensation in the European market. Teak and ebony were imported from the Far East and highly valued in the West. Yet the major furnishing rage was for lacquered goods, usually in the form of small chests of cabinets. The cabinets sat on top of stands, which were built to measure in Europe.

Antique furniture is a hot collector's item. True Chinese antique furniture is defined by purity of form, with decorative and interpretive patterns carved into the sides or backs. Dealers and collectors alike scour the shops and auction houses. It is better to find an unfinished piece and oversee its restoration than to find one that has already been restored. If it has been restored, find out who did the work and what was done. Some unknowing dealers bleach the fine woods and ruin their value. Others put a polyurethane-like gloss on the pieces and make them unnaturally shiny.

Because Asian furniture is used to the local climate, be certain that your hometown weather will not damage the furniture you buy and that you have the proper humidifiers. Many shoppers say it's better to buy furniture from cities farther south in China and Asia, and not to buy in Beijing.

If you decide to buy, decide beforehand how you will get the piece home. If you are having the shop ship it, verify the quality of the shipper and insurance. If you are shipping it yourself, call a shipper and get details before you begin to negotiate the price of the piece. Ask about duty. I once paid $250 for a small piece and ended up paying an additional $425 to get it to my door—the shipping wasn't very expensive, but the duty was.

Horn

Tortoise shell is illegal to buy and import into the U.S., but most Asian tortoisey-looking items are made out of buffalo horn. Ask.

Ivory

One word of warning: Articles made from raw ivory will not be allowed into the United States. Only antique pieces made from carved ivory are allowed in, and only if the dealer provides the proper paperwork and provenance. It is not smart to try to run raw ivory. It's risky on several levels, so you may want to forget this category of goods.

Another word of warning: New items that look like ivory are made of other materials, including walrus bone and even nut. Carvers in Hong Kong are currently using dentin from walruses, hippopotamuses, boars, and whales as substitutes for elephant ivory. If you want to make sure you are not buying elephant ivory, look for a network of fine lines that is visible to the naked eye. If the piece you are buying is made of bone, it will not have any visible grain or luster. Bone also weighs less than ivory. Imitation ivory is made of plastic but can be colored to look quite good. It is a softer material and less dense than real ivory.

Jade

The term *jade* is used to signify two different stones: jadeite and nephrite. The written character for jade signifies purity, nobility, and beauty. Some consider it a magical stone, protecting the health of the wearer. The scholar always carried a piece of jade in his pocket for health and wisdom. Jade is also reported to pull impurities out of the body; old, red-brown jade reputedly has absorbed the blood and impurities of its deceased former owner.

Jadeite is chemically different from nephrite and tends to be more translucent. For this reason, jadeite is often considered to be more valuable. Furthermore, really good jade—sometimes called "imperial jade"—is white, not green.

In Chinese, *chen yu* is real jade, and *fu yu* is false jade. Jadeite comes in many colors, including lavender, yellow, black, orange, red, pink, white, and many shades of green. Nephrite comes in varying shades of green only.

The value of both is determined by translucence, quality of carving, and color. Assume that an inexpensive carving is not jade. "Jade" factories work in soapstone or other less valuable stones. Poor-quality white jade can be dyed into valuable-looking shades of green. Let the buyer beware.

Jade should be ice-cold to the touch and so hard it cannot be scratched by steel. Some shoppers make it common practice to quick-touch or lick-touch a piece. This is not a real test of good jade, although stone will certainly feel different to the tongue than plastic. You may also want to "ring" a piece, because jade, just like fine crystal, has its own tone when struck.

If you are interested in carved jade figures, bring out your own jeweler's loupe and watch the dealer quake. If the carving is smooth and uniform, it was done with modern tools. Gotcha! A fine piece and an old piece are hand-cut and should be slightly jagged on the edges.

What are those green circles you see in the market and often in the street? They are nephrite and should cost no more than $1 per circle. These "jade doughnuts" make fabulous gifts when tied to a long silken cord and turned into a necklace.

Kites

On one of my trips to China, I bought two very similar kites: One cost $26 in a hotel gift shop, and one cost $2 in Tiananmen Square. If you are buying the kite for a child who will most likely destroy it, get smart.

It is believed that kites appeared about 2,400 years ago, first made of wood and bamboo and later refined in silk or paper, which had better draft. While kite flying is a hobby and an entertainment, it is also a science based on aeronautical engineering. In fact, early kites were used for military purposes, but around the year 784 and the start of the Tang dynasty, people began to fly kites for entertainment.

Among the most common folk motifs in kites are dragons and bats—bats being a figure for good luck, based on a pun with the Chinese word *fu,* which means "bat" and "blessing."

The value of a kite depends on the construction of the frame, the fabric, and the artistic merit of the designs.

Lacquer

No, I don't mean nail varnish. I'm talking about an ancient art form dating as far back as 85 B.C. Baskets, boxes, cups, bowls, and jars are coated with up to 30 layers of lacquer in order to make them waterproof. Each layer must be dried thoroughly and polished before another layer can be applied. After the lacquer is finished, decoration may be applied. Black (on the outside) and red (on the inside) is the most common color combination.

You may be able to date an item by the colors used; metallics in the decorative painting were used by the Han dynasty. Modern (post-1650) versions of lacquer may be European-inspired chinoiserie: beware.

Lanterns

Several styles of lanterns are for sale in Hong Kong and China. Because they have become a fashion statement in home style lately, reproduction lanterns abound. Antique lanterns are available in some markets in Beijing and Shanghai; they are most often made from wire with red fabric inserts.

Plastic lanterns are popular in Hong Kong during the Mid-Autumn Festival and are sold on the street for the night parades.

Monochromatic Wares

You may adore blue-and-white porcelain, but remember that it was created for export because locals thought it was ugly. The good stuff was usually monochromatic. Go to a museum and study the best and brightest before you start shopping, because fakes abound.

Celadon is perhaps the best known of the Chinese porcelain monochromes. It is pale gray-green and gained popularity because of the (false) assumption that poisoned food would cause a piece of celadon pottery to change color. The amount of iron in the glaze determines the amount of green in the piece.

Mooncakes

Just as Anglo-Saxons associate Christmas with fruitcake, the Chinese give mooncakes for the Mid-Autumn Festival. The mooncake is the food that inspired Americans to invent the fortune cookie. It dates to a successful revolt against Mongol warlords. The Chinese communicated with messages that were baked into the little cakes. Now the cakes are a form of celebration, and the design and packaging play a big part of the shopping process and the price.

More than 30 brands are sold in Hong Kong; one large department store sells 10,000 mooncakes a day. Types include those made with lotus flour, bean paste, and even with a hard-boiled duck egg as the prize in the center.

Opals

Hong Kong is the opal-cutting capital of Asia. Dealers buy opals, which are mined mainly in Australia, in their rough state and bring them to their factories in Hong Kong. There they are judged for quality and cut either for wholesale export or for use in local jewelry making. Black opals are the rarest and most expensive. White opals are the most available; they are not actually white, but varying shades of sparkling color.

The opal has minuscule spheres of cristobalite layered inside; this causes the light to refract and the gem to look iridescent. The more cristobalite, the more "fire." An opal can contain up to 30% water, which makes it very difficult to cut.

Dishonest dealers will sell sliced stones, called doublets or triplets, depending upon the number of slices of stone layered together. If the salesperson will not show you the back of the stone, suspect that it is layered.

Paper Cuts

An art form still practiced in China, paper cuts are hand-painted and hand-cut drawings of butterflies, animals, birds, flowers, and human figures. Often they are mounted on cards; sometimes they are sold in packs of six, delicately wrapped in tissue. I buy them in quantity and use them as decorations on cards and stationery.

Pearls

Pearls have been appreciated and all but worshiped in both Eastern and Western cultures for centuries. Numerous famous women in history have had enviable pearl collections: Queen Elizabeth I, Queen Elizabeth II, Elizabeth Taylor, Coco Chanel, and Barbara Hutton, whose pearls were once owned by Marie Antoinette.

The first thing to know about shopping for pearls in Hong Kong is that the best ones come from Japan. If you are looking for a serious set of pearls, find a dealer who will show you the Japanese government inspection certification that accompanies every legally exported pearl. Many pearls cross the border without one, and for a reason.

Pearls are usually sold loosely strung and are weighed by the *momme* (pronounced like "mom"). Each momme is equal to 3.75 grams (¹⁄₁₀ oz.). The size of the pearl is measured in millimeters. Size 3s are small, like caviar, and 10s are large, like mothballs. The average buyer is looking for something between 6 and 7 millimeters (about ¼ in.). The price usually doubles every half-millimeter after 6. Therefore, if a 6-millimeter pearl is $10, a 6.5-millimeter pearl would be $20, a 7-millimeter pearl $40, and so on. When the pearl gets very large, prices often triple and quadruple with each half millimeter.

Most pearls you will encounter are cultured. The pearl grower introduces a small piece of mussel shell into the oyster and then hopes that Mother Nature will do her stuff. The annoyed oyster coats the "intruder" with *nacre,* the lustrous substance that creates the pearl. The layers of nacre determine the luster and size. It takes about 5 years for an oyster to create a pearl. The oysters are protected from predators in wire baskets in carefully controlled oyster beds.

There are five basic varieties of pearls: freshwater, South Sea, *akoya,* black, and *mabe* (pronounced *maw*-bay). Freshwater pearls, also known as Biwa pearls, are Rice Krispies–shaped and come in shades of pink, lavender, cream, tangerine, blue, and blue-green. Many of the pearls that are larger than 10 millimeters are known as South Sea pearls. They are produced in the South Seas, where the water is warmer and the oysters larger: The silver-lipped oyster produces large, magnificent silver pearls, while the golden-lipped oyster produces large golden-colored pearls.

The pearls you are probably most familiar with are akoya pearls. They range from 2 to 10 millimeters in size. The shapes are more round than not, and the colors range from shades of cream to pink. Some of these pearls have a bluish tone.

The rarest pearl is the black pearl, which is actually a deep blue or blue-green. Black-lipped oysters in the waters surrounding Tahiti and Okinawa produce these gems, which range in size from 8 to 15 millimeters. Putting together a perfectly matched set is difficult and costly.

Mabe pearls have flat backs and are considered "blister" pearls because of the way they are attached to the shell. They are distinguished by their silvery bluish tone and rainbow luster.

Pearls are judged by their luster, nacre, color, shape, and surface quality. The more perfect the pearl in all respects, the more valuable. Test pearls by rolling them—cultured pearls are more likely to be perfectly round and will, therefore, roll more smoothly.

You needn't be interested in serious pearls, whether natural or fake. In fact, prices being what they are, I'm in favor of fakes. Fake versions of cultured pearls are readily available in Hong Kong; specialty items such as baroque-style or gray pearls are hard to come by. Chanel-style pearl items may be found in fashion stores, but not at pearl dealers.

Silk

Anthropologists will tell you that silk is China's single greatest contribution to world culture. The quality of Chinese silk has always been so superior that no substitute has ever been deemed acceptable. The trade routes that brought silk around the world also brought cultural secrets from ancient worlds into Europe.

The art of weaving silk originated some 4,000 years ago in China and has spread throughout Asia and the world. China, however, remains the largest exporter of silk cloth and garments. Hong Kong receives most of its silk fabric directly from China. Fabric shops in the markets sell rolls of silk for reasonable prices, although silk is not dirt-cheap and may be priced competitively in your home market.

When buying silk, be sure that it is real. Many wonderful copies are on the market. Real silk thread burns like human hair and leaves a fine ash. Synthetic silk curls or melts as it burns. If you are not sure, remove a thread and light a match. If the dealer has a fit, ask him to do it or walk out. Vendors who are proud of their merchandise will often do the test for you. Ask.

Snuff Bottles

A favorite collector's item, snuff bottles come in porcelain, glass, stone, metal, bamboo, bronze, and jade. They also come in old and new old-style versions. They are hard to distinguish from perfume bottles, especially if they have no tops. In short, watch out; because of tourist demand, fakes flood this category.

A top-of-the-line collectible snuff bottle can go for $100,000; if you think you are buying a fine example of the art form for $10, think again. Glass bottles with carved overlays are rare and magnificent, one of the specific schools of design and style in snuff bottles that are especially valuable to collectors.

You can find more ordinary examples in any market. If you just want a few ornaments for the house (or Christmas tree), the markets or shops on Hollywood Road in Hong Kong will have plenty.

Soy Sauce

Ongoing disputes about soy-sauce manufacturing have become a big brouhaha for grocery shoppers in the U.S., where Japan is demanding specific labels and a possible name change. The real thing must be made from real soy products and fermented for at least 3 months.

Spirit Money

Colorful fake paper money that is to be burned for the dead, spirit money is sold in old-fashioned paper shops, which are (sadly) fast fading out. You can still find a string of such paper shops lining Shanghai Street in Kowloon, in Causeway Bay near Jardine's Bazaar, and in Macau, in the antiques-stores neighborhood.

Tea

The **Museum of Tea Ware in Flagstaff House,** 10 Cotton Tree Dr., Hong Kong (© **852/2869-0690;** www.lcsd.gov.hk), is a good place to start exploring the mysteries of tea. Tea has been cultivated in China for more than 2,000 years and reflects the climate and soil where it is grown, much as European wines do. Three categories make up the tea market: unfermented, fermented, and semifermented.

It is customary to drink Chinese tea black, with no milk, sugar, or lemon. Cups do not have a handle, but often do have a fitted lid to keep the contents hot and to strain the leaves as you sip. Because Hong Kong was a British colony, many hotel lobbies and restaurants serve English high tea (a great opportunity to rest your feet and gear up for a few more hours of shopping).

Because tea is relatively inexpensive and often comes in an attractive package or tin, it makes an excellent gift, whether you choose high-priced, well-packaged goods or those from a grocery store or herbal or medicine shop. All the Chinese department stores have a wide selection of teas and tea containers.

All About Bubble Tea

Bubble tea originally began as a Taiwanese craze but has steadily invaded most of Southeast Asia. It is frequently available in Hong Kong and has also created quite a sensation in U.S. cities that have large Asian populations, such as San Francisco, New York, Honolulu, and Seattle. Available in hot or cold formats, the beverage can be made with tea (sometimes you can choose between green or black), coffee, or fruit juice. A bubble tea is something like a creamy smoothie (particularly the ones made with juice), but it also includes "bubbles"—marble-sized balls of (usually black) tapioca (*sego* in Chinese). The gimmicky treat comes complete with an over-sized straw you need to use to slurp up the so-called bubbles. I order the ingredient kits online and make mine as a novelty for parties or serve it to teens. Flavors range from the more exotic (taro root and litchi) to those more suitable to the traditional palette (strawberry and coconut).

Chapter Four

....

HONG KONG

WELCOME TO HONG KONG

....

Oh my Buddha! That's all I can say. In my 20-plus years of visiting this destination, I have never, I mean *never*, seen anything like what is going on now. Construction everywhere, talk of a united Hong Kong—Shenzhen metroplex, feng shui to the wind. I am an earth rat!

Hong Kong is the center of the universe, the diamond in the Asian crown. It was the first of the Asian markets to come back from the slump; last fall's auctions at Christie's and Sotheby's Hong Kong branches set record prices for specialty sales in Asian art. Real estate is back up; the stores are cookin'. McDonald's is expanding, and Disneyland Asia is open. More and more flights are winging into town; Kong wows visitors with its future—not to mention the fact that English is readily spoken and understood, a rarity in most of Asia. Oh wait, what's happening over there? You say the old airport is becoming the new cruise port? That the new Western Tunnel has changed two neighborhoods to a chop suey of luxe? Oh my, but Hong Kong has come out of all of this as a star.

I REMEMBER MAMASAN

Use Hong Kong as your base for exploring the new China. Remember these facts:

- Designer goods are 20% less expensive in Hong Kong than in mainland China.
- Hong Kong has been doing luxury and customer service for so long that they are second nature.
- For 99 years, English was the official language.
- If you are looking for Chinese atmosphere, you may find it more readily in parts of Hong Kong than in China's big cities, where the past is being torn down at an alarming rate. Hong Kong is a lot more than the Star Ferry and the skyline you've seen on billboards—there are scads of nearby islands and destinations that will send you over the mooncake when it comes to charm.

The Lay of the Land

Hong Kong encompasses Hong Kong Island, the city of Kowloon, the New Territories, and a few hundred islands. Technically speaking, what we commonly refer to as Hong Kong is now part of the People's Republic of China (PRC), but because it has separate but equal status, its address is written as "Separate Administrative Region," or "SAR" (not to be confused with SARS, the disease).

When people discuss addresses in the Hong Kong area, they may cite a particular number on a particular street, but more often than not, you'll hear your fellow travelers simplifying directions by just naming a building and a neighborhood. And they play fast and loose with what constitutes a neighborhood. Some people call all of Victoria Island "Central" and all of the Kowloon Peninsula "Kowloon."

Shopping in Hong Kong concentrates heavily on two areas: Central, the main business "downtown" area on the Hong Kong Island side, and Tsim Sha Tsui in Kowloon. Central is very

Hong Kong Orientation

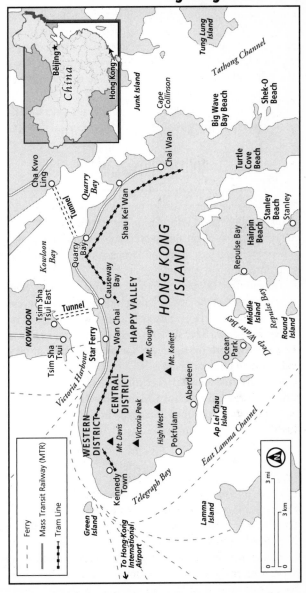

upscale, civilized, businesslike, and modern. Tsim Sha Tsui (often written TST) is grittier and more frenetic. As real estate continues to sky rocket, there is new interest in Mong Kok, the area of Kowloon beyond TST, which now has some luxury hotels, a mall, and Elements, a new deluxe mall in the Western-Tunnel side of Kowloon.

See "Shopping Neighborhoods" (p. 73) for a detailed discussion of Hong Kong's shopping and commercial districts.

BOOKING HONG KONG

The Hong Kong Tourist Association (www.hkta.org) provides a great deal of useful information for travelers at no cost. It publishes pamphlets on almost every subject imaginable, many of which you can pick up as you exit passport control at Hong Kong International Airport.

The monthly *Official Hong Kong Guide* contains general information about the city, including listings of festivals, events, and exhibits. The HKTA also publishes a weekly newspaper called *Hong Kong This Week*. It contains news on events and shows, along with the usual ads for shops. It's free at major hotels and in HKTA offices.

Inside the free tourist packet you can pick up at the airport is the A-O-A Map Directory. Maps show both building and street location—helpful for finding addresses that include the building, street, and area names.

GETTING THERE

When it comes to booking your plane tickets, you'll encounter a confusing number of possibilities, deals, routes, and reasons to go with any number of different plans (or planes). (**Note:** Remember that you can often add on a single city for very little extra money.)

Ticket Deals

Because they buy in bulk, wholesalers often get better prices and pass their savings on to their customers. See p. 24 for a recommended agency in the U.S. and one in Paris. Both offer discounted deals.

Other thoughts:

- If you're flying to Hong Kong from the West Coast, look into a Circle Pacific fare or an All Asia ticket. Most American carriers, and many international ones, allow you to make your own itinerary, traveling to several cities in Asia at package-tour prices. You do not join a group; you set your own pace, but you get a break on the price because you fly all legs with the same carrier. I just saw a Cathay Pacific deal for $999 (when bought online) that offered a choice of some 17 cities.
- Watch for gateway deals. When Cathay added a second daily flight between Hong Kong and San Francisco, they offered excellent prices. American Airlines is asking for support for their proposed nonstop from Chicago to Beijing, which would launch in March 2009.
- If you're pricing airfares on several carriers, it is imperative that you understand the quality of the service and what you are getting. Virgin has made quite a splash with its extra perks and great entertainment system, but it offers real value only to those travelers able to pay extra for Upper Class service (double beds?!). The non–Upper Class seats don't compete with other airlines for comfort or price.
- If you must fly in a coach seat, look for ways to break up the travel. You can get a discounted seat from the U.S. to London or Paris for $300 to $400, and a seat to Hong Kong for $600 to $700, leaving you enough money for a refreshing layover, and a bigger adventure.
- Package tours often offer the best deals financially, especially if they include airport transfers and some extras. Check them out, especially when you can stay at luxury hotels. Likewise,

add-on tours offered by cruise lines sometimes have fabulous prices that include promotional events and benefits.
- Those 55 and over may qualify for special flight deals for seniors. Cathay has an offer for two seniors traveling together that provides for fare to Hong Kong and then one of several other cities that you get to pick.
- If you are planning big-time shopping, consider buying your ticket by class of service and excess baggage rules/costs. Find out if you qualify for perks when you are a premium member of a certain airline or what the weight allowances are with the various classes of service. Know if your carrier goes on the weight system or the per-piece system since more and more airlines are now switching over to a weight system, even if you are flying into the U.S. from Asia.

PROMOTIONAL DEALS

All airlines have promotional deals. Deals to Asia are sometimes harder to find and often aren't advertised in America, but you can find them by calling the airlines' toll-free numbers in the United States or by going online. You may also find a promotional deal through your favorite credit card.

And keep in touch with locals who can tip you off to promotional deals: Friends in Hong Kong recently told me about flights between Hong Kong and London that cost £200 roundtrip. They were available only for 3 days; all local carriers (Virgin, Cathay Pacific, and British Airways) matched the deal. The savings were for coach seats only—but, hey, what a deal.

An especially interesting new promotion called **Fly Via HK** (www.flyviahk.com) offers some amazingly low fares if you plan to make Hong Kong your hub. It includes various Chinese and Pacific Rim destinations and big-name carriers such as Cathay Pacific, Thai Airways, Philippine Airlines, and Dragonair. Fares are most often posted in U.S. dollars and include deals to nearby Cambodia and even Australia (for just $363—reason enough to put another shrimp on the barbie).

Don't forget Disney deals, which offer packages to the newest Magic Kingdom and the happiest place in Asia.

Disneyland Asia (www.hongkongdisneyland.com) is near the airport on Lantau; you can take the train into the major shopping districts of Hong Kong and Kowloon. Of course, shopping abounds in the kingdom.

ARRIVING IN HONG KONG

The gorgeous Hong Kong International Airport (HKIA), designed by Sir Norman Foster, is like a metallic crab sunning itself on Lantau Island. It's modern and easy to use; you whisk along electric carpets, onto trains, and through to the main terminal. If you have arranged car service from your hotel, look for the hotel desks in the center of the arrivals hall. Someone will escort you through the rest of the process, taking your baggage and meeting you at your car.

Car Service

Traveling from the airport in the swank car your hotel sends for you is a delightfully elegant way to arrive—and an expensive one. Although public transport is simple and inexpensive, part of the fun of being in Hong Kong is settling into the hotel's Rolls, Daimler, or Mercedes-Benz. Expect to pay $95 to $150 (it varies from hotel to hotel) each way for the luxury, but do try to find it in your budget. Hotels in the Central district— the main shopping and business area—may charge more than those in Kowloon.

Airport Bus & Train

AirBuses run every 15 minutes or so, but another bus option is Executive Coach. The seating is nicer than the first-class cabin of any airline, with tons of legroom for you, your wheelchair, and your carry-on. You can reserve your seat through your hotel or go to the bus desk in the arrivals hall, section A. The fare to Central is HK$140 ($18).

The train (Airport Express) is for those who have little to no luggage. It whooshes right through the airport terminal; you can hop on and be at the main station in Central in 22 minutes. From there, you take a taxi to your hotel. You can buy a tourist package for HK$220 ($29) that includes the one-way Airport Express fare and a 3-day MTR Octopus Card (see "Getting Around," below). For HK$300 ($39), it includes the round-trip fare to the airport. You can even buy the pass from the duty-free on some airlines. If you don't buy the package, the bus costs HK$154 ($20) each way.

Taxis on Arrival

Taxi stands are near the arrivals lounge. A large sign lists approximate fares to different areas of Hong Kong and Kowloon. Taxis usually charge a flat rate of approximately $45—it is a long drive to town. I took a taxi once and never did it again. I saved half the price of a hotel car, but the bus is so much fun that I prefer to save even more and float in executive luxury.

GETTING AROUND

Hong Kong is an easy city to navigate because its transportation options are excellent. It's a good city for walking, true, but you'll also want to enjoy its ferries, *kaidos* (bigger ferries), trams, double-decker buses, and superb MTR (Mass Transit Railway).

Most rides on the MTR take less than 20 minutes; you can cross the harbor in approximately 5 minutes.

Crossing the harbor by car or taxi during rush hour is difficult, but it's a breeze on the MTR. The Star Ferry is much changed (see below).

MTR

The MTR stop at Central will get you to most locations in Hong Kong, and the Tsim Sha Tsui (TST) stop is convenient to most locations in Kowloon. *For a detailed map of Hong Kong regional transportation, see the inside back cover of this book.*

The MTR is half the fun of getting to great shopping. Three lines connect the New Territories to industrial Kwun Tong, to business Central, to shopping Tsim Sha Tsui, and to the residential eastern part of the island. Each station is color-coded, and signs are in English and Chinese.

The longest trip takes less than an hour, and the cost is based on the distance you travel; one-stop journeys usually cost HK$4 (50¢) to HK$10 ($1.30). Buy your ticket at the station vending machines by looking for your destination and punching in the price code. You will need exact change, which you can get from a machine nearby. Ticket windows sell multiple-journey tickets.

If you're visiting Hong Kong from overseas, the best value is a 1-day unlimited MTR ticket, available at any HKTA office, any MTR station, select Hang Seng banks, and MTR Travel Services Centres. It costs HK$50 ($6.50). You must buy your ticket within 2 weeks of your arrival and show your passport at the time you purchase it.

Stored-value cards are called **Octopus Cards.** They cost HK$70 ($9.10), HK$100 ($13), and HK$200 ($26). Cards are electronic and can be read through your wallet or handbag; just place yours on the pad. Flash it again to depart the station at your destination. To use single-journey tickets, insert and retrieve. You need the ticket to exit the station, at which time it will be "eaten."

The MTR runs between 6am and 1am.

Taxis

Taxis in Hong Kong are cheap. The meter starts at HK$15 ($1.95); after that, the charge is HK$1.30 (20¢) per 200m (656 ft.). Taking the Cross-Harbour Tunnel costs an extra HK$10 ($1.30) each way, making the total additional fees HK$20 ($2.60). I tend to avoid taking a taxi through the Cross-Harbour Tunnel unless I'm loaded down with packages and have

Stop! The Taxi Guide

In any major Hong Kong bookstore, you can buy a single edition or boxed set of three books called *Stop! The Taxi Guides,* which contains a Hong Kong Taxi Guide, Shanghai Taxi Guide, and Beijing Taxi Guide. The guides, organized by topic, are in English, Pinyin, and Chinese. You just point and the driver reads . . . and drives.

had a long, hard day of shopping. Surcharges apply for luggage, waiting time, and radio calls.

If a taxi is in Central and has a sign saying KOWLOON, it means that the driver would like a fare going back to Kowloon and will not charge the extra HK$10 ($1.30) tunnel fee if he gets such a fare. It is sometimes hard to find a cab during the 4pm shift change. If a taxi doesn't stop for you on a busy road, it is probably because the driver is not allowed to stop.

Look for a taxi stand where you can pick up a cab. Hotels are always good places to find a taxi. Even if you are not a guest, the doorman will help you. Tip him HK$5 (65¢).

English is still an official language, but it's always nice insurance to have your destination written in Chinese. Hotels have preprinted cards, one side of which tells the driver how to reach the hotel. Get a card ahead of time; otherwise, drivers simply put a map book in your hand and ask you to find the address.

Trains

The Kowloon-Canton Railway (KCR) has just merged with the MTR, making one smooth ride direct to Shenzhen, increasing routes for local commuters and lowering fares for all Because you can't get into China without a visa, chances are you won't be traveling as far as the border. But do hop onboard, because you should take this chance to get out into the New Territories and see some of the real world.

The TST East station allows you to step out of the Peninsula or InterContinental hotel and into a luxury train that whisks you to China in less than an hour. For tips on visits across the border, see p. 17. You can use the Hung Hom station for travel deeper into the Pearl Delta.

Ferries

The most famous of the Hong Kong ferries is the Star Ferry, "the least expensive tourist attraction in the world," with service from Kowloon to Central and back. The green-and-white ferries have connected the island to the peninsula since 1898, and the 8-minute ride is one of the most scenic in the world. You can see the splendor of Hong Kong Island's architecture and the sprawl of Kowloon's shore.

However, if you know Hong Kong, you may be shocked to know that the ferry terminal on the Victoria side has moved! I personally don't feel quite the same way about the Star Ferry and don't find the new terminal location to be very convenient. And I am being polite here . . . careful and polite.

That said, the Star Ferry can be a small piece of magic for no more than pocket change. First class costs HK$2.20 (30¢); tourist class is HK$1.75 (25¢). The difference is minimal except at rush hour, when the upper deck (first class) is less crowded, or if you want to take pictures: you get a much better view from the upper deck. The Central/Tsim Sha Tsui (TST) service runs daily from 6:30am to 11:30pm.

Trams

Watch out crossing the streets of Central, or you're likely to be run over by a double-decker tram. Victoria Island trams have operated for more than 85 years, from far western Kennedy Town to Shau Kei Wan in the east. They travel in a straight line, except for a detour around Happy Valley. The fare is HK$1 (10¢) for adults, half-price for children. You pay as you enter. Many trams do not go the full distance east to west, so note destination signs before getting on. Antique trams are available for tours and charters, as are the regular ones.

The **Peak Tram** (www.thepeak.com.hk) has been in operation for more than 100 years. It is a must for any visitor to Hong Kong—unless you are afraid of heights. You can catch the tram on Garden Road. A free shuttle bus will take you from the Star Ferry or Central MTR station (Chater Garden exit) to the Peak Tram terminal. The tram runs to the Peak every 10 minutes starting at 7am and ending at midnight. The trip takes 8 minutes. The best time to make this trip is just before dusk; you can see the island scenery on the trip up, walk around to various viewing points or peek in on some of the expensive mansions and high-rises, watch the spectacular sunset, and then ride down as all the city lights are twinkling.

Rickshaws

It's over, folks. Rickshaws are *fini, kaput,* anachronistic, socially incorrect, gone with the wind.

SLEEPING IN HONG KONG

I can't think of any other city in the world—and that includes Paris—where your choice of hotel is a more integral part of your stay than in Hong Kong.

Although I'm incredibly picky about hotels, I've found several in Hong Kong that offer the most important factor in a shopping hotel—location—and still have all the luxury I lust for. Asian hotels are famous for their deluxe standards and fabulous service; enjoying these perks is part of the pleasure of staying in Hong Kong.

Hotel Tips

I find hotels' official rack rates irritating and refuse to quote them in these pages. Few people pay the official rates, and deals can almost always be made; Hong Kong is deal city.

Promotional rates can be as low as $149 a night at the Marco Polo Gateway (Kowloon); I once saw a Mandarin Oriental ad touting Oriental Interlude Leisure breaks, with a price per room (not per person) of HK$1,100 ($143). Rates are on the rise in Hong Kong, however, and rooms can be dear, especially when trade fairs are in town and hotels are full of convention-goers. It pays to shop around for rates and for the right time of year to visit since prices change with the seasons.

Tricks of the Trade

Some secrets that might make booking your hotel easier:

- Ask about packages, which may include breakfast, airport transfers, and other items that usually incur an extra charge. Almost every luxury hotel in the world offers a honeymoon package. As long as you don't show up with the kids, you're on your honeymoon.
- Mileage awards can be used to pay for hotel rooms, to obtain discounts on rooms, or to accrue more mileage for your favorite frequent-flier account.
- Always ask whether the hotel offers weekend or 5-day rates. Almost all hotels discount rooms during the off sea-son or when not a lot of trade shows are in town. In fact, Hong Kong has so many conventions that you may get a low-price convention rate if you ask and rooms are available.
- Check on prices on Club Floors or Lounge Floors—these rooms usually cost about $50 a night more but have a ton of perks from free breakfast to free Internet and cocktails. Even at $100 a night extra, you can often save money by spending money.
- There is no more high or low season in Hong Kong. Sum-mer rates are usually the least expensive, but watch out for Mainland or Japanese visitors who pay top dollar.
- In fact, mind your Japanese and Chinese holidays, which are usually not on U.S. and U.K. calendars; Hong Kong hotels fill up at these times.

- Check the big chains for promotional rates. Often you can prepay in U.S. dollars and save, or the chain will have a deal in the computer that your travel agent doesn't know about. A Hilton telephone operator told me about an exceptional value at the Conrad, which at the time saved me about $100. InterContinental has totally reinvented itself; find out what it offers. I do a Shop & Spa tour for InterContinental every year, which is a package deal with great prices. Join us! (For details, see www.suzygershman.com.)

Hong Kong's Best Shopping Hotels

CENTRAL

I've found three hotels that serve as one because they're in the same location: **Pacific Place,** right above the mall of the same name. They all have entrances within the mall as well as front doors on the street.

CONRAD HOTEL
88 Queensway, Central (MTS: Admiralty)

This is the hotel that made me fall in love with the Conrad brand, which specializes in hotels all over Asia (although the division of Hilton has spiffy hotels worldwide, even in places like Brussels, where the Conrad is one of the fanciest hotels in town). But I digress. Conrad in Hong Kong is one of the three anchor hotels at the Pacific Place Mall, which instantly makes it a shopper's delight.

The hotel has a pathway that leads directly to the mall. It also has several famous restaurants and incredible views of the peak and the harbor. Plus, Conrad gives a little extra in order to woo luxury and business travelers—you get a robe, you get a rubber ducky in your tub, and some stays include airport transfer fees. You can get a price break for booking further in advance and may even pick up a promotion—say, a king deluxe room with ocean view and included breakfast buffet for $500 per night.

U.S. and Canada reservations © 800-445-8667. www.conrad hotels.hilton.com.

FOUR SEASONS HOTEL HONG KONG
8 Finance St., Central (MTR: Central)

Four Seasons returned to Hong Kong with this wow-'em hotel in the IFC Tower, overlooking the water, Kowloon, and the new Star Ferry terminal. The IFC Tower also houses a multi-level luxury shopping mall and cinema complex, and the Airport Express train station. The hotel has drop-dead fabu restaurants, direct entry into the mall, and makes the Star Ferry seem viable one more time. Rates begin around $600.

U.S. and Canada reservations © 800/819-5053. Local © 852/ 3196-8888; fax 852/3196-8050. www.fourseasons.com/ hongkong.

WAN CHAI

GRAND HYATT
1 Harbour Road, Wanchai (MTS: Wanchai)

I have shied away from this hotel for years thinking that the location was too oddball for me: boy, was I wrong! Attached to the Convention Center, with direct ferry service to TST East, adjacent to a large Chinese Arts & Crafts store, and famous for its restaurants and its spa, this hotel is one of the best in town. The hallways are decorated with dramatic black-and-white photos; most of the rooms have views; and, while the rooms are not gigantic, they are technologically equipped to offer amenities at the push of a button. The pool, garden, and spa transport you to another world, making it impossible to believe you are in downtown Hong Kong.

The spa is named Plateau: here, you may book treatments (request the June Jacobs products) or book the entire lifestyle and take a room with a futon bed, a view of the harbor, and a specialty health-food menu. Rooms with a view of the harbor begin around $450.

US and Canada reservations © 800/492-8809. Local © 852/ 2588-1234. www.hongkong.grand.hyatt.com

KOWLOON

GRAND STANFORD INTERCONTINENTAL
78 Mody Rd., TST East (MTR: TST East)

TST East is a location popular with business travelers who want to get into China easily. It's essentially right on top of the KRC Hung Hom train station, and an escalator ride from the new TST East train station.

InterContinental has this hotel in its constellation for those who don't need the luxury of the flagship property (see below) and are happy to get a room with the usual InterConti perks for about $150 to $185.

Just enough shopping is in the area to satisfy your needs, and you can walk to TST or take the ferry directly to Central.

U.S. and Canada reservations © 888/303-1758. Local © 852/2721-5161; fax 852/2732-2233. www.interconti.com.

INTERCONTINENTAL HOTEL HONG KONG
18 Salisbury Rd., Kowloon (MTR: TST)

To me, it will always be the Regent, but locals have adapted to the change and call this hotel the InterConti. In one of the most scenic locations in Hong Kong, the hotel occupies the tip of Kowloon Peninsula. The views from the lobby bar at night are nothing short of spectacular.

The tricks and treats are also incredible—an Alain Ducasse restaurant; a club membership that provides for tons of perks, making it a bargain shopper's best buy; a Feng Shui spa; and now Nobu, which is worth the scratch.. Downstairs is one of my favorite quick-bite places—the coffee shop, Harbourside.

Rates here vary enormously; I have heard of $199 rooms during very low season. However, the average is closer to $300 and up (harbor views cost more, of course).

U.S. and Canada reservations © 888/303-1758 or 770/604-2000. Local © 852/2721-1211; fax 852/2739-4546. www.interconti.com.

LANGHAM HOTEL
8 Peking Rd., Tsim Sha Tsui (MTR: TST)

If you know the London hotel scene, you are familiar with the Langham Hotel, a former Hilton a block from Regent Street. This hotel—and its sister (Langham Place) in Mong Kok—shares the same ownership. You can spot the similarity as soon as you enter the Kowloon hotel; the lobby has a barrel-vaulted ceiling so Victorian in style that you can scarcely remember you are in Hong Kong.

The Langham is relatively new to the five-star scene, after a $30-million renovation that made it a luxury property aimed at business travelers. The hotel is in the Leading Hotels of the World bible (from which I book most of my hotels), so you end up comparing it to the Peninsula, across the street. In reality, this hotel competes with the InterConti and the recently spruced-up Sheraton.

The hotel is gorgeous; the 488 modern, plush rooms have every amenity. The Club floor offers even more perks, such as one-way airport transfer (included in the room rate).

Opposite the Ocean Terminal mall and the Hong Kong China City ferry terminal, the hotel is 1 block from the Star Ferry. It has several restaurants, including a New York–style deli and the Chinese restaurant, **T'ang Court.** Rooms begin at $450 and increase with the view.

U.S. reservations © 800/457-4000, or book through Leading Hotels of the World (© 800/223-6800). Local © 852/2375-1133. www.langhamhotels.com.

THE PENINSULA HOTEL
Salisbury Rd., Kowloon (MTR: TST)

The Pen, as it is called, is the most famous hotel in Hong Kong. In the ever-changing world of hotel competition, this *grande dame* keeps ahead with new and imaginative programs. The latest development, the Peninsula Academy, allows you to take exclusive classes, hear lectures, meet with specialists, or eat in the chef's private kitchen. The newer part of the hotel, a tower with superb views, a health club, a pool, and a Philippe Starck–designed restaurant (Felix), provides the modern foil to the old-world 1928 fancy. A helicopter pad on the roof and the Rolls-Royce transfer service to or from the airport provide luxe transport.

Not only does the hotel have a complete shopping mall, but the wonderful health club and the new E-Spa, which is the most dramatic spa I have seen in my entire career. I now book myself into the spa shortly after arrival. In fact, the perfect way to get acclimated is to shop in the hotel arcade and then slip into E-Spa. Finish up with tea in the famed lobby.

With these extras, you already know this is the most expensive hotel in town. A bargain rate would be in the low $400s, but sometimes you'll find promotions that offer a free night or some other nicety.

U.S. reservations © 800/262-9467, or book through Leading Hotels of the World (© 800/223-6800). Local © 852/ 2920-2888; fax 852/2722-4170. www.peninsula.com.

DINING IN HONG KONG

If you think Hong Kong is most famous for shopping, think again. The number one attraction is culinary pleasures—from five-star restaurants in the most elegant hotels to Chinese eateries off the beaten path. Certain places are so fabulous that you just have to try them to complete your Hong Kong experience. True foodies may even want to book a trip to coincide with the Hong Kong Food Festival in August.

Because this is a small town and food is so important to the culture, Hong Kong has a number of private dining clubs. If you don't know a member, ask your hotel concierge if he can book you a table at either **Kee Club** or **China Club.**

Please note that in the last year or two Hong Kong has opened eateries from many of the world's most famous chefs: Alain Ducasse, Pierre Gagnaire, Joel Robuchon, Nobu, and so on. Macau, with its big-name Las Vegas hotels, also has a lot of fancy eats and famous toques. Did someone say *bon apetit?*

Legends & Landmarks

When I pick a restaurant for this category, I consider the length of time the establishment has been in operation, the quality of its food, location, and ambience.

Some places so typify what is special about Hong Kong that I consider them "don't miss" experiences. A few (such as Jumbo) are good for the family, for first-timers, or for people who want an entire experience that includes food. In fact, all of the places in this section are legends, landmarks, or both, and are worthy of a memory-making meal.

GADDI'S
The Peninsula Hotel, Salisbury Rd., Kowloon (MTR: TST)

Visitors and locals alike know Gaddi's as the best French restaurant in town, and serious foodies wouldn't consider a trip to Hong Kong complete without a visit. It's much like a private club of local and visiting professionals.

If you are looking for something special, you may want to book lunch or dinner at the chef's private table in the kitchen. You can ask the chef to create a menu for you, or you can pick from the regular menu. If the kitchen table is booked, note that some people request the kitchen menu for lunch in the restaurant. Lunch and dinner are both popular; lunch is less expensive. The house offers a set dinner menu of five courses, each with its own wine, for approximately $125 a person, an excellent value. Reservations are a must; call © 852/2366-6251.

JUMBO KINGDOM
Shum Wan, Aberdeen (no nearby MTR)

My first thought about Jumbo was that only tour groups go here, and it wasn't worth my time. It took me years to come here, and now that I've done it . . . why did I wait so long? If ever there was a fantasy place to bring your kids, this is it.

Jumbo is the most famous of the floating restaurants in Aberdeen Harbour. It is best seen at night when all the lights are aglow, but you can go for lunch and take advantage of the souvenir vendors who set up shop in junks and on the pier that provides service from Aberdeen Harbour to the floating restaurant. (More shopping is to be had when you get into the restaurant, but all the prices are marked in yen.)

The place is enormous and has a fun, almost silly atmosphere. This is not intimate dining, but if dressing up in a mandarin's outfit and having your photo taken sounds like fun to you (or your kids), this is the place. Menus feature pictures, so you just point to what you want. The food is American-style Chinese. Dinner for two with beer is about $40. For reservations, call © 852/2553-9111.

LUK YU TEAHOUSE
24 Stanley St. (MTR: Central)

It's not the teahouse of the August Moon, but Luk Yu—a landmark eatery in the center of Central—could be a movie set. Order dim sum from the menu in Chinese, and try not to take pictures, because that's what everyone else is doing. Go for an early lunch (locals eat between 1 and 4pm, so if you're there by noon, you should be able to get a table without much of a wait) or at teatime, when you can get a table easily.

Dim sum is served until 5pm. A perfect location in Central makes this a good stop for shoppers; it's halfway to Hollywood Road and not that far from the Landmark.

Do note that waiters at Luk Yu make it a policy to be rude to Westerners unless they know you. On the other hand, it's rude for you to ask about the recent gang-land shoot-'em-up. Dim sum will run about $20 per person; full meals cost more. For reservations, call © **852/2523-5464.** Cash only.

Snack & Shop

It's quite easy to get a snack while shopping in Hong Kong. It's simply a question of how adventurous you are. *Dai pai dong* is the Chinese name for the street vendors who cook food from carts in street markets or on corners. Although I have pictures of my sister, the late great Dr. Debbie, eating from assorted *dai pai dong,* her advice to me on how to stay healthy has remained in the back of my head: "Always eat lunch in the best hotel in town." Hong Kong has lots of great hotels, and each has several restaurants, so you'll have no trouble following this simple advice.

Even the most expensive hotels usually have a coffee shop or a moderately priced restaurant amid their galaxy of four or five eateries. For a shopper's lunch, I'm often at one of the following.

HARBOURSIDE
InterContinental Hong Kong, 18 Salisbury Rd., Kowloon (MTR: TST)

Incredible edible buffet. If you want to order a la carte, make that clear so you are not charged for the buffet. One floor below the main lobby, the cafe is a fancy coffee shop for meals and snacks. Expect to spend about $15 per person, or you can do the buffet for about $50 per person. © **852/2721-1211.**

THE LOBBY
The Peninsula Hotel, Salisbury Rd., Kowloon (MTR: TST)

The Pen is known for its other famous eateries (Felix, Gaddi's, and lunch at the chef's table in the kitchens), but The Lobby is a great place for a light bite and an opportunity to "do" the

Pen, even on a budget. Tea is the big deal, and people do wait in line. I often come here for dinner; spaghetti or a salad is about $20. Easy, well-priced, and near the Nathan Road shopping district. © 852/2920-2888.

SHOPPING HONG KONG

Shopping Hours

Generally, shops open late morning and stay open until late in the evening. Most specialty stores open at 10am and close at 6:30pm. However, these are just guidelines. Some stores open whenever they feel like it. Central businesses tend to open later than those in Kowloon.

For the most part, stores close at 6:30pm in Central, 7:30pm in Tsim Sha Tsui, and 9pm on Nathan Road in Yau Ma Tei and in Mong Kok. In all honesty, I've been in the stores on Granville Road until 11pm at night. I think that as long as traffic keeps up, the stores are willing to stay open.

Mall stores are open during regular business hours on Sunday. Most shops in the main shopping areas of Tsim Sha Tsui and Causeway Bay are open daily. Those in Central close on Sunday.

Many shops close on major public holidays. Everything closes on Chinese New Year; some stores are closed for 2 days, others for 2 weeks. Do not plan to be in Hong Kong and do any shopping at this time.

Store hours are affected by the following public holidays:

- January 1 (New Year's Day)
- January/February (Chinese New Year)
- March/April (Good Friday, Easter Sunday and Monday)
- June (Dragon Boat Festival)
- August 25 (Liberation Day)
- December 25 (Christmas) and December 26 (Boxing Day)

On public holidays, banks and offices close, and shops may close as well. Factory outlets will definitely not be open. Many holiday dates change from year to year. For specific dates, contact the HKTA (p. 52) before you plan your trip.

If you are planning a tour of the factory outlets, remember that lunch hour can fall anywhere between noon and 2pm, although 1 to 2pm is most common. Outlet shops will close for 1 hour, along with the factory. Because of this practice, you might as well plan to have lunch then, too.

Department store hours differ from store to store. The larger ones, like Lane Crawford and Chinese Arts & Crafts, maintain regular business hours: 10am to 5pm. The Japanese department stores in Causeway Bay open between 10 and 10:30am and close between 9 and 9:30pm. They're all closed on different days one day of the week, however, which can be confusing. Don't assume because one department store is closed that they all are.

Market hours are pretty standard. Only food markets (sometimes called "wet markets") open very early in the morning. Don't bother arriving in Stanley before 9am. Even 9:30am is slow; many vendors are still opening up. The Jade Market opens at 10am every day, including Sunday, and closes around 3pm. The weekend outdoor market on Reclamation Street is a local affair, so it opens earlier; plenty is going on at 9am.

Christmas in Hong Kong

Even when I'm in Hong Kong in July, I start thinking about Christmas. Christmas decorations go up in Kowloon (it's hard to spot the neon amid all the neon) in mid-November, when stores begin their Christmas promotions.

Christmas permeates the air; even street markets sell decorations—plastic wreaths, silk flowers, ornaments, and more. You'll also be thrilled to find Victorian-style embroidered tree ornaments in stores in Hong Kong.

Among the best deals in town at this time of year is the free shipping many department stores offer. It covers shipping to the United Kingdom or to anyplace in the world, depending on the store, for purchases that cost more than a certain amount.

Better yet, Hong Kong is the perfect place to load up on inexpensive presents. What can you find at home that's fabulous for less than $1? Not much! Go to the Jade Market and you'll find plenty.

New Year in Hong Kong

I don't mean Western New Year's; I mean Chinese New Year, and when it comes, you may go crazy if you want to shop. Expect most stores to be closed a minimum of 2 to 3 days, but some stores close for weeks. The date of the new year varies because it is based on a lunar calendar; the danger zone falls somewhere between the end of January and mid-February. In 2008, the big day is February 10; in 2009, it's January 26.

Hong Kong on Sale

The sales in Hong Kong are the best time to get regular retail merchandise—and designer brands—at the lowest prices. The real bargains in Hong Kong are not in retail stores; the real bargains in Hong Kong may not be in perfect condition. So if you insist on brand-new, clean, undamaged goods, you should feel safe buying them on sale. If you have teens or are on a limited clothing budget, shop Hong Kong during the sale periods. Check the advertisements in the *South China Morning Post* for special sale announcements.

Fakes for Sale

New York's streets teem with vendors selling faux Chanel earrings, T-shirts, and scarves and the worst-made Goyard fakes you have ever seen. These goods are easy to differentiate from the real thing and really don't compete with them anyway because they are so ugly.

While Hong Kong doesn't have a lot of fake Chanel on the streets (it's hidden), there are many items for sale— especially at markets—that appear to be real. But they aren't.

They usually hold up in the same way you'd expect a fake to hold up—not well. But for trendy items, you could be very impressed with these look-alikes.

I once bought a canvas-and-leather book bag from a street market for the high (for Hong Kong) price of $20. It had a big, perfect Gap label on the front. It fell apart 36 hours later. Both buckles and one leather strap broke so quickly (in three different incidents) that I am convinced that real Gap labels were sewn onto shoddy canvas bags. Let the buyer beware.

In an attempt to make China perfect for the Olympics, the government has ensured that many sources for fakes are drying up. It's pretty much business as usual in Shenzhen (see p. 146), but some things appear to be totally cleaned up.

Fakes don't just apply to handbags or DVDs. I swear I just paid a lot of money for a prescription drug that is made of chalk and simply doesn't work.

Remember that when you buy fake merchandise, the person who gets cheated is you.

SHOPPING NEIGHBORHOODS

The island of Hong Kong (Central) and Kowloon (TST), on the Kowloon Peninsula, are the most popular areas and the two basic shopping neighborhoods.

Just because they are the best-known and the handiest areas doesn't mean you should stop learning your neighborhoods. I will send you everywhere, from TST East to the New Territories; I'll also tell you how to reach some factory districts and a lot of other neighborhoods.

The more I visit Hong Kong, the more comfortable I am with getting away from tourists and the commercial main streets of Central and Kowloon. I define a successful visit to Hong Kong as one in which I've spent at least a little bit of time in the real-people neighborhoods. But I also have to admit that during my last trip to Hong Kong, with only 4 full days in town, anything in an out-of-the-way neighborhood quickly disappeared from my must-do list.

Getting Around the Neighborhoods

The MTR will get you almost everywhere, or at least into the main neighborhoods and basic shopping areas. Unless I specifically note otherwise in an address, the MTR stop at Central gets you to most locations in Hong Kong; use the MTR stop at Tsim Sha Tsui (TST) for most shopping in Kowloon.

Excellent bus and ferry service goes to outlying islands where you can roam around upon arrival. Getting to specific addresses in the New Territories can be difficult without a car; consider hiring a taxi or a car (with driver) from your hotel.

If your time is limited and you want to see a lot, a car and driver is an economical luxury. The price ranges from $250 to $350 per day. If you can't afford the whole day, hire the car and driver until lunch, and finish on foot. The time you'll save with a chauffeur will permit you to get to a number of out-of-the-way neighborhoods and enhance your enjoyment of the shopping time you have.

A Word About Addresses

An address is most often the name of the building and not the street address. I want to stress that when street addresses are written out, they may designate a specific door or portion of a building. So you may see different addresses for the same building, like the **Landmark, Swire House,** or **Prince's Building.** Don't assume it's an error. Simply check your trusty map. If an office building takes up a city block, as many do, shops can list different street addresses on all four sides!

The same is true when cruising the boutiques in a shopping center like the **Landmark:** Often the shop's address will simply be the name of the building. The easiest way to find what you're looking for is to check the directory on the main floor of the mall.

Hong Kong Island Neighborhoods

The island of Hong Kong makes up only a portion of what most tourists refer to as Hong Kong. While government, business, and "downtown" functions take place on the island, much of the local population lives elsewhere in neighborhoods that do not seriously feature shopping and, therefore, do not appear in these pages.

A ridge of hills topped by the famous Peak divides the island. The rich and famous live in villas lining the road to the Peak; the almost rich and famous (as well as the upper-middle class) live in what's called the "Mid-Levels," the area of the hills above Central but below the Peak.

To get to most other portions of the island, you can either go through a tunnel under the hills toward Aberdeen, or take the tram or MTR along the shoreline to the housing estates, where middle-class people live in housing blocks and "mansion" or "estate" developments.

CENTRAL

Central is the part of Hong Kong that refers to what we used to call "downtown" when I was growing up. It's the main business and shopping part of town, and the core of Hong Kong Island.

Shopping in Central is mostly Westernized and even glitzy. But wait, you round a corner and, *voilà*—it's the **Lanes**: real people galore. You walk up Pottinger to Hollywood Road, and, again—the real thing. Central seems to house the ridiculous and the sublime within the same city block; it's your opportunity to mix Westernized shopping with Eastern lifestyles. Call it China Lite.

The **Landmark** (see map on p. 77), a shopping mall of mythic proportions, houses five floors of shopping, including stores in the basement, at street level, on a mezzanine, and in two towers that rise above the main floors. European designers have their shops here or across the street in **Swire House**, the **Prince's Building**, or the **Mandarin Oriental Hotel**. Giorgio Armani, across the street from the **Landmark,** is a knockout and brings a good bit of energy to this corner of Central.

The **Lanes** are two little alleys (Li Yuen West and Li Yuen East; see map) half a block apart and teeming with people and products. They are lined with storefronts and filled with stalls, so you have to look behind the stalls and poke into nooks and crannies to get the full flavor. One lane specializes in handbags (mostly imitations of famous brands and styles, few of good quality), the other, underwear.

The **Pedder Building** (p. 120) is conveniently located across the street from the Landmark and in every shopper's direct path. There are a handful of factory outlets and jobbers here, as well as the tony **Blanc de Chine. Shanghai Tang** is also here, alongside the outlet building: This is the single best stop if you need a pick-me-up and a piece of oh-wow retailing.

WESTERN

The Western District is adjacent to Central and can be reached on foot or by MTR. Take the MTR to Sheung Wan to get to central Western. Despite the decidedly touristy flavor in the renovation of **Western Market,** the Western District is a lot more Chinese, in both appearance and attitude, than Central. This is the district to see before it is ruined; as modernization continues, Western in its current form will disappear within the next few years.

Going west from Central, the area begins shortly after **Central Market,** at Possession Street, and continues to Kennedy Town, where most of the local working people live. Western includes the famous **Man Wa Lane,** where you can purchase your own personalized chop (p. 100), the **Shun Tak Centre** (where you take the ferry to Macau), and **Bonham Strand East,** where you'll find scores of Chinese herbalists. The farther west you wander, the more exotic the area becomes.

My best way of "doing" Western is to combine it with a trip to Hollywood Road; if you walk downhill from Hollywood Road, you'll end up in Western. Then you can take in

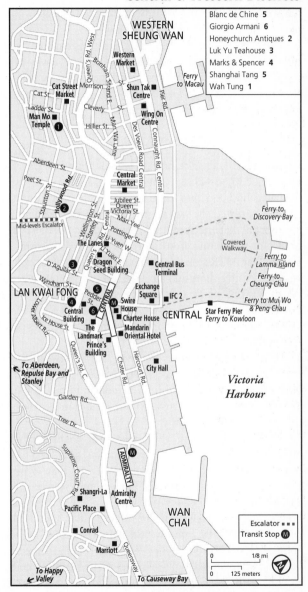

Central & Western Districts

Blanc de Chine **5**
Giorgio Armani **6**
Honeychurch Antiques **2**
Luk Yu Teahouse **3**
Marks & Spencer **4**
Shanghai Tang **5**
Wah Tung **1**

WESTERN
SHEUNG WAN

Western
Market

Ferry
to Macau

Shun Tak
Centre

Wing On
Centre

Cat Street
Market

Cat St.

Ladder St.

Man Mo
Temple ❶

Queen's Rd. West

Bonham Strand W.

Morrison

Cleverly

St.

Hillier St.

Man Wa Lane

Des Voeux Road Central

Connaught Rd. Central

Pier Rd.

Aberdeen St.

Peel St.

Staunton St.

Hollywood Rd.

Central
Market

Ferry to
Discovery Bay

Jubilee St.

Queen
Victoria St.

Man Yee

Pottinger St.

Mid-levels Escalator

❷

The Lanes

Li Yuen W.

Li Yuen E.

Wellington St.

Stanley St.

Queen's Rd. Central

Covered
Walkway

Ferry to
Lamma Island

Ferry to
Cheung Chau

D'Aguilar St.

❸

Dragon
Seed Building

Central Bus
Terminal

Exchange
Square

IFC 2

Ferry to Mui Wo
& Peng Chau

Wyndham St.

LAN KWAI FONG

❹

Central
Building

Pedder
St.

❺

CENTRAL

Ⓜ

❻

Swire
House

Charter House

Star Ferry Pier
Ferry to Kowloon

Lower Albert Rd.

Ice House St.

The
Landmark

Mandarin
Oriental Hotel

CENTRAL

To Aberdeen,
Repulse Bay and
Stanley

Prince's
Building

City Hall

Queen's Rd. C.

Chater Rd.

Harcourt Rd.

Victoria
Harbour

Garden Rd.

Tree Dr.

Supreme Court Rd.

ADMIRALTY

Ⓜ

Shangri-La

Admiralty
Centre

Pacific Place

WAN
CHAI

Conrad

Marriott

Queensway

To Happy
Valley

To Causeway Bay

Escalator ■ ■ ■
Transit Stop Ⓜ

0   1/8 mi
0   125 meters

the **Western Market** before walking back to Central or hopping on the MTR at Shun Tak station.

One of the most interesting things about Western is the 'new' tunnel which costs more and is slightly out of the way from the Cross Harbour Tunnel but which gets those willing to spend a buck to save an hour. New hotels and retail are sprouting on the Kowloon side of this tunnel.

HOLLYWOOD ROAD

Up above Central, and technically within the Central District, Hollywood Road—Hong Kong's antiques district—is a shopping neighborhood unto itself. It isn't hard to get to, but it is not necessarily on the way to anywhere else you're going, so it's essential that you specifically plan your day or half a day to include this outing. You can reach it from the Central or Sheung Wan MTR stop. It's within walking distance if you're wearing sensible shoes and have the feet of a mountain goat; you can also tell your taxi driver *"By Fa Gai"* (meaning "white flower") and be dropped off in the core of the antiques area, in what used to be the neighborhood where the prostitutes plied their trade.

There are antiques stores elsewhere, but Hollywood Road is still a great place to get to know. The idea is to walk the 3 blocks of Hollywood Road from Wyndham to the Man Mo Temple. Then you'll hit Cat Street and the flea market before descending into Western.

As charming as this area is, I must warn you upfront that much of what is in these shops is imitation, or at least faux. If you are looking to do anything more serious than browse, I suggest you make your first stop **Honeychurch Antiques** (no. 29). Expatriate American owners Glenn and Lucille Vessa are bright, honest, and always willing to help. They know who's who and what's what in their world of dealers and will tell you about their stock and everyone else's. Their look is an eclectic blend of antiques from around the Orient (kind of country chinoiserie); however, they know who has the more formal pieces. In fact, they know who has everything. If you are spending big bucks, it is imperative that you buy from a reputable shop. Ask Glenn and Lucille for guidance.

But wait! **Wah Tung,** the porcelain shop, has a showroom on Hollywood Road (no. 148), and although I think it is overpriced, there's a lot to be said for convenience. The entrance is small and not very warm; you may be put off. Go upstairs.

WAN CHAI

Wan Chai these days means "Convention Center," but it is also a showcase for the cutting-edge set. The area that was once known as the home of Susie Wong and then better known for the Hyatt hotel is now getting trendy. Start with **Fine Man,** 123 Wan Chai Rd., and work your way to **Conrad,** 288 Wan Chai Rd. Stores are also popping up on Hennessy Road, in the Wan Chai district but not on Wan Chai Road.

Note that if you are at a convention in the Convention Center, you have a lot of walking to do to get to any decent shopping. The **Chinese Arts & Crafts** store, China Resources Building, 26 Harbour Rd. (© 2827-852/6667), is nearest; everything else is a big schlep.

The Star Ferry provides direct access from Kowloon Peninsula: It travels from Tsim Sha Tsui to Wan Chai Pier. Old Wan Chai has been pushed back from the waterfront and will continue to be developed. If you want to see some original architecture and shops, prowl Queen's Road East and the lanes connecting it to Johnston Road. Shopping in the convention center is decidedly unexciting, but if you move on to the Hopewell Building, there is a fabulous **street market** on nearby Fenwick Street—no other tourists in sight, and a great place for taking pictures.

CAUSEWAY BAY

This area is so crowded, so fast-paced, so hip, and so much fun that I feel 20 years younger when I wander the streets wondering why I've been such a stick-in-the-mud to stay in more established areas. Causeway Bay features one deluxe hotel (the **Excelsior**) and many tourist package–style hotels. It has several fancy Western malls, a street of outlet stores (Lee Gardens Rd.), some curving little alleys and streets filled with funk and glory, and countless shoppers, pushing their way to low-priced copies of the latest fashions.

This area is far funkier than Central, but it does have **Chanel** and a branch of every other designer, if that's your thing. The MTR stop is Causeway Bay. Note that Causeway Bay is directly across the bay from Tsim Sha Tsui East, so getting through the Cross Harbour Tunnel is a tad easier.

Why do I love Causeway Bay?

- Funky street shopping, with a nod toward fashion, just-starting-out talent, and Japanese designers.
- Jardine's Bazaar, a small warren of street stalls.
- Fashion Walk, a gathering of designer and up-and-coming designer shops in three adjoining buildings.
- Times Square, a relatively new giant mall that has taken the town by storm because it has four floors of local and Western brands. My favorite store there is City Super.
- The Japanese department stores, which are less and less Japanese and more and more global. The two best are **Sogo** and **Mitsokoshi. Seibu,** the Bergdorf Goodman of Japanese department stores, is in the Pacific Place mall.

AP LEI CHAU

Some people think that this neighborhood is part of Aberdeen, but it is a place unto itself, connected to Aberdeen by a bridge. One high-rise building is home to many outlets, including the **Joyce Warehouse** (closed Mon) and the **Lane Crawford Warehouse.** For more furniture, try **Beijing Antiques Shop,** on the 20th floor, which has the kind of furniture many people cross into China to buy; it looks antique but is mostly refinished. Nearby is a Prada outlet, **Space.**

This is mostly a residential area, popular for its water views. Take a taxi and either have the driver wait or get the number of a taxi company so you can arrange a pickup.

Causeway Bay

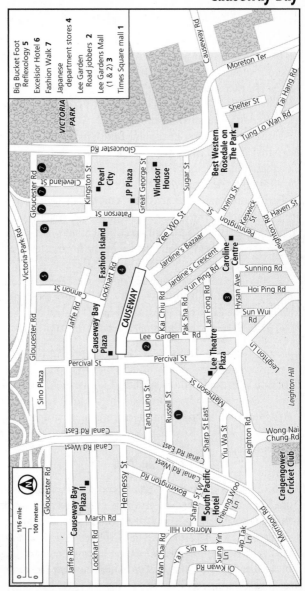

Big Bucket Foot Reflexology **5**
Excelsior Hotel **6**
Fashion Walk **7**
Japanese department stores **4**
Lee Garden Road jobbers **2**
Lee Gardens Mall (1 & 2) **3**
Times Square mall **1**

STANLEY/REPULSE BAY/OCEAN PARK

It seems to be very "in" to bash **Stanley Market** and say it isn't up to the old standards. I have a love-hate relationship with this tourist trap, which sits in the heart of downtown Stanley (no MTR; take a taxi or bus no. 6). Last trip, I loathed it. I actually had tears streaming down my face. It's very touristy, and I couldn't find anything to buy.

However, when I spoke to some British first-timers a week later, they couldn't stop raving about Stanley. And my Hong Kong shopping friends still claim to find bargains here. Maybe it's a matter of perspective.

Part of the pleasure of a visit to Stanley is the drive across the island, especially the view as you go around some of those coastal curves. If you agree with me about Stanley, simply get back in the taxi, go to Repulse Bay, shop the snazzy stores, eat lunch, and then return to Hong Kong proper.

Stanley is exceedingly crowded on the weekends, delightfully quiet midweek. Note that Stanley is not one of those markets where the early bird gets the worm. The early bird gets to sit and sulk until the shops open around 9:30am.

Kowloon Neighborhoods

Kowloon is packed with shops, hotels, excitement, and bargains. You can shop its more than 10 sq. km (4 sq. miles) for days and still feel that you haven't even made a dent. Like Hong Kong Island, Kowloon is the sum of many distinct neighborhoods.

TSIM SHA TSUI

The tip of Kowloon Peninsula consists of two neighborhoods: Tsim Sha Tsui and Tsim Sha Tsui East. It is home to most of Hong Kong's fine hotels and to Kowloon's serious tourist shopping. The MTR's Tsim Sha Tsui (TST) station is in the heart of things. Use the Jordan Road station when you're traveling a bit farther into Kowloon and working your way out of the tourist neighborhoods.

The Kowloon Peninsula

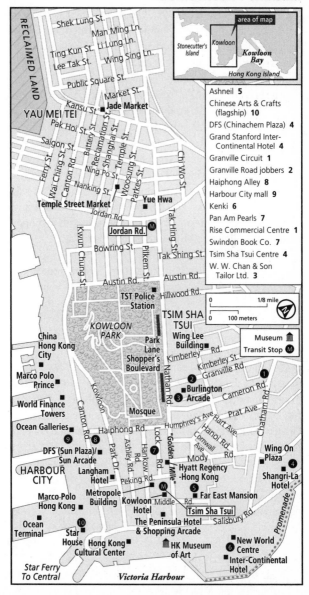

Shek Lung St.
Man Ming Ln.
Ting Kun St. Li Lung Ln.
Lee Tak St. Wing Sing Ln.
RECLAIMED LAND
Public Square St.
Market St.
Kansu St. Jade Market
YAU MEI TEI
Pak Hoi St.
Saigon St.
Ferry
Battery St.
Reclamation St.
Shanghai St.
Temple St.
Wai Ching St.
Canton Rd.
Ning Po St.
Woosung St.
Nanking St.
Parkes St.
Temple Street Market
Yue Wha
Jordan Rd.
Chi Wo St.
Tak Hing St.
Jordan Rd. M
Kwun Chung Rd.
Bowring St.
Pilkem St.
Tak Shing St.
Austin Rd.
Austin Rd.
Hillwood Rd.
TST Police Station
TSIM SHA TSUI
KOWLOON PARK
Park Lane Shopper's Boulevard
Wing Lee Building
Kimberley Rd.
Kimberley St.
Granville Rd.
China Hong Kong City
Nathan Rd.
Burlington Arcade
Cameron Rd.
Chatham Rd.
Marco Polo Prince
World Finance Towers
Kowloon
Mosque
Humphrey's Ave
Hart Ave.
Prat Ave.
Ocean Galleries
Haiphong Rd.
Hanoi Rd.
Cornwall Ave.
Wing On Plaza
DFS (Sun Plaza)/ Sun Arcade
Canton Rd.
Park Dr.
Ashley Rd.
Harkow Rd.
Lock Rd.
Golden Mile
Mody Rd.
Hyatt Regency -Hong Kong
Shangri-La Hotel
HARBOUR CITY
Langham Hotel
Peking Rd.
Metropole Building
Kowloon Hotel
Middle Rd.
M
Far East Mansion
Marco Polo Hong Kong
Ocean Terminal
Star House
Hong Kong Cultural Center
The Peninsula Hotel & Shopping Arcade
Tsim Sha Tsui
Salisbury Rd.
HK Museum of Art
New World Centre
Inter-Continental Hotel
Promenade
Star Ferry To Central
Victoria Harbour

area of map
Stonecutter's Island Kowloon
Kowloon Bay
Hong Kong Island

Ashneil **5**
Chinese Arts & Crafts (flagship) **10**
DFS (Chinachem Plaza) **4**
Grand Stanford Inter-Continental Hotel **4**
Granville Circuit **1**
Granville Road jobbers **2**
Haiphong Alley **8**
Harbour City mall **9**
Kenki **6**
Pan Am Pearls **7**
Rise Commercial Centre **1**
Swindon Book Co. **7**
Tsim Sha Tsui Centre **4**
W. W. Chan & Son Tailor Ltd. **3**

0   1/8 mile
0   100 meters

Museum 🏛
Transit Stop Ⓜ

At the very tip of Tsim Sha Tsui are the Star Ferry Terminal and the Harbour City Complex. This western harborfront includes Ocean Terminal, Ocean Galleries, Ocean Centre, the Marco Polo Gateway Hotel, the Marco Polo Hong Kong Hotel, and the Marco Polo Prince Hotel.

The heart of Tsim Sha Tsui is **Nathan Road,** Kowloon's main shopping drag; it's the equivalent of London's Oxford Street. Nathan Road stretches from the waterfront for quite some distance and works its way into the "real people" part of Kowloon in no time at all. The most concentrated shopping is in the area called the **Golden Mile,** which begins on Nathan Road perpendicular to Salisbury Road. Both sides of this busy street are jampacked with stores, arcades, covered alleys, and street vendors. There are also some hotels here, each with a shopping mall and enough neon to make Las Vegas blush.

If you are walking north (away from the harbor), you'll pass the Golden Mile. Then you reach a mosque on your left and then the **Park Lane Shopper's Boulevard,** also on your left. To your right, across the street from the Park Lane, is **Burlington Arcade.** The next street on your right is **Granville Road,** which was once famous for its jobbers, although the bargain ops on this street have been going downhill.

Nathan Road is the core of Kowloon, but my favorite part of Tsim Sha Tsui is a bit off the beaten path—though directly in sight. In the Golden Mile section of Tsim Sha Tsui, two streets run parallel to Nathan Road and are centered between the Golden Mile and Ocean Terminal: Hankow Road and **Haiphong Road.** They have some outlets, some jobbers, and several stores that sell DVDs and legal VCDs (video compact discs). Also check out Lock Road, which runs perpendicular to these streets. Once you become an old China hand, you'll note that prices on Nathan Road are for tourists, and you may disdain the whole Golden Mile area. On the other hand, so much of Lock Road and the area where the Hyatt Hotel once stood has been destroyed that the new tenants may be fun.

Near Jordan Road, the atmosphere is more real. Be sure to get to the **Temple Street Market** (p. 130). And you can't miss the **Jade Market.** If you have a true spirit of shopping and adventure, you'll also make sure you get to Fa Yuen Street (see below).

HARBOUR CITY

Although it's technically part of Tsim Sha Tsui, I count the western portion of Kowloon as a separate neighborhood because it is basically one giant shopping mall, in the form of several huge interconnected malls. I call the whole entire stretch of Canton Road—from the Star Ferry to China Hong Kong City—Harbour City. This definition includes the buildings across the street on Canton Road, like **Silvercord** and the **Sun Plaza Arcade.**

The denser shopping is on the Ocean Terminal side, where (walking away from the Star Ferry) the buildings, in order, are: **Star House, Ocean Terminal, Ocean Galleries, Ocean Centre, Marco Polo Prince Hotel,** and **China Hong Kong City,** which is a mall-and-towers complex and ferry terminal. This entire stretch of shopping buildings also includes office space and residential towers, as well as some of the well-known tourist hotels in this area: Marco Polo Gateway, Marco Polo Hong Kong Hotel, and Marco Polo Prince Hotel.

TSIM SHA TSUI EAST

If you have Hong Kong Harbour at your back, Ocean Terminal to your left, and the InterContinental to your right, you're looking at the heart of Kowloon, or Tsim Sha Tsui. As the Kowloon peninsula curves around the harbor and the land juts away from Kowloon and the InterContinental, the area just east of Tsim Sha Tsui but before Hung Hom and the old airport is known as Tsim Sha Tsui East. Because it's waterfront property and just about on top of the KCR train station to China, it has a string of luxury hotels and a few shops.

Tsim Sha Tsui East fascinates me; I see it as a miniature version of greater Hong Kong. You can find almost everything you need right here. Mobbed on weekends by local shoppers, its various buildings include **Auto Plaza, Houston Centre,** and the enclosed mall itself, **Tsim Sha Tsui Centre.** There is street-level shopping all along Mody Road, in the various buildings, in the mall, and at street level of the buildings behind the Great Stafford and Nikko hotels. There is also some shopping in each hotel. My favorite store in this area is **DFS**, which has terrific souvenir, food, and traditional medicine departments.

YAU MA TEI

The most famous shopping site in the area is the well-known **Jade Market** at Kansu and Battery streets; look for the overpass of the highway, and you'll spot the market right below it. The experience is just short of mind-boggling. Here you can shop from 10am until 2:30pm, going from stall to stall, negotiating for all the jade (p. 127) that you might fancy. There are two tents filled with vendors. You'll never be strong enough to do both tents.

Alongside the Jade Market, on Shanghai Street, is a "wet market"—a real live Chinese **green market** (farmers market) worthy of exploration with or without a camera. As the street stretches to the south, it has some old-fashioned paper stores.

At night you will want to visit the **Temple Street Market,** also in this district but not as far north as the Jade Market. As you push your way through the shoulder-to-shoulder crowds, you can buy from the carts, have your fortune told, or enjoy an open-air meal.

HUNG HOM

Home of Hong Kong's original outlets, this part of town will disappear once the real estate here goes up in value, due to the change in airports, scarcity of land, and opening of the new arts and culture center. Already the factory outlets here have gone downhill, and shopping visitors no longer feel compelled to visit. In fact, factories have already moved out, and the outlet scene is bad. If you have tons of time on your hands, maybe check it out. Most agree with me, though: Don't waste your time checking this out unless you are doing a dissertation on Hong Kong real estate.

The most famous address in Hung Hom is **Kaiser Estates,** an industrial development of factories and factory-outlet stores with a few fancy outlets—when you look at **JBH/Fashions of Seventh Avenue,** you'll be seeing a boutique as smart as anything in Central.

PRINCE EDWARD & FA YUEN

Even though Fa Yuen is just a street and not a true neighborhood, it's enough of an event that it should be considered a separate destination. It's my favorite new neighborhood in Hong Kong. On a recent visit, I bought so much I truly could not fit the stairwell to the MTR station.

In a nutshell, Fa Yuen is the newer version of Granville Road. It's farther "uptown," deeper into the real Hong Kong, and a good bit cheaper than Granville Road, while offering much the same style of shopping—storefront after storefront of racks and bins filled with no-name and designer clothing for as little as $10 an item. Silk blouses cost a tad more.

Fa Yuen has been blossoming for several years now; no doubt it will become too commercial, and a new place will sprout. Until then, what are you waiting for? Bring plenty of cash because most of these stores do not take plastic. Consider bringing airline wheels—or a donkey. It is time to shop 'til you drop, Hong Kong style.

If you need a jumping-off place, head for **Come True,** 146 Fa Yuen St. Then there's **Kwong Shui Hong,** 190 Fa Yuen St. These 2 blocks are dense with great stores that sell overruns (mostly clothes) from the nearby factories; just walk from one to the next. They truly all look alike, but you'll be getting used to this kind of thing by now. Besides, after you've done Granville Road, this will come naturally to you.

From here, you can wander over to the nearby **Ladies' Market** (see below). It's 2 blocks away on Tung Choi Street and opens around 4pm. Don't confuse these two shopping venues. This Ladies' Market is mostly a street market with stalls on

Prince Edward, Mong Kok & Fa Yuen Street

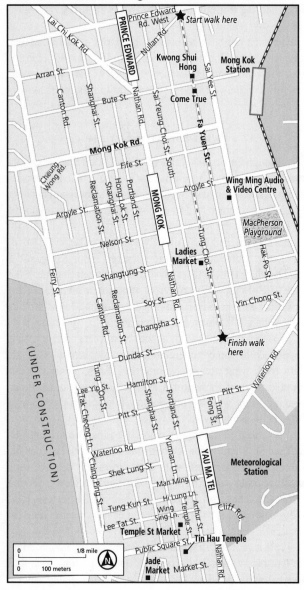

the road, while Fa Yuen Street consists of traditional retail with actual shops. Look at a map. Also note that the **Bird Market** is in this neighborhood, on Yuen Po Street. To get there, take the MTR to Prince Edward.

MONG KOK

Mong Kok is having a huge image makeover with the arrival of its first luxury hotel, the **Langham Place,** which comes complete with designer shopping mall. This is a real-people part of town and great fun—it's filled with shopping ops. There's **Mong Kok Market** at Tung Choi Street, an afternoon market that is also called the **Ladies' Market** (see map). If you have evening plans and can't make it to the **Temple Street Market,** then Mong Kok is the afternoon market you should plan to visit. In addition to stands selling alarm clocks that cluck, blaring Canto-pop, and fake designer scarves, you'll find everything else you could ever need.

To get there: Depart the MTR at Mong Kok station and find Hong Lok Street, which is more of an alley, on the south side of Argyle Street. It's 2 blocks west of Nathan Road (if your back is to the harbor, then west is to your left).

Chapter Five

....

HONG KONG RESOURCES A TO Z

ANTIQUES

....

Hong Kong is home to many places where you can buy art and antiques. Two important things to remember:

- Internationally famous dealers do business in London, New York, Tokyo, Vancouver, Taipei, Brussels, and other places besides Hong Kong; buy according to reputation and trust, not location.
- The number of fakes and frauds in the art business is infamous and truly frightening, especially in Hong Kong.

Buy what you know; if you don't know much, buy what you love, regardless of its real value. Bring your own expert if you are truly serious, or hire one in Hong Kong. If you are considering something pricey, get a second opinion. Many dealers on Hollywood Road will appraise an item from another source for a flat fee.

Bear in mind that the truly wonderful pieces are usually put away. Most dealers have warehouses or back rooms where they keep their best wares; many are open only by appointment.

ARCH ANGEL
53-55 Hollywood Rd., Central (MTR: Central).

I can't tell you how many personal recommendations I have received from readers who love this source. Prices are high, but the name can be trusted. Open daily for furniture, statuary, and tabletop items. A second shop sells art.

HONEYCHURCH ANTIQUES
29 Hollywood Rd. (MTR: Central).

Honeychurch Antiques has been my home base on Hollywood Road since the beginning of the *Born to Shop* series. I know you will be well taken care of by American expat owners Glenn and Lucille Vessa. They have held court for over 25 years and know everything and everyone; stop by and ask whatever pops into your mind . . . but don't ask if you can call home.

The store carries a wide variety of merchandise. The look is sort of Oriental Country. There are goods from Japan and other exotic locations besides basic Chinese antiques. Try both floors in the main shop and a warehouse floor next door (ask to be taken over), with larger pieces of furniture and a few other goodies. Yes, they have blue-and-white; yes, they'll let you smell the opium pipes. If you ask nicely, they will even let you use the bathroom.

P.C. LU & SONS LTD.
Ocean Terminal, Harbour City, the Silk Road, Canton Rd., Kowloon (MTR: TST).

A fine antiques dealer with showrooms in the major hotels, P. C. Lu is owned by a family that has been in the business for four generations. It's one of the finest resources for antique ivory and jade, porcelain, and decorative work. The three sons who run the business work closely together. Stop in at any of the galleries and browse, or get a look when you're prowling the Silk Road.

ARTS & CRAFTS

....

The Chinese look hasn't been so fashionable in years, certainly not since The Beatles took to wearing Mao jackets. Now everything's coming up ethnic so Chinese classics are more chic than ever. You can buy them in markets, at souvenir shops, and at **Chinese Arts & Crafts** (p. 105).

KENKI
Shop 126 & 127, Basement 1, New World Center, 20 Salisbury Rd., Kowloon (MTR: TST).

This store has a few branches around town—they differ enormously so I try to visit as many as possible. I always start at the mall adjacent to the InterContinental Hotel because two different branches are actually there. Hmmm, technically speaking, the **smaller shop** (© 852/2368-0921) is shop #L055 under the InterConti. For a store in Central, on Victoria Island, head to Pottinger House, 24 Pottinger Street, Central © 852/2523-9993.

Best Buys: Kenki sells embroidered shirts and blouses, reversible silk-to-velvet or cotton and silk Chinese coolie shirts, brocade vests with and without fur—I'd call it the poor man's Shanghai Tang. Prices are excellent—about $40 for a shirt, $100 for an elaborately embroidered jacket.

The website will give you addresses and maps and tell you all about the firm. © **2367-8908.** www.kenki.cc.

RIBBON EMPORIUM
33A Haiphong Rd., Kowloon (MTR: TST), and other locations.

I'm not sure which is funnier, the name of the store or my calling it a resource for arts and crafts . . . or the fact that some of these stores are in the process of changing their names, which is eternally confusing. Never mind. You'll recognize the store immediately. It's what many people would call a jobber and, despite the name, does not sell ribbon. But it does sell many arts and crafts items—from clothes to handbags to zip sacs—at unbeatable low prices. There are heaps of stuff everywhere. Not all of the stores are the same; there are several branches around town.

X-Quisit
Shop L141, Mall Place, InterContinental Hotel, Salisbury Rd., Kowloon (MTR: TST).

This store is behind the hotel's grand staircase and may seem to be hiding from you. It also seems to have several names in the front window. The selection of crafted goods, from jewelry to notebooks to hostess gifts to robes, is very chic and very expensive. This is the kind of place that should be your first stop: You stare at and touch everything and then sigh.

BATH & BEAUTY

See the "Spas" section (p. 137) for more information, and remember that this is a city where the InterContinental Hotel has a 24-hour "bath butler"—all sorts of beauty products for the tub (and shower) are readily available. For brands you may not be familiar with, high-tail it to any of the big malls. For color cosmetics, see page 101.

I am quite fond of Japanese bath salts. You can buy them in any drug- or grocery store and can tell the scent by the pictures—since the package is entirely in Japanese; I buy mine at City Super (p. 112).

Aesop
52-60 Lyndhurst Terrace, Central (MTR: Central).

This Australian brand of skin care is an excellent line of all-natural products. Unfortunately for travelers, almost everything is packaged in glass, which makes items heavier. You can buy this product in the U.S., but the store is sensational to look at, and this brand is very much in keeping with the new Pacific Rim. They open at 11am daily. © 852/2544-4489.

HARVEY NICHOLS
The Landmark Mall, 15 Queen's Rd., Central (MTR: Central).

Although listed elsewhere in this book (p. 94), Harvey Nicks is great when it comes to cult beauty brands. © 852/3695-3388. www.harveynichols.com.

JURLIQUE
Landmark Atrium, 16 Des Voeux Rd. (MTR: Central); Times Square mall (MTR: Causeway Bay).

Say "Jur-*leak*," then celebrate Australia and this terrific brand. Lavender hand cream is the most famous of Jurlique's numerous products. I fly with Herbal Recovery Mist in my purse, and I like the silk dust (instead of powder) for really sweaty summer days. The line is also sold at Faces, the beauty portion of Lane Crawford in Ocean Terminal, Kowloon. Prices may be lower in the U.S., but the line is not easy to find there.

LUSH
Shop 40, Festival Walk (MTR: Causeway Bay); Shop 3315, Harbour City (MTR: TST); Hong Kong International Airport, arrivals hall.

You can almost smell a Lush shop before you see it; asthmatics need not apply. Despite the high prices, the British firm (which is spreading through the U.S.) is onto something charming. The deli-counter environment features beauty and bath products, soaps that are sliced like deli cheeses, and bath bombs as large as tennis balls, ready to lob into a hot tub. The concepts and scents are the same throughout the world, but ingredients may be different in some international stores.

MGA
Lane Crawford Pacific Place, 88 Queensway (MTR: Admiralty).

The letters stand for Men's Grooming Area, and this is one of the newest trends to hit town—products and grooming just for guys. Shop for fragrance, skin care, and hair-grooming supplies. © 852/2118-3333. www.lanecrawford.com.

BOOKS

Because English is still used as a second language in Hong Kong, it isn't hard to find books in English. True, they are pricey, but not as expensive as in other cities in China.

COSMOS
96 Nathan Rd., Kowloon (MTR: TST).

I stop in this bookstore because it is at the corner of Nathan and Granville roads, where I shop in the bins for closeouts. English-language books and stationery supplies are downstairs.

DYMOCKS
IFC mall (MTR: Central).

I have good news and bad news here. Since the Star Ferry terminal has moved, my favorite branch of Dymocks is now gone. But plenty of branches of this famous bookstore still exist; about half of the chain's stores are in areas where tourists will shop and the others are farther out where locals live. You'll find local guidebooks, cultural information, and new releases as well as fiction by author, international magazines, some stationery items, and plenty of nonfiction in English. Other locations include Peak Galleria, Prince's Building, and Harbour Centre. © 852/2117-0360. www.dymocks.com.hk.

PAGEONE THE BOOKSHOP
Lower level, Times Square mall, 1 Matheson St., Causeway Bay (MTR: Causeway Bay).

This is a firm based in Singapore with stores dotted around Southeast Asia. Branches of this chain are often in malls alongside the grocery store City Super. Books are in Chinese and in English, and the magazine selection is huge. Part of the house specialty is art and design. They stock a few nonbook items; the trophy of one of my sprees was an eight-lens camera for $50. They carry office supplies, paper goods, and novelty items, too. Sometimes they host author events in English. Other stores around town are in malls such as Festival Walk, Harbour City, and Century Square. © 852/ 2506-0381. www.pageonegroup.com.

SWINDON BOOK CO. LTD.
13-15 Lock Rd. (behind the Peninsula Hotel), Tsim Sha Tsui, Kowloon (MTR: TST).

Although this medium-size store carries everything, the most impressive range is the selection of art books and books on Chinese culture.

CAMERAS

Forget it. If you're talking serious money, buy at home. And for heaven's sake, avoid those guys on Nathan Road.

If you're talking inexpensive, look around but don't get suckered. And please remember this little tale: I decided I needed a credit card–size digital camera and tried to buy one for $59 on my flight from Hong Kong to Shanghai, but they were sold out. The same camera cost $149 on the flight from Hong Kong to Paris.

CHAMPAGNE COURT
Off Granville Rd., Tsim Sha Tsui, Kowloon (MTR: TST).

This is a destination, not a single store. All of the dealers in this courtyard sell professional cameras to knowing photographers. They also carry many secondhand parts.

KING DRAGON
33 Mody Rd. (behind the Holiday Inn), Tsim Sha Tsui, Kowloon (MTR: TST).

This shop is for pros and those who know a lot about cameras. Ask for Alan.

CASHMERE

Cashmere from the Orient is not of the same quality as that which comes out of Scotland or Italy because of how the yarn is combed and milled. Meanwhile, Iranian cashmere, which is of even lower quality than Chinese, is flooding the market. Price should be related to the ply number (from 1, the lowest quality, to 4); 2 is the usual number available in Hong Kong.

You can find cashmere in many of the outlet stores in the **Pedder Building,** in several stores at the **Peninsula Hotel Shopping Arcade,** at **Stanley Market,** and at the Chinese department stores. Quality will be a big issue here—it affects the hand (feel) as well as the price. Most likely, you can get cashmere at home for prices similar to those in Hong Kong. But wait: Did I tell you about the **Tse Cashmere** outlet sale?

PEARLS AND CASHMERE
The Peninsula Hotel, Salisbury Rd., Kowloon (MTR: TST).

The selection of colors is excellent. Prices are not dirt-cheap but are competitive with low-end prices in the U.S., meaning you get more quality than usual for the price, which is close to $200 per sweater. Some sweaters cost less; the store also carries other items.

TSE CASHMERE
Peninsula Hotel Shopping Arcade, Salisbury Rd., Kowloon (MTR: TST).

Tse (say "say") is a luxury brand with expensive merchandise sold at fancy stores around the world. Once a year, usually before Christmas, an outlet sale takes place at an address announced in the *South China Post* newspaper. When I went, the floor was dirty, but the merchandise (organized by size and color) was fabulous. The staff took credit cards and spoke English. Just about everything cost less than $100. It was a heart-stopping shopping moment, especially good for those who need luxury labels in their bargains.

CDs, VCDs & DVDs

CDs and VCDs (video compact discs) are sold on the street, in the usual music stores and chains (such as HMV), and in Shenzhen.

Note that VCDs are not DVDs—DVDs are more expensive and are said to have better quality, although I have had no problem with the quality of VCDs. DVDs also hold more information, so a movie fits on one disc, as opposed to two (or more) VCDs.

The average price for a VCD in Hong Kong is HK$50 (US$7). However, when I last tested, VCDs did not play on a U.S. machine—though they do play on my U.S. laptop. Hong Kong has really cracked down on fake DVDs; most of the stores that sell low-cost movies sell them in VCD format, which is less expensive and legal. You can get a legal DVD in the U.S. for $10 to 20, so it's not worth the risk here.

CERAMICS

Chinese crafts stores carry a selection of china. And yes, assume that blue-and-white is fake unless guaranteed otherwise.

OVERJOY
Kwai Hing Industrial Building, 10-18 Chun Pin St., Block B, 1st floor, Kwai Chung, New Territories (MTR: Kwai Hing, then taxi).

Located in the heart of Hong Kong's shipping and container district, where there are a few other porcelain showrooms, Overjoy is worth the trouble. Although it's not a replacement for the lost wonders of Wah Tung (see the next listing), it is a good source. The selection includes both Western and Chinese patterns. I bought ginger jars for $5, mugs with lids for $10, and lamps for $40. The store offers international shipping (rates are posted) and free delivery to Hong Kong hotels. There is also a showroom in Wan Chai. When you are ready to leave, the staff will give you a small piece of paper asking your taxi driver (in English and Chinese) to take you to the MTR station. Taxis are readily available out front.

WAH TUNG CHINA COMPANY
Wholesale showroom: Grand Marine Industrial Building, 3 Yue Fung St., Tin Wan, Aberdeen; call ahead.

Stores: 57 Hollywood Rd. (MTR: Central); 8 Queen's Rd. E. (MTR: Admiralty).

I have bad news for old China hands: Wah Tung, which for years was fabulous, has been sold. The selection is different (the new owners are pushing "European style") and the prices much higher. I've bought tons here in the past and loved every minute of it, but I am sorry to say that I don't feel the same now. But wait! The factory will still allow tourists to shop there, and it can be a lot of fun. It's the new store on Queensway that I don't really like.

The new shop is within walking distance of the Pacific Place mall but is otherwise in the middle of nowhere Wan Chai and, to me, not worth it. A coupon in *Where* magazine gets you 15% off your purchases.

All of the retail stores have the same hours: 11am to 7pm daily. The factory is open Monday through Saturday from 9am to 5pm. Take a taxi, but call first before schlepping out there to see whether the staff is expecting customers; they seem to be directing trade to their retail stores: © 852/2873-2272.

CHOPS

In China a *chop* is a form of signature stamp on which a symbol for a person's name is carved. The chop is dipped in dry dye (not pressed onto an ink pad) and then placed on paper to create a signature stamp, much like a rubber stamp—though chops are not made of rubber.

Although chops vary in size, they are traditionally as big as a chess piece, with a square or round base. Up to four Chinese characters or three Western initials can be inscribed on the base.

Quality varies greatly, depending on the ability of the person who does the carving. We have done enough chop shopping to know that the very best place to get a chop, if you crave atmosphere, lies in **Man Wa Lane,** deep inside the Western District. It's also the worst place because it is so confusing—you may never find your way back to the proper vendor when you need to pick up your finished chop. Nevertheless, Man Wa feels very authentic, and you may enjoy the entire experience.

Every hotel has at least one gift shop that will have your chop engraved. Allow at least 24 hours. Many shops will provide 1-hour service. A variety of dealers at **Stanley Market** offer while-you-wait service.

You may buy the chop a la carte or in a set or gift box. The boxed set comes with your chop and the inkpot in a silk-covered (or faux silk) box with an adorable clasp; expect to pay about HK$100 (US$13) for a boxed set at Stanley Market.

COMPUTERS & ELECTRONICS

I am nervous about buying computers and most other electronics in Hong Kong—too much can go wrong. On the other hand, my greatest delight has been buying small DVD players to give as gifts in the U.S. They play DVDs, VCDs, and discs from all zones. Well, they play DVD-9 all over the world.

I shop for electronics at **Broadway,** a reputable chain with stores all over Hong Kong, and buy either the brands we all know or Shinco. Make sure the instructions are in English and that voltage is 110–220. You will also have to buy plugs. Another reliable chain is **Fortress,** which has stores in all trading areas. There are computer buildings, streets, and fairs (even a flea market) for locals who know what they are doing. Shop at your own risk.

BROADWAY
Times Square mall, 7th floor (MTR: Causeway Bay); 28 Soy St. (MTR: Mong Kok); and many other locations.

I've had my share of bad experiences buying electronics in Hong Kong, so it's a pleasure to find a store I can trust. This chain has locations everywhere. I won't shop anywhere else.

FORTRESS
5 Peking Rd., Kowloon (MTR: TST), and many other locations.

The other trusted name in electronics, with stores all over town. This one is behind the Pen. The downstairs (ground floor) area is smallish; go upstairs.

COSMETICS & FRAGRANCE SUPERMARKETS

The best buys in this category are noteworthy in terms of availability, not price—check out scents that have been introduced in Europe but not in the U.S. And I am not going to mention a brand just because it's new or hot in Hong Kong, such as Kiehl's (the latest thing), because you can easily get Kiehl's for less money in the U.S.

Many big-name cosmetics companies manufacture for the Far East in and around Hong Kong; often they will have a product with the same name as the one you use at home, but it will be slightly different. They may also have a product or shade that you have never heard of and will never find again anywhere else in the world.

If you just wander through any of the malls, especially **Harbour City,** you will finds tons of little shops selling brands that may interest you—a few local labels, some European brands that don't have good distribution in the U.S., and many Japanese products.

BONJOUR
Locations all over town.

This is a chain possibly devised for adolescent girls; I'm not crazy for it, but your 12-year-old might enjoy it. It's a knock-off of the SaSa concept (see below).

BOOTS
IFC mall, Central (MTR: Central).

Boots is a British chemist that sells several of its own brands of makeup and treatments, among other things. Some Watson's stores carry the line at in-store boutiques, but there is a growing trend toward free-standing stores for beauty items only (these are not Boots stores as we know them in the U.K.), with an emphasis on well-being products. The line No. 7—a riff on No. 5, as in Chanel—is an excellent color cosmetics selection at a moderate price.

SASA COSMETIC COMPANY
Locations all over town.

SaSa has emerged as one of the leading discounters in Hong Kong, with branch stores everywhere. Note that all branches are not created equal; some have more stock than others.

Many goods come directly from sources in the U.S., which makes them much cheaper locally—but not cheaper than at home, if you are American. Shop carefully. Also note that some items are closeouts and discontinued lines.

WATSON'S, THE CHEMIST
24-28 Queen's Rd. (MTR: Central), and many other locations.

There's a Watson's on almost every big, busy block and mall in Hong Kong; I stop in all of them because they're not all the same. Selected stores have a Boots department (see above). Watson's is actually a drugstore-cum-general-store that sells many things, including other lines of makeup and treatments.

DEPARTMENT STORES
....

European-Style

HARVEY NICHOLS
The Landmark, 16 Des Voeux Rd. (MTR: Central).

Just when you thought the British had left Hong Kong, London's best department store arrives at the city's fanciest mall. Harvey Nicks has a bit of a Barney's feel to it and is excellent in its selection of cult brands in fashion and makeup. The cafe is a good place for people-watching and getting your cool down pat. Part of the store's cachet is that they carry brands not found elsewhere, even by Joyce (p. 119)—such as Goyard from France.

LANE CRAWFORD
IFC2 Mall (MTR: Central); Mall at Pacific Place, 88 Queensway, Central (MTR: Admiralty); Times Square mall (MTR: Causeway Bay).

Lane Crawford is the most prestigious Western-style department store in Hong Kong. It's a jewel to those who work and live here but crave the elegance of old-world charm in a retail setting. Lane Crawford is not huge by American standards, but you'll find all the familiar top-quality brands. It is not really for tourists, but it does offer the guarantee that you are not getting fakes, seconds, or inferior merchandise. Snobs often buy their jewelry and their lifestyle here.

The newest branch, some 8,361 sq. m (90,000 sq. ft.) of razzle-dazzle, is in the IFC mall. If you stay at the Four Seasons hotel, you are practically adjacent to the IFC mall and Lane Crawford and will get to know it as a friend. Though actually, I like the outlet store (p. 109) better.

Also note that Lane Crawford is in the same retail group now as the Joyce Ma stores and City Super. Give these guys a hand—they are the best stores in town.

LCX
Ocean Terminal, Harbour City, Tsim Sha Tsui, Kowloon (MTR: TST).

The concept is one big warehouse, so it's a department store within a mall—and one that has no walls. Brands have different identity areas, clearly delineated, but you wander from one to the next as if sailing from island to island. A few of them are names you know (Gap, Banana Republic), some are names you have been dying to meet, and others are totally unknown even to the savviest shopper. The space is young and hip, but it's also interesting if you just want to see something very different from an old-fashioned department store or mall.

MARKS & SPENCER
Harbour City Ocean Galleries, 25-27 Canton Rd., Kowloon (MTR: TST); Mall at Pacific Place, 88 Queensway, Central (MTR: Admiralty); The Landmark, 16 Des Voeux Rd. (MTR: Central); Cityplaza III, 1111 King's Rd., Quarry Bay (MTR: Tai Koo).

I love M&S, but there are no great bargains here. Being in the store, especially the grocery department, is just fun. It also offers a chance to buy Western sizes and larger sizes. Need a brassiere? Need shoes? Can't get a fit elsewhere? This is your source. Just watch out for clothes marked "Asian fit," which probably will not fit you. Women's shoes go up to size 42 (U.S. size 11).

Chinese-Style

CHINESE ARTS & CRAFTS STORES (H.K.) LTD.
Flagship: Star House, next to Star Ferry, Canton Rd., Kowloon (MTR: TST); branches throughout town.

This is the most Western of the Chinese department stores. By American standards, the prices are good, although the David Tang look-alike merchandise is just as expensive as his! Ouch! The stores are clean, easy to use, and tourist friendly, but you pay for these luxuries.

The silk-fabric (yard goods) department is fun, although the prices are cheaper in markets. I've been told this is a reputable place to buy jade. There's no imitation passed off as real here. *Be warned, however:* Real jade is quite pricey.

The store will ship for you; the sales help has been very pleasant to me—unusual for some Chinese stores. This is a good place for souvenirs. Hours in all stores are basically Monday to Saturday from 10am to 6:30pm; Sunday hours vary with the location.

YUE HWA CHINESE PRODUCTS EMPORIUM
Main store: 301-309 Nathan Rd., Yau Ma Tei, Kowloon (MTR: Jordan Rd.); also Park Lane Shopper's Blvd., 143-161 Nathan Rd., Kowloon (MTR: TST) and Peking Road, Kowloon (MTR: TST).

This is a real Chinese department store, with many convenient branches. Unfortunately, the newer the store, the more Western it is, which is not my favorite style of Chinese department store. Buy from the "Great Wall of China," as I call the china department; get silk pj's; get silk by the yard.

The main store is rather jampacked and junky and absolutely divine. If this is too hard for your system to digest, the newer Park Lane store is almost as nice as Macy's.

Best Buy: I just bought a silk ancestor's coat (in other words, a men's-style dressing gown) on sale for $99 in size XXXL; it is divine.

Ignore the Western goods and buy Chinese. The stores mail to the United States. Hours are daily from 9:30 or 10am to 8 or 9pm. © 852/2739-3888.

Japanese-Style

Most of the large **Japanese department stores** are in Causeway Bay and aren't very different from U.S. department stores. Seibu, the most upscale of all Japanese department stores, bucked the trend by opening in the Pacific Place mall. Hard times have forced cutbacks, but the store is still open.

SEIBU
The Mall at Pacific Place, 88 Queensway, Central (MTR: Admiralty); Langham Place, Kowloon (MTR: Mong Kok, Nathan Road, Kowloon (MTR: TST)).

Once one of the best department stores in the world, Seibu is now cutting back a tad but still has two very stylish outposts in Honkers. The store has many brands and strives to introduce brands that no one else has. They specialize in The Antwerp Gang, the Belgian designers who get so much coverage in the fashion press. They also opened the first **Diesel StyleLab** in town and were among the first to see the potential in Mong Kok. *Insider's tip:* The two branch stores pale compared to Pacific Place. © 852/2269-1888.

DESIGNER GOODS

Hong Kong gains designer shops every day; I cannot come to town without being annoyed that so many new ones have opened. Who in the world is shopping at these places? Did any of us come to Hong Kong to buy big-name designer clothes

Up-and-Coming Talent

More and more young designers are finding that Hong Kong is a fine place to be discovered. Although many of the young designers in town are not yet represented in boutiques, they are busy designing private-label goods for large stores. You may never have heard their names, but you may dig their designs.

You'll find the latest and wildest designs by hot young talents in the shops that line **Kimberley Road** and **Austin Avenue.** These two streets, in the northern end of Tsim Sha Tsui, have become the SoHo of Hong Kong. The shops' decor is avantgarde; the prices are affordable. Start at the corner of Austin and Nathan roads, walking east. Austin Road turns a corner and becomes Austin Avenue, which turns again and becomes Kimberley Road, heading back toward Nathan Road. Also in this area is the **Rise Commercial Building** on Granville Circuit, a small, hard-to-find alley off Granville Road.

at regular retail prices? Or to buy at prices higher than at home? I mean, *really.*

Every now and then you can get a break on designer goods, but not often. Some Chanel items (such as makeup) are cheaper than in the U.S. or at the airport duty-free shop. Most items, however, are not. If you are interested in a certain designer line, I suggest you shop for it at home and come to Hong Kong with notes in hand. Don't be surprised if designer prices are totally out of line; Ferragamo may just give you heart failure. But wait: I just read an article in a Toronto newspaper by the fashion editor who went to Hong Kong this past summer, hit some sales, found Prada to be half her hometown prices, and felt that designer goods were all but growing on trees. Maybe there's hope yet.

If confused, go for brands or selection in Hong Kong that have not yet come to the U.S. or that you do not know, so that you can be the first on your block to wear a certain style.

DISCOUNTS & DEALS

....

Most manufacturing is done outside of Hong Kong, so there are few genuine factory outlets these days. Still, there are some jobbers in the **Pedder Building** (p. 120) and a handful of good sources elsewhere. Changes at **Horizons Plaza** make it worth the trip, and there's usually a line of taxis waiting to whisk you home—a recent improvement.

With the exception of Lok Wah, none of these establishments is near the MTR; take a taxi.

JOYCE WAREHOUSE
Horizons Plaza, 2 Li Wing St., 21st floor, Ap Lei Chau.

Joyce has been the most famous name in European luxury brands in Hong Kong for over 25 years. She's had a number of stores and has suffered the usual ups and downs of retail in hard times. All of her stores are now owned by Lane Crawford (see above). Her warehouse and outlet store sells off goods that don't move out of her stores. I saw an Armani blazer for $50 (US!) and other designer bargains that left me breathless. Sizes tend to run so small that I get depressed easily.

KAISER ESTATES
Phases 1, 2 & 3, Man Yue Rd., Hung Hom.

This is a formerly famous shopping district that I find very boring and somewhat overpriced. A Donna Karan DKNY blazer for $250 is not my idea of a bargain. I did, however, luck into the Adidas outlet sale—shoes at $30 a pair were a good bargain. Most of the outlets are in Phase 1, with a few in Phase 2. Frankly, I think you can give this area a miss, but I got a note from readers who loved it here. Go figure.

LANE CRAWFORD WAREHOUSE
Horizons Plaza, 2 Li Wing St., 25th floor, Ap Lei Chau.

Better than any other Hong Kong outlet I've recently been to. Armani jackets for under $200, suits for $400. Shoes, accessories, home style, menswear. Gorgeous stuff. Maybe I got lucky, but it sure was more fun than the Joyce Warehouse. They have a greater variety of sizes, and you can buy nice gifts if you find nothing for yourself.

LOK WAH
Lok Wah Bo, 193 Fa Yuen St. (MTR: Mong Kok); Lok Wah Top World, 175 Fa Yuen St. (MTR: Mong Kok); Lok Wah Top Place, 53 and 55 Granville Rd., Kowloon (MTR: TST); Lok Wah City, 11 Lee Garden Rd. (MTR: Causeway Bay).

This small chain of jobbers operates stores that sell clothes—often including big-name brands—out of bins. Each major shopping area has a store, which can be your jumping-off point in its neighborhood. I'm not saying it's the best of the jobbers, but I have done well on repeat visits and found a variety of merchandise and sizes at low everyday prices.

SPACE
Marina Sq. E., 2F Commercial Block, South Horizons, Ap Lei Chau.

Space is the name the Prada Group gives to its warehouses selling all its lines—Prada, Miu Miu, Jil Sander, Helmut Lang, and so on. With all the fake Prada in China, it's hard to suggest that you visit, but this *is* the real thing, and it carries clothes, shoes, and accessories, too. This outlet is in Ap Lei Chau but not in Horizons Plaza (though it is nearby). Ask your hotel concierge to call © 852/2814-9576 for directions, then have him write them in Chinese.

ETHNIC STYLE

Costumey Chinese dresses, jackets, and shirts are for sale just about everywhere in Hong Kong, from souvenir stores to **Chinese Arts & Crafts** to the chicest of them all, **Shanghai Tang** (p. 121). However, if you prefer the look that qualifies more as boho chic, you will need a good eye and some luck. The fanciest Asian chic is from **Blanc de Chine** (p. 118). For the wannabes that are quite affordable, try **Kenki** (p. 92).

FABRICS

As a rule, don't think that just because you are close to the silkworms, you can walk away with bargains. Silk is usually about $15 a meter.

Buying fabrics from tailors in the PRC can be tricky (they may lie about the origin of the goods), but you can trust the fine tailors in Hong Kong to offer European fabrics for suits, shirts, and other clothing. If you don't know your tailor, don't let him sell you European fabric without showing you the bolt or sample book. Low-class tailors have been known to do a switcheroo—or just fib.

The second floor of the **Western Market** (p. 131) is home to a fabric market. You may get a kick out of **Excellent Silk Mill,** 17 Cameron Rd., second floor, Kowloon (MTR: TST), which takes only cash but has vintage fabrics for sale off the bolt. It's near Nathan and Granville roads.

Shanghai Tang sells gorgeous silks and fabrics, but the prices may kill you. For similar fabrics, try a branch of **Chinese Arts & Crafts.**

Shenzhen, across the border (see chapter 6), is a good place to shop for silk; there is an entire fabric market located in the main shopping mall at the border. **Li Yuen West,** in The Lanes (p. 128), is more convenient.

FURS

Just when you thought it was safe to go out into the cold, fur is back. Fun fur—cheap, funky, colorful, and possibly fashion forward—is the latest trend and can be found in Hong Kong in the winter. There's also a fair amount of fake fur around, even in markets. The most trusted name in real fur is **Siberian Furs** on Chatham Road in Kowloon.

GLASSES

The days of truly inexpensive eyeglasses are over, but many people do find considerable savings in Hong Kong.

EYE'N-I
1 Lan Fong Rd. (MTS: Causeway Bay).

With an optometrist in the shop and more designer frames than you can imagine, this is one of the hipper spots for eyewear in a very trendy neighborhood.

NEW FEI OPTICAL SUPPLY LTD.
Lucky Horse Industrial Building, 64 Tong Mi Rd., 1-7 Bute St., 12th floor, Kowloon (MTR: Prince Edward, then shuttle bus or taxi).

This source comes from my friend Louis, who is chief concierge at the InterConti and wears glasses (I had Lasik). Louis knows everything and everyone. This is one of the best sources he has ever given me.

It's is a factory in an industrial part of town. You pick your frames, you have your eyes tested, and you wait 10 minutes. If your prescription is more complicated, you may wait a half-hour while they make your glasses.

You can buy reading glasses, eyeglasses, or sunglasses prescriptions; children have their own selection. There are thousands of frames, many from big-name Euro designers. The eye test is free. The setup is sort of supermarket-style, then you sit at a table with a mirror and try on frames all day. Cold drinks are served.

I have had about a dozen pairs of glasses made here in the past few years. Prices average about $100 per pair. Note that you will not only need your Rx but something called the PD (pupillary distance measurements). If you are having glasses made for someone who is not with you, make sure you have the PD!

You can take the shuttle bus or a taxi from the MTR; the area is industrial but not frightening. To arrange for the shuttle bus before you head out, have a hotel staff member call © 852/2398-2088. Avoid weekends if you can; some 400 people a day pass through on Saturday and Sunday. Hours are daily from 10:30am to 8pm.

GROCERY STORES

The best grocery stores in Hong Kong are more like department stores. Indeed, one of my favorite stores in town is called **City Super**—it sells everything. **Marks & Spencer** stores sell some packaged (not fresh) foodstuffs; the local grocery store chains, **Wellcome** and **Park 'N Shop,** have small branches all over.

CITY SUPER
Times Square mall (MTR: Causeway Bay); IFC2 Mall (MTR: Central); Ocean Terminal, Kowloon (MTR: TST).

I'm not sure if I am more in love with the wide selection of Japanese bath products, the gadgets department, the international foodstuffs, or simply the people who shop here—but this is a great business and a really fun concept. It's the modern version of the general store.

GrEAT
Mall at Pacific Place, 88 Queensway, Central, downstairs from Seibu (MTR: Admiralty).

I don't like GrEAT as much as City Super because it's more of a gourmet grocery and less of a department store. But baby, what a grocery store. There's a fancy food court and all sorts of international grocery and gourmet products. Branch stores are opening in Kowloon.

NEEDS
New World Centre, Salisbury Rd., Kowloon (MTR: TST).

Every time I check in to the InterConti next door, I make this my next stop. I'm not saying you should make a special trip here (as I would suggest for any branch of City Super), but the Kmart-type establishment is a great grocery store. You can also buy health and beauty aids, electronics, and more.

SUPER WELLCOME
Causeway Bay (MTR: Causeway Bay).

Wellcome is a well-known grocery chain; this location is almost a superstore in the heart of crowded Causeway Bay, near the big hotels there. You can buy snacks and real-people needs, and browse in a fun, modern supermarket.

HANDBAGS

ASHNEIL
Far East Mansions, 5-6 Middle Rd., Shop 114 (up the stairs), Tsim Sha Tsui, Kowloon (MTR: TST).

My heart goes pitter-pat every time I walk into this closet-size store. I've never seen so many bags that I couldn't live without. As Ashneil himself says, "The quality has to be good; we have no logos."

These bags are not copies—they do not have designer logos or anything illegal. They just coincidentally look a lot like the handbags in the fashion magazines. These bags are not cheap, but they cost less than the designer versions. The company does private trunk shows across America, but you have to sign up to be invited while you are in Hong Kong. It is also possible to choose and pay for your bags in Hong Kong and have them sent from the U.S.—you save space in your luggage and don't worry about Customs or duties.

Shopper beware: We have had a few notes from readers who have not been happy with the repair service offered—although they admit that all the bags were over 18 months old and repairs were honored.

Ashneil is off Nathan Road, a half-block from the Inter-Conti, right behind the Sheraton. However, the building is what you might call funky, so first-timers may feel nervous. Don't be. Walk up one flight of stairs to the first floor and follow the signs to room 114.

MAYLIN
Peninsula Hotel Shopping Arcade, Salisbury Rd., Kowloon (MTR: TST).

Big changes in this store! They've expanded, remodeled, and totally changed their stock so there's nary a Birkin to be seen. Insiders always knew this as a great source for well-made Hermes-like styles, but no more! They have expanded their shoe department, still take custom orders for shoes and bags, and specialize now in woven-leather handbags that are very, very good looking and fairly priced, beginning around $250. Think major Italian brand you wish you could afford.

SAM WO
41-47 Queen's Rd., basement, Central (MTR: Central).

Sam Wo is an old source who has been on and off these pages for years. I am very conflicted about sending you here because it takes a very good eye in order to score. When I look at all the bags, they seem to jump off the wall and race toward me. I get dizzy, and the sans-logo bags look cheap. However, when I see a single bag worn by a stylish woman, I am always shocked when she tells me her treasure came from Sam Wo. For the same sort of thing, I like Shenzhen better. If you can't get to Shenzhen, you may have a ball here.

Expect to pay about $75 to $100 for a decent designer copy. Some bags are leather, some are PVC—they will tell you which is which if you can't tell the dif. Sam Wo has two shops: a tiny, stall-like location in The Lanes (p. 128) and a larger basement store, which has a door in The Lanes but an official Queen's Road address.

HOME STYLE

....

GOD
48 Hollywood Rd. (MTR: Central); Hong Kong Hotel, 3rd floor, Kowloon (MTR: TST); Leighton Centre, Sharp St. E. (MTR: Causeway Bay).

The name means Goods of Desire, thank you. This store is also listed below for its home items, but I shop here for accessories (like wallets) and gift items. Locals, however, load up on furniture, home style, and more. © 852/2890-5555. www.god.com.hk.

KOU
Fung House, 20 Connaught Rd., Central (MTS: Central).

The offerings at KOU are more lifestyle than home style, and everything here is within the range of one woman's vision. It feels so well done that you could truly move right in. Great for wedding gifts. Store opens 11am. © 852/2530-2234. www. kouconcept.com.

JADE

Books have been written on jade, and there is a small section about it in chapter 3. The news here is that I now have a contact in the Jade Market, so you can ask for Erica and have her guide you to the more honest dealers and help with your negotiations. She runs her business, **Jade Butterfly**, out of Booth no. 63. Her mobile phone, if you want to call from your hotel before you head over: ✆ 852/9042-3872.

JEWELRY & GEMSTONES

The jewelry and gemstone businesses are separate and converge only at the wholesale level, where you will never be admitted without a bona fide dealer. If you are serious about buying stones, you should be introduced to the wholesale dealers. This requires personal contact from a dealer in Hong Kong or from a friend who is Chinese and living in Hong Kong. It is a very tight business. Don't expect to just walk into a shop off the street and see the best stones or get the best prices.

There is risk in every purchase, but if you are dealing with a reputable jeweler, that risk is minimized. Reputation is everything. If you are looking for good pearls, diamonds, opals, jade, or ivory, educate yourself. Take the time to learn before you leap.

If you are into creating your own necklaces, you need to meet Jenny. You pick and buy the beads from her, tell her what you want, and she will string them and deliver to your hotel. **Jenny Gems Company**, No. 364–65 and 410 Jade Market, Yau Ma Tei (MTR: Jordan Rd.) or jennystore@hotmail.com.

LEADING CO. JEWEL & WATCH
New World Centre, #L066, Salisbury Rd. (MTR: TST).

This is the jeweler that my friend Richard has been using for years: James Ma. I have never had anything made here but have enjoyed the bling that Richard's friends and family have shown

me. His shop is adjacent to the InterContinental Hotel.
© 852/2369-9727.

PAN AM PEARLS
9 Lock Rd., Kowloon (MTR: TST).

I sometimes buy my faux pearls here, and I consider this as
one of my single best sources in Hong Kong. The faux pearls
I've bought here are about the best I've seen at these prices. I
have seen fluctuations in quality according to stock, and I have
yet to match the quality of the double-strand, 8-millimeter set
that cost me $40, 5 years ago. A strand of pearls runs about
$20; the staff will string together several strands into a single
necklace with a new clasp as you wait. Baroque pearls are also
available.

THE SHOWROOM
Central Building, Pedder St., 12th floor (MTR: Central).

I run with an expatriate crowd in Hong Kong that seems to
do everything in groups; everyone knows everyone and shares
the same resources. Many of those resources have become
regulars in these pages. According to my sources, the place for
jewelry these days is a small place simply called The Showroom,
where a woman named Claire Wadsworth holds court. Good
work at excellent prices is the general opinion, backed up by
many I trust.

LEATHER GOODS

Hong Kong is a big handbag and shoe destination for several
reasons:

- If you go to Shenzhen, you might buy a dozen handbags—
fakes but also inspirations; see p. 152.
- Almost all American and European designer brands have
shops in Hong Kong; you will find brands you've never heard

of and models your neighbors haven't got. Take a look at **Etienne Aigner,** which is just coming back to HKG and the fashion scene as a hot ticket.

- If you go for quality but don't need a brand name, you will be floored by the number of Kelly, Birkin, and Bollido bags in Hong Kong, usually in the $100-to-$300 price range. Hotel arcades (p. 125) are a good source for these items. Note that Hermes has just gone the Chanel route and begun to prosecute, so there are fewer Hermes copies out there.
- The major malls and hotel shopping centers usually have stores representing European brands that often don't have distribution in the U.S.

LOCAL HEROES

....

BLANC DE CHINE
Pedder Building, 12 Pedder St; The Landmark, Central (MTR: Central).

The original showroom in the Pedder Building was still open as we went to press, but the brand-new boutique across the street in The Landmark is quite sleek and spiffy. Blanc de Chine is one of the best stores in Hong Kong: chic Chinese clothes for men and women, and home style . . . sort of Armani goes classic Asian. Expect to pay about $500 for a blazer. ✆ 852/2524-7875.

GOD
48 Hollywood Rd. (MTR: Central); Hong Kong Hotel, 3rd floor, Kowloon (MTR: TST); Leighton Centre, Sharp St. E. (MTR: Causeway Bay).

This store does not personify any deity—the name is an acronym for "Goods of Desire." It sells everything from furniture to soft furnishings to home style. This is a great place for gift items. ✆ 852/2890-5555. www.god.com.hk.

JOYCE
2106 Canton Rd., Kowloon (MTR: TST).

Joyce is my personal saint. She is the most brilliant and successful woman in Hong Kong retail; joining up with a big-time holding company has ended her financial woes and she continues as a beacon of good taste and great ideas. Her main store is just as eye-catching and fabulous as any other Joyce project. For information about the Joyce Warehouse in Ap Lei Chau, see p. 108. © 852/2367-8128.

WALTER MA
49A Kimberley Rd., Kowloon (MTR: TST).

Ma is in the category of designers who have been "up-and-coming" for 20 years. Nonetheless, his clothing is easy to wear and different from other brands that make you feel you look like everyone else. Much of it is for the young, but a lot of it is so imaginative that you have to grin.

MALLS

Hong Kong is totally overrun with shopping centers. It's as though a contagious disease has spread to all architects, who now feel compelled to equip hotels and office buildings with three floors of retail shops.

Central

IFC2
1 Harbourview St. (MTR: Central).

Hot damn, this is the new center of the world. It's the tallest building in town, the location of the new Four Seasons Hotel, and home to a very nice mall, complete with a **City Super.** It's also where the Star Ferry now comes to port. The package is all rounded out by a cinema, an MTR station, and an Airport Express stop as well as a great view to Kowloon. Just about every major store has a branch here; **Lane Crawford**'s new flagship is here. And, yup, **Starbucks**, too. © 852/2295-3308.

THE LANDMARK
16 Des Voeux Rd. (MTR: Central).

The most famous of the Central malls, The Landmark has the reputation and the big names in luxury retail, and it stays ahead of the game by adding new stores and concepts. The latest innovations are a **Mandarin Oriental** boutique hotel and the first Asian branch of the London department store **Harvey Nichols**. I suggest this mall as a jumping-off place for Westerners who want to see something but aren't quite ready for Kowloon. After a quick survey, you'll probably find that everything is gorgeous but very expensive, and that you are ready to move on. A few cafes here offer lunch options. © 852/2525-4142.

THE MALL AT PACIFIC PLACE
88 Queensway, Central (MTR: Admiralty).

If you are staying in one of the many hotels built next to the mall, this place is a natural for you. If you are in a hurry, you may want to come by because you can pack a lot in. Note that the official name of this place is the Mall at Pacific Place, but everyone calls it **Pacific Place**. Technically speaking, Pacific Place includes the office tower above the mall and the fancy hotels grouped around the tower (Marriott, Conrad, Island Shangri-La). It also includes a branch of every store you want to visit, and you can do it here in Western fashion—it's not quaint, but it's handy. You'll have plenty of choices for lunch (or dinner) and a good opportunity to have a look-see at some big hotels. © 852/2844-8988.

PEDDER BUILDING
12 Pedder St. (MTR: Central).

Well, the Pedder Building is looking downright spiffy. My bet is that rents have risen, which explains why almost all the old favorites have moved out. Although it's across the street from **The Landmark,** it offers the opposite in shopping appeal—outlet stores on one side and the famed **Shanghai Tang** at street level. Most of the outlets in the Pedder Building have dried up. There are two reliable destinations: **Shopper's Safari** and **Blanc de Chine** (p. 118). Note that Blanc de Chine is not discount or inexpensive or anything other than Armani with an Oriental twist.

PRINCE'S BUILDING
Chater Rd. (MTR: Central).

This office building with five levels of shopping has so many big names now that it competes with **The Landmark** and the **Central Building,** both of which are across the street. The Prince's Building connects by bridge to the Mandarin Oriental Hotel (don't miss shopping there, either) and may be more fun than The Landmark. It is not mind-boggling like The Landmark, so you can shop and enjoy yourself, and it houses many other big names in international deluxe brands.

Causeway Bay

FASHION WALK
Gloucester Rd., Causeway Bay (MTR: Causeway Bay).

Not technically a mall, Fashion Walk is a shopping concept. The street level of several adjacent buildings—three of them in sort of a triangle—houses up-and-coming designers, cutting-edge designers, Japanese designers, hopeful designers, and the likes of Vivienne Tam. There are also several cafes. On the Victoria Park side of the Excelsior Hotel, this destination is extremely refreshing because the stores are unique and you aren't inside a mall too much of the time.

LEE GARDENS 1 & 2
*Leighton Centre and Hennessy Centre, 111 Leighton Rd.
(MTR: Causeway Bay).*

This mall has so many fancy designer shops that you'll forget you are in Causeway Bay. The two buildings lie perpendicular to each other: Lee Gardens 1 is on Hysan Avenue, and Lee Gardens 2 is between Yun Ping Road and Jardine's Crescent. The two malls have brands such as Chanel, Hermès, Vuitton, Paul Smith, Prada, Cartier, Longchamp, Gucci, Bottega Veneta, and so forth. You get the picture. Philippe Starck designed the new Jean-Paul Gaultier shop.

TIMES SQUARE
1 Matheson Rd. (MTR: Causeway Bay).

The mall is divided by category of goods, which simplifies life for someone shopping for a specific item; it combines Western chains and big names with local dealers and small firms. There are four floors of restaurants. This is a destination, not merely a mall, and it attracts a lot of young people. My favorite shop is **City Super,** a grocery store and department store in one (enter through Lane Crawford).

Aberdeen

HORIZONS PLAZA
2 Lee Wing St., Ap Lei Chau (no nearby MTR).

This is not a mall, but it functions like one. The high-rise tower houses many furniture showrooms, wholesale sources, outlet stores, carpet stores, and gift sources. It's worth the trip because of the selection.

The **Joyce Warehouse** is in this building; I've never done well with Joyce in outlet stores, but hey, you never know. The **Lane Crawford** outlet is here; I found it great. **Tequila Kola** is sort of a large version of Pier 1 Imports: It carries tabletop accessories, bed linens, curtains, and small decorative items, but it's known for furniture. That makes it more of a source for locals—unless you want to ship (which you can) or are just looking for ideas. The large space holds a number of room sets. The tenants change frequently, but there are so many of them that you can still have fun. Each store keeps its own hours. There's a free directory at the welcome desk. Taxis wait out front.

TST

HARBOUR CITY
Canton Rd., Kowloon (MTR: TST).

The shopping complex that occupies most of Tsim Sha Tsui's western shore is generally known as Harbour City. It includes **Ocean Terminal, Ocean Centre,** and **Ocean Galleries** along with the **Hong Kong Hotel,** the **Marco Polo Hotel,** and the **Prince Hotel.** There are four levels of shopping, and if you can successfully negotiate your way from end to end, you won't even have to come up for air. All luxury brands have stores here, as do most chains. © **852/2118-8601.**

NEW WORLD CENTRE
18-24 Salisbury Rd., Kowloon (MTR: TST).

The New World Centre is yet another massive, multilevel, spick-and-span, concrete-and-cold-floor shopping center filled with little shops, 1-hour photo stands, and ice-cream vendors. It has a cute Japanese department store (**Tokyu**—open Fri–Wed 10am–9pm) at street level, but really, don't waste your time on my account. If you are a guest at the adjoining InterConti— or any nearby hotel—the grocery store, **Needs,** is a lot of fun and sells all sorts of things besides groceries.

PARK LANE SHOPPER'S BOULEVARD
Nathan Rd., Kowloon (MTR: TST).

This architecturally unique strip mall will certainly catch your eye (and maybe your credit card) as you stroll the infamous

Nathan Road. **Yue Hwa,** a Chinese department store, occupies about half of the space. There's also an **American Express.**

Kowloon

APM
Millennium City 5, 418 Kwun Tong Rd., Kowloon.

This is a convenience mall for those who live out here, and— oh my!—what a lifestyle. This is a fun evening of sociology— go for a meal (huge food court and many restaurants), shop, and take in a movie. This mall really gets going at night, with the action keeping up almost until midnight. © 852/2267-0500.

Festival Walk
88 Tat Chee Ave., Kowloon Tong (MTR: Kowloon Tong).

This is the local go-to mall for young people and foodies, with 30 restaurants plus a food court. It's not that well known by tourists, which makes it all the more attractive. © 852/2844-2228.

Mong Kok

Langham Place
8 Argyle St. (MTR: Mong Kok).

With 300 stores, this is the hot new place in town for the younger crowd, as well as an attempt by the city to rejuvenate the area. Part of the mall is the snazzy new Langham Place Hotel. There are also the usual Cineplex and food court. This mall is not a destination for tourists, so it's a great place to get a look at the future—Mong Kok is arriving, the young people from China are arriving, and the trendy clothes and concepts are already here. And it's not at all downmarket or funky: There's a branch of the posh Japanese department store **Seibu** as well as a huge branch of **Muji.**

Hotel Arcades/Hotel Malls

The fanciest hotels have the most trustworthy shops. Certainly the shops in the **Peninsula** are the most expensive and most exclusive. But that doesn't mean there's anything wrong with the shops in the **Holiday Inn,** which happen to be touristy but fine if you want a TT (tourist trap).

THE INTERCONTINENTAL HOTEL
18 Salisbury Rd., Kowloon (MTR: TST).

As the hotel arcade/shopping center/mall sweepstakes heats up, this small mall offers one of every big name (including **Chanel**) *and* adjoins the New World Centre. This is not a destination mall but a convenience for hotel guests. More interesting is the new **Shanghai Tang** in the hotel lobby.

THE PENINSULA HOTEL
Salisbury Rd., Kowloon (MTR: TST).

Small shops fill the eastern and western wings of the hotel, with more on the mezzanine and still more in the basement. Every big name in the world has a shop here. The shopping arcade is being renovated as we go to press, so you'll just have to show up and explore. A free handout lists all the stores in the arcade, so don't miss out.

MARKETS

Markets offer a real slice of life and one of the few less-than-glamorous looks at the real China. Some are not pretty or fancy. If you are squeamish, avoid the food markets that sell live chickens or ducks and slaughter them on the spot.

Merchandise markets are busy and hectic. Each has its own clientele and its own personality. There are no spacious aisles or racks of organized clothing. Some markets exist only at certain hours of the day or night. At a preappointed time, people appear from nowhere, pushing carts laden with merchandise. They set up shop along the street and sell their goods until the crowds start to dissipate, at which time they disappear into the night.

Most markets have no specific street address but are known by the streets that bound them or that intersect in the middle of the market area. Most cabdrivers know where the markets are by name. However, it is always a good idea to have your concierge write the name of the market and location in Chinese. You probably won't need it, but it can't hurt. Buses, trolleys, and the MTR usually serve the markets as well. Take a hotel business card with you so you'll have the address in Chinese. The following markets are open daily.

BIRD MARKET
Yuen Po St. Bird Garden, next to the Mong Kok stadium (MTR: Prince Edward).

The Bird Market is really just an alley that sells birds and bird supplies, but it's also an experience you will never forget. The sound of the chirping is overwhelming. I just want to know if the noise is made by birds chirping or grasshoppers chirping. The vendors sell bird supplies (including grasshoppers); you will be surprised at how many bird cages you suddenly want. You won't buy much here, but it is fun. Forget it during outbreaks of bird flu.

CAT STREET MARKET
Cat St., just below Hollywood Rd. (MTR: Central).

Cat Street Market is Hong Kong's answer to a flea market: Vendors sell used merchandise of the tag-sale variety from blankets and a few stalls on a 2-block stretch of pedestrian pavement just below Hollywood Road. One guy sells only used typewriters and used sewing machines. A few dealers sell old jade, which I like. One vendor has Chinese sunglasses from the 1930s. The shops behind and around the market specialize in formal antiques; some of these stores are reputable and even famous.

FA YUEN MARKET (FLOWER MARKET)
Fa Yuen St., Kowloon (MTR: Prince Edward).

This is not the Ladies' Market, although the two very different markets are close enough to be a single destination. Some people call this the Flower Market only because a few vendors sell fruit and flowers in baskets. A nearby flower market sells flowers, plants, and plastic greenery. You're here for the fun fashions, however, and will be walking toward Argyle Street. With Prince Edward to your rear, walk toward Kowloon.

The jobbers on Fa Yuen Street (p. 109) are open during the day when the market is closed. But at about 4pm, the street becomes a pedestrian mall, filled with fruits and veggies, handbags and brassieres. The jobbers remain open, so this is a mad case of too many bins, not enough money.

You will not see many tourists in these parts; the rummaging through bins may not be to everyone's liking. This is my favorite kind of shopping, and I always find deals. You'll see men's, women's and children's clothing as well as plus sizes in various jobbers' stores on both sides of Fa Yuen running for about 3 blocks. Cash only. ATMs are not that easy to find, so be prepared.

JADE MARKET
Kansu and Battery sts., Yau Ma Tei, Kowloon (MTR: Jordan Rd. and walk a bit or take a taxi).

The market is in two free-standing tents under the highway overpass at Kansu and Battery streets.

The Jade Market is an official market organized by the Hong Kong and Kowloon Jade Merchants Workers' and Hawkers' Union Association. Each merchant inside the fence is licensed to sell jade and should display his or her license above the stall. It is a good idea when buying to note the number next to your purchase, just in case you have a problem later on and the jade turns out to be plastic.

If you are not willing to bargain here, don't buy. The merchants in the Jade Market expect to lower their price by 20% to 40%, depending on your bargaining skill and their need to sell. Market hours are 10am to 3pm, although many of the vendors close up at 2pm. Go early rather than late.

LADIES' MARKET (MONG KOK MARKET)
Argyle St. and Nathan Rd. (MTR: Mong Kok).

The market sets up a short distance away from the Mong Kok MTR station; it begins around 4pm and goes into the evening, until about 10pm or so. It really gets going after work and seems to be a date spot. Watch your handbag.

The streets have the feeling of a carnival, with lots of people parading by the stands, stopping to examine shirts, socks, sewing sets, buttons, and bras. There are some toys and sunglasses—mostly lots of trinkets, clothing, everyday goods, and the usual ringing alarm clocks, fake designer goods, electrical doodads that flash and whirr—no live snakes or chickens. It's very different from Fa Yuen Street, so visit them both, if at all possible.

THE LANES
Li Yuen East and Li Yuen West, Central (MTR: Central).

The Lanes are twin alleys, about 50m (164 ft.) apart from each other, darting between Queen's Road and Des Voeux Road in Central. I had given up on them for several years, but a friend asked me to reconsider for this revision. I had a ball. Furthermore, the women I took here all liked it a lot.

The general layout of each lane is the same—stores along the thoroughfare, and a center aisle of stalls. One lane specializes in Chinese arts and crafts, T-shirts, fabric off the bolt, and blinking electronic toys that make annoying sounds. This is also a good place for reading glasses that fold up into a slim tube.

The other lane specializes in handbags and padded bras. (Could I make this up?) Bra Lane also has several jobbers; I personally have never met a jobber I could walk past. On my last foray, I bought a pair of Nautica khakis for $10 and a T-shirt for $4. There is also a branch of the **Ribbon Emporium** (p. 92), that crazy source. *Hint:* It doesn't sell ribbons.

The stores and stalls are crowded and active; you are pestered and pursued and pressured to buy. Haggle until dusk. Who needs a trip to mainland China when you can shop here? Also note that this is an excellent neighborhood to snoop around in—1 block from Shanghai Tang and The Landmark, yet in another world. Queen's Road has many branches of favorite stores, even the Chinese department store **Yue Hwa**. And there are lots of banks with ATMs.

LUEN WO MARKET
Luen Wo, New Territories (KCR from TST East to Fanling, then bus no. 78 or taxi).

This is an authentic local food market quite near the border with China. The market and the merchandise are not enormously different from what you'd see in town, so the trip may not be worth your time. On the other hand, if you crave a peek into the real China or a world gone by, this is your Sunday adventure. The market fills a square city block. The shoppers are far more rural-looking than those you might find in downtown Central. You go here for the total experience, for the fact that it's real. You might want to give it a miss if there have been avian flu outbreaks.

MID-LEVELS MARKET
20 Borrett Rd., Mid-Levels (take escalator).

This is more of a Sunday-stroll, easygoing neighborhood kind of thing but it offers a little bit of everything. It is held the second Sunday of each month only, from 10am to 5pm.

STANLEY MARKET

Stanley Main St., Stanley Village, Hong Kong (public tran-sit: bus no. 6 from Exchange Sq. in Central or no. 20 from Star Ferry).

Any tourist coming to Hong Kong knows about Stanley: Shop-ping legends abound about bargains in this village-cum-market-cum-tourist-trap. Some people love Stanley; they are mostly first-timers. Stanley has become so touristy that I can barely cope—and I go there often, just to make sure I am up-to-date. I found no retail stock and no fake designer mer-chandise (oh, woe!). All I found were tourist goods—white linens, Chinese pajamas, knickknacks, and cheap gifts. Not bad if you want that sort of thing, but I wanted deals. Actually, I bought three "van Gogh" oil paintings for $6.50 each. The market is open daily from 10am to 7pm. A taxi will cost about $15 each way; the bus from Star Ferry takes about an hour.

TEMPLE STREET MARKET

Temple St. and Jordan Rd., Kowloon (MTR: Jordan Rd.).

This night market has grown a lot over the years, and as it spreads, the charm is diluted, making it yet just another street market. You have to know where the Chinese opera singers and the fortunetellers are in order to find them.

Exit the MTR onto Nathan Road toward **Yue Hwa Chi-nese Products Emporium.** You will see Yue Hwa; you can't miss it. Stay on the Yue Hwa side of the street (this is still Nathan Rd.). With the harbor to your back, it's the left side. Walk north on Nathan Road for 2 or 3 blocks. Keep looking to your left. You are searching for a tiny entryway, a small alley crammed with people. This is where the opera singers do their thing on little patios. When you spot the alley, turn left into the crowd.

This alley is only about 45m (148 ft.) long. When you emerge from the alley, you will be on Temple Street, at the cor-ner of a real temple. Walk forward 1 block, keeping the side-walk that borders the grounds of the temple yard on your right side. On this sidewalk you'll see a long row of fortunetellers, each with his (they're all men) own gimmick. One or two may speak English. The market itself begins thereafter.

WESTERN MARKET
323 Des Voeux Rd., Central (MTR: Sheung Wan).

Once upon a time, Western Market was a dump. Then along came a developer who turned the space into a festival market. It has a branch of **Fook Ming Tong,** the fancy tea broker; there are toy soldiers and plenty for kids to see and buy. Many of the cloth merchants who were disenfranchised when Cloth Alley was destroyed have taken space on the second floor of Western Market. Flags fly, banners flap, people shop. The space has a lot of energy and a number of unique stalls that sell merchandise I haven't seen anywhere else in town. True to its name, this market is much farther west than the rest of Central's basic shopping areas.

MEN'S SHIRTS: MADE-TO-MEASURE

There are a lot of choices to be made: the fit of the body, the type of collar and cuffs, the fabric, and the possible use of contrast fabric. Prices usually depend on the fabric: 100% cotton costs more than a poly blend; Sea Island cotton costs more than regular cotton. Expect to pay about $75 for a Sea Island custom-made cotton shirt, although such a shirt can cost more, depending on the maker. For custom shirts, two fittings are necessary—one for the measurements and one with the garment.

Many shirt houses have a minimum order; most tailors make shirts as well as suits. If you are buying the shirt and the suit from the same tailor, there is usually no minimum shirt order. Most shirt houses also make pajamas and boxer shorts.

Ascot Chang Co. Ltd.
The Peninsula Hotel, Salisbury Rd., Kowloon (MTR: TST);
InterContinental Hotel, 18 Salisbury Rd., Kowloon (MTR:
TST); Prince's Building, Chater Rd. (MTR: Central).

Perhaps the best known of the internationally famous shirt dealers, Ascot Chang advertises heavily in the U.S. and stresses its
quality and devotion to fit. This shirt maker has many branches
in Hong Kong and Kowloon. The shops are filled with wonderful fabrics imported from Switzerland and France. Prices
are competitive with **David's** (see below); mail order is available once your measurements have been taken. Shirts run
between $40 and $125, depending on the fabric and style. Top
of the line. Ascot Chang also has a shop in Manhattan.

David's Shirts
Victoria Hotel, Unit 201, Shun Tak Centre (MTR: Sheung
Wan); Mandarin Oriental Hotel, 5 Connaught Rd. (MTR:
Central); Wing Lee Building, 33 Kimberley Rd., ground
floor, Kowloon (MTR: TST).

David's is the other most popular of the custom shirt shops in
Hong Kong. It's less glitzy than **Ascot Chang** (see above) but
just as famous to those in the know. David's also has a branch
in New York City. The main shop in Hong Kong is in Kowloon
on Kimberley Road. But there are more convenient branches,
mostly in hotels like the Regent and the Mandarin Oriental.

David's will copy any shirt you like; just bring it with you
and plan to leave it. The shop also has a framed illustration
of collar and cuff styles you can choose from. Mail order is
not only possible but common with repeat customers. If you
cannot get to Hong Kong, ask for a current swatch and price
list. Return a shirt that fits you perfectly and a check, along
with fabric and collar and cuff choices. Approximately 4 to 6
weeks later, a box of new shirts will arrive.

MEN'S SUITS: MADE-TO-MEASURE

Probably the most famous Hong Kong fantasy is that made-to-measure suits grow on trees or that they are easily and inexpensively obtained with a snap of the fingers and a few hundred dollars. No way. Remember the first law of Hong Kong custom-made suits: A bargain is not a bargain if it doesn't fit. Furthermore, the whole point of a bespoke suit is psychological—you must feel (and look) like a king in it. Its impact derives from the fact that it was made for your body, that it moves with you as no off-the-rack garment can.

- Start your search for a tailor the minute you arrive. Leave yourself time for three fittings while in Hong Kong. The first will be for measurements and choice of fabrics; the second will involve a partially finished suit with only one sleeve in place; the third will be to detail the finished garment. Good tailors usually have everything wrapped up by the third fitting.
- If at all possible, choose your tailor before you leave home and fax ahead for an appointment so you can meet shortly after arrival in Hong Kong. For the two best men's tailors in Hong Kong, see below. After you check in to your hotel, the tailor should be your first stop. You may want to choose your hotel based on the convenience to your tailor.
- Most tailors carry a full line of imported fabrics from Italy, England, and France. If your tailor is not one of the top two, ask whether the thread is imported also. If it is not, ask to see the quality, and test it for durability. Remember all those horror stories you have heard about suits falling apart? It wasn't the fabric, it was the thread. You do not need to worry about quality at the two biggies.
- Well-made suits from a Hong Kong tailor are not inexpensive. Imported fabrics run about $20 to $80 per yard, and an average-size suit will take 3½ yards. Silk-wool blends and cashmeres cost more. The finished price for a top-quality, killer suit runs $550 to $800. You could do better in some cases

with an off-the-rack suit in the U.S., but the quality would not be the same. Your suit should be the equal of a $3,000 Savile Row suit.

- The tailor will want a 50% deposit to start the work. You may be able to pay with a check in U.S. dollars or pounds sterling. Ask ahead of time.

- If you are having the tailor ship the suits to you, remember to figure in the Customs charges and shipping. On average, air freight costs $20 per suit. Shirts can be shipped for $30 per dozen. U.S. Customs charges about $75 in duty on a single new suit. Once you have established an account with a tailor or a shirt maker and he or she has your measurements on file, you can simply get fabric swatches sent to you and do your shopping through the mail—or in a local hotel, if your tailor visits major U.S. cities.

- Check to see if the tailor you have chosen travels to the U.S. to visit customers. Chances are, if you live in a major city (New York, Washington, San Francisco, Los Angeles, or Chicago), he or she will. Most of the tailors I recommend either come in person once a year or send a representative with fabric books and order forms. At that time, new measurements can be taken in case you have lost or gained weight.

The Big Names: Hong Kong's Finest Tailors

A-MAN HING CHEONG CO. LTD.
Mandarin Oriental Hotel, 5 Connaught Rd. (MTR: Central).

Fondly referred to as "Ah-men," this shop turns out quite a few garments for the rich-tourist-and-businessman trade and, therefore, has become adept at relating to the European-cut suit. The tailors don't even blink twice when you ask for an extra pair of trousers. They just smile and ask for more money. The prices here are on the higher side, with a suit beginning around $650.

A-Man will also do custom shirts for approximately $50 to $150. © **852/2522-3336.** Fax 852/2523-4707.

W. W. CHAN & SONS TAILOR LTD.
*Burlington House, 92-94 Nathan Rd., 2nd floor, Kowloon
(MTR: TST).*

Peter Chan carries on a family business, which he has built and
expanded over the years. He also has two shops in Shanghai
(p. 268) and is personally based there. In Hong Kong, men want
to see Eric and women want to see Danny. The average price
for a suit is $650 to $800; mink-cashmere blends can cost more.
The W. W. Chan showroom is decidedly more relaxed than other
big-time contenders' spaces. The showroom is neat, clean,
modern, and even spacious, which is hard to find in Hong Kong.
But the location in Kowloon and the approach to the actual
showroom are not so swank; businessmen who are used to wall-
to-wall carpet may need a moment to adjust. © 852/2366-2634.

RESALE

This is somewhat of a new category in Hong Kong (and
Kowloon). It follows a major trend in London, Paris, and
New York: Many socialites take their year-old designer clothes
and accessories to resale shops, which sell them to the public
for less than full cost. Ah, the consummate Hong Kong Hob-
son's choice: to buy used or fake? Used is more expensive.

FRANCE STATION
80 Russell St. (MTR: Causeway Bay).

Heads up—this will be on the final. The resale shops related
to the next listing (Paris Station) are all named after cities, so
Milan Station is part of that family. This store, however, is part
of a different group, with a name chosen to confuse or blend
with the concept. This store's main specialty is designer bags.

PARIS STATION
Metropole Building, 12 Hankow Rd., Kowloon (MTR: TST).

This is one shop in a growing chain—other stores have names such as Milan Station and so on. Paris Station sells designer handbags and accessories. It's around the corner from the Kowloon Hotel and behind the Pen, so you're going to be in the area anyway. There are no bargains, but it's fun to poke around. For information about the newest shops, call ✆ 852/8200-7588.

VIP STATION
61 Granville Rd. (MTR: TST East).

I think this is a third chain getting into the action—its business cards list another store near Times Square. I like this one because after you've been bin shopping at the jobbers on Granville Road, it's fun to finish up here. Mostly designer handbags in good condition, but pricey.

SOUVENIRS

It's not hard to find gifts or souvenirs in Hong Kong—they are everywhere. Actually giving the gifts to your friends will be harder; I always want to keep everything for myself. I included some gift suggestions in chapter 1. Below are a few stores that specifically sell great gifts.

CITY SUPER
Times Square mall, Causeway Bay (MTR: Causeway Bay); Harbour City, Kowloon (MTR: TST); IFC2 mall (MTR: Central).

I listed City Super under "Grocery Stores," but it is really a department store of goodies with a complete section of dry goods separate from the foodstuffs. Tons of inexpensive novelty items—especially beauty supplies and bath items—make great souvenirs and gifts. I bought many in packaging that I could not even understand.

DFS (DUTY FREE SHOPPERS)
DFS Galleria at Sun Plaza, 28 Canton Rd., Kowloon (MTR: TST); DFS Galleria at Chinachem Plaza, 77 Mody Rd. (MTR: TST East).

This is a department store meant mostly for Japanese shoppers but handy to all. I don't like it for normal designer shopping only because it bores me. When it comes to souvenirs, however, DFS may have the best in town.

A department in each store sells Chinese meds, foods, and souvenirs—I'd head there, ignoring the Burberry and Chanel. Don't miss the key chains, including one that allows you to insert your own photo into the body of a Chinese warlord.

DFS sells in bulk units, with prices discounted according to how much you buy. It has shuttle bus service that makes a loop from a few major hotels to the stores, and will deliver your purchases to your hotel so you can continue shopping with free hands.

SPAS

Most of the swank hotels in Hong Kong have had spas for quite some time, and they have all refurbished their spas to take on the competition. Especially with the problems caused by jet lag—or the general need for detoxification—a trip here is no longer complete without some sort of treatment.

Note: All of the spas listed in this section require a reservation. Most hotels let nonguests test the spa waters.

The latest trend is foot treatments. Hawkers on the street will hand you brochures or try to lure you into alleys for a treatment. One of the nicest evenings I spent in town was an early dinner with friends and then a trip (for all four of us) to a foot spa.

E-SPA AT THE PENINSULA
Peninsula Hotel, Salisbury Rd., Kowloon (MTR: TST).

I have been to many spas in my time, but I gotta tell you: this isn't a spa—this is paradise. I'm talking about the architecture, the cocooning feel, the cozy little room where you sip tea and stare at the wild blue yonder, the steam room. Yes, the treatments are excellent, too. I always come for the cure to my jet lag and spring for ESPA products to carry along on my travels; they're just good, and I'm worth it. Pick your treatment from the spa menu online and book ahead of your arrival. © 852/2315-3271; www.peninsula.com.

I-SPA
InterContinental Hotel, 18 Salisbury Rd., 3rd floor, Tsim Sha Tsui, Kowloon (MTR: TST).

Not to be confused with the E-SPA brand of spa products, I-Spa will cure whatever else ails you. I always do a spa treatment after my long-haul flight and tried "Ancient Rituals of the Orient" recently. It was amazing, right down to the part when my neck and arms were stretched against tension and sprung free from their pins and needles and jet-lag woes. The treatment was so successful in helping me get acclimated to local time that I also booked a treatment for my evening of departure. This time I did a face treatment that actually aerated my skin. It wasn't so relaxing, but it was therapeutic. I could see the difference immediately after the treatment and felt it was a smart thing to do before spending 12 hours in a tin can flying across the world.

Note: If you book a Born to Shop & Spa Tour, you have an I-Spa treatment included in the package. © 852/2721-1211, ext. 81.

PLATEAU
Grand Hyatt Hotel, 1 Harbour Rd. (MTR: Wan Chai).

While Hyatt Hotels are internationally renowned for spa facilities, no other Hyatt has anything quite like this. A new addition includes a 23-room section of the hotel that is dedicated as a "spa lifestyle program." The city's most incredible spa, constantly voted one of the best in the world by various travel magazines, is where I discovered the June Jacobs brand of spa treatments, which you can also buy in the U.S. ✆ 852/2588-1234.

Foot Spas/Reflexology

Foot spas are everywhere. I am always reluctant to try just any old place (I am still Dr. Kalter's daughter), so the ones I list here were suggested by friends and tested by my tootsies. Wherever you go, if there is no disinfectant process as you begin, grab your shoes walk out.

BIG BUCKET FOOT
Shops 1 and 2, Hoi Kung Court, 264 Gloucester Rd. (MTR: Causeway Bay).

I will always have a soft spot for this place, my first foot spa, because I first thought it was a shoe store for large sizes. It's half a block from the Excelsior Hotel and not too swish—but it is clean. Your feet soak in a big bucket, hence the name. The 90-minute treatment costs about $20; I tipped HK$20 ($2.60) afterward. I did a treatment before leaving for the airport on departure eve and swear it helped me. ✆ 852/2572-8611.

HENG LAM FONG
Star House, 3 Salisbury Rd., 18th floor, Kowloon (MTR: TST).

When I told Louis, the chief concierge at the InterConti, that I was researching reputable foot and reflexology treatments, he suggested this establishment. Located right at the Star Ferry, it provides traditional Chinese medicine as well as reflexology and massage treatments. The staff's English can be spotty. ✆ 852/2376-3648.

TAI PAN FOOT SOAKED BATH
18 Middle Rd., Tsim Sha Tsui, Kowloon (MTR: TST).

This is one of the fancy, clean, and swank places, as befits its address right behind the Pen. You take off your shoes and socks and put them in a locker, soak your feet to disinfect them, and then settle into a first-class airline seat for a treatment that will have you floating. Prices begin at $20. © **852/2301-3820.**

TEA

Some of the best tea in China is sold in Hong Kong. In fact, it's sold everywhere, and it makes a great gift. The packaging seems to be the main attraction—to me, anyway—but there are many tastes you won't find at home, and they're far more exotic than Lipton Yellow Label. Not that I'm knocking Lipton. If you do not know the Yellow Label line, which I don't think is sold in the U.S., you might want to try it. It makes excellent iced tea.

The listings below include individual brands and retail chains. Don't forget that every supermarket has a large selection.

BOJENMI
Chinese supermarkets such as Needs, New World Centre, Kowloon (MTR: TST).

The red-and-white Bojenmi brand box has an illustration of a girl playing the lute. I find that the tea smells like dead fish and tastes worse. But I have several friends in Hong Kong who swear by it. They claim you get used to it and then eventually like it, and that in 6 months, the cholesterol numbers will drop and life will be much more healthy. So I am doing my three cups a day. But I am nursing the same tea bag through the three cups because it tastes better when it's weak.

CHINESE HEALING TEA
Locations in major MTR concourses, including TST (near exit B), Central (exit A), and Admiralty MTR (exit A).

About a dozen of these little shops—all clean and white and spiffy—operate in MTR stations. They're selling their packaging, their hype, and their marketing skills. The shops have tea, jellied tea, and a line of health products made from tea. You can taste brewed teas. I can't tell you whether any of the teas work, but for $10 you can get a cute gift package.

FOOK MING TONG
Western Market, 323 Des Voeux Rd., Central (MTR: Sheung Wan); Ocean Terminal, Harbour City, Tsim Sha Tsui, Kowloon (MTR: TST); IFC mall (MTR: Central); and many other locations.

This is the leading chain of tourist-oriented (excuse me) tea shops, selling tea and teapots. The shops are adorable, the selection is exotic, and there is nothing too unusual about it. The packaging is so perfect that you will be comfortable and willing to buy all your gifts here.

YING KEE TEA CO.
151 Queen's Rd. Central (MTR: Central); Shop G8, 28 Hankow Rd., TST, Kowloon (MTR: TST); and other locations.

This is a small chain with a store in just about every major shopping district in Hong Kong.

TEENS & TWEENS

All of Causeway Bay—the area behind the Excelsior Hotel and between Times Square mall and Lee Gardens—is a hive of teen, tween, young, and hip fashion. It's mobbed but exhilarating. Try to avoid the hours when the kids get off work in the evenings, unless you want to observe the phenom rather than shop.

THE ALLEY
New Territories (MTR: Lai Chi Kok).

A garmento friend from the U.S. brought me here—I never would have found it on my own! It's possible that "The Alley" is the name given to it by Americans who work this space looking for hot new ideas—there are no signs that say THE ALLEY. Do we care? This is a trade building with a ground-level floor filled with stall after stall of shops selling teen and tween fashions at *grrreat* prices. It's an amazing social phenom just to be here and watch it going on swirling around you, but it's not for princesses. You walk down a center aisle that gives you the feeling of being in an alley, hence the name. It is indoors; it is truly incredible.

To get here, take the B2 exit from the MTR, walk away from the green and yellow towers, and turn right at the Hong Kong Industrial Center. Enter through parts B/C.

SUN ARCADE
78 Canton Rd., Kowloon (MTR: TST).

This small mall is underground, as is the fashion—which is mostly Japanese. Sizes are small, but the clothes are so fabulous that creativity freaks will be drooling. The crowds are also fun. Located beneath DFS.

WATCHES

As they say on the street, "Copy watch, lady?" Indeed, you can buy a fake Rolex or save money on a real Rolex. The trick is finding the right watch at the right price. You can pay anything from $50 to $10,000 and still not know what you have bought. Furthermore, the savings seem to be on high-end merchandise, so, yes, you can save $3,000 on a $15,000 Rolex—but did you really want a $15,000 Rolex in the first place?

Some things to be aware of before you buy:

- Check to see that the whole watch and not just the movement was made by the manufacturer. A common practice in Hong Kong is to sell a Swiss watch face and movement with a Hong Kong–made bracelet. The bracelet is probably silver with gold plating. This can work to your advantage if you do not want to spend $5,000 for a solid-gold watch but want the look. A reputable dealer will tell you that this is what you are buying and will price the watch accordingly. These watches cost $150 to $400.
- Check the serial number on the inside movement against the serial number on your guarantee.
- If you do not receive a worldwide guarantee, don't buy the watch.
- Do the same careful checking at brand-name dealers that you would do at a no-name shop. We know of someone who bought a brand-name watch from a reputable dealer, got the watch home, and had problems. When she turned to the brand's U.S. dealer, she learned that, yes, indeed, she had bought one of their watches, but the movement was 5 years old. She had bought a current body with a used movement!

If you are simply looking for something unusual and fun, try **City Chain,** a huge chain with a branch in every mall and shopping district. It carries Seiko, Bulova, and Zenith, among other name brands, as well as fashion watches like Smash (a takeoff of Swatch).

Copy watches are sold in every market and on the streets of Nathan Road. Far better copies are for sale in Shenzhen, although quality varies and the whole process can be overwhelming. Expect a Triple-A quality (the best fake possible) version of a Cartier watch to cost about $150. Prices for watches in Shenzhen begin at $10.

WOMEN'S CLOTHING: MADE-TO-MEASURE

I started going to **W. W. Chan** for the simple reason that Peter Chan made my husband's clothes. Of the top two tailors, only W. W. Chan has a women's division.

Women are charged a flat rate for the making of the garment (no matter what size or how complicated); you pay for the fabric by the yard or provide your own. A woman's suit totals about $750, depending on the fabric. French wools (the same ones used at Chanel, and so on) bring the cost up. A dress costs about $170 for labor alone, a jacket, $175. See p. 135 for the W. W. Chan address and coordinates. To make an appointment or send a message directly to Danny Chen, who makes my clothes, write danny@wwchan.com.

Chapter Six

·················

PEARL RIVER DELTA: SHENZHEN, CANTON, DONGGUAN & MACAU

WELCOME TO THE PRD

·······································

You can get a small taste of China with a day trip, overnight visit, or weekend in the nearby Pearl River Delta, or PRD. This is one of the fastest-growing areas in China, and once you really get into it, you can participate in the new China. The main shopping cities are Shenzhen, Canton (Guangzhou, sometimes spelled Quangzhou), and Macau; they encircle Hong Kong. The entire area is part of the Guangdong Province. Do not confuse Guangzhou (say "Gwan-*joe*"), the city, with Guangdong, the province.

With Hong Kong as your base, you can do a circle tour, plan a series of days out or nights away, or even arrive through one of the area's flashy new airports—which often offer less expensive flights than those that go direct to Hong Kong. All sorts of adventures are out there, waiting for those who dare to do something a little bit different.

Local Lingo

Once you cross into China, you can expect the ability to speak or understand English to plummet. One morning I asked for "two eggs, poached" and got two eggs, toast. They sound amazingly similar when you think about it. Learn to speak Chinese or get a grip.

Tourist Guides

Because very few American tourists go into the PRD, few tourist guides cover the area. For specific information, often in Chinese and English (very helpful when dealing with taxi drivers), check bookstores in Hong Kong, which carry several locally printed guidebooks. Shop carefully—many guides are out of date.

WELCOME TO SHENZHEN

....

There is talk by politicos that by the year 2013, Shenzhen and Hong Kong will be united into one giant metroplex. As crazy as this sounds (to me, anyway), insiders say that this idea makes a lot of sense. Time will tell.

I've seen Shenzhen described as "the new Hong Kong," which sort of puts Shanghai in an awkward position. To me, Shenzhen is the new Shenzhen. It was once a fishing village without history or locals, and now it is a card-carrying part of the New China: a massive city of apartments, theme parks, shopping malls, and factories. While I used to come just as a day trip, or maybe an overnight to ease the shopping burdens, I've now discovered how amazing this huge city has become and love it for a weekend getaway.

For those on a first excursion, Shenzhen (say *Shum*-sum in Cantonese) is actually a visit to one building—a sort of giant mall where the merchants sell a lot of copy merchandise. The day trip to Shenzhen is as good as a trip to the far side of the moon, but I have to say right upfront that I do not condone fake merchandise. For the most part, I think you get what you pay for—fake is fake. It won't last, it usually looks cheap, and it tarnishes your reputation. But then, I am referring to fake handbags, shoes, ties, and, well, fashion. I have something totally different to say about fake art—see p. 138.

In the years that I have been doing this day trip, it has gotten enormously easier—there are now signs in English. I understand that once you know your way around, anything is easy (this being a life lesson) . . . so perhaps I am not the one to ask. But to my eye, things are an awful lot easier.

- The new TST East train station makes it possible to jump onboard right in front of the InterContinental Hotel in Kowloon, and *vroom vroom*—you are soon walking across the border into China. If you're making Shenzhen an overnight or weekend destination, you have a choice of several international hotel chains, including a brand-new Inter-Continental that is built right into a theme park!
- The new organization at the immigration center makes the lines go more quickly, the transition more smooth, and the wait less annoying.

Serious Shopper Notes

Consider taking a rolling suitcase for all your purchases. Wear comfortable shoes. Wimps and wusses need not apply. Have plenty of cash and patience. Prices are now in RMB; if you want to pay in Hong Kong dollars, not yuan, there is a 6% surcharge. There are ATMs and exchange booths all over the immigration center.

Rush Hour

Stores in Shenzhen don't open until 10am (in the Mall, they open at 11AM), giving you plenty of time to arrive. Allow 1 hour from Kowloon to the Mall. Rush hour is 7 to 9am heading inbound, and 5 to 8pm heading outbound. Try to leave Shenzhen by 4pm if you are on a day trip.

Avoid holidays, Fridays, and weekends.

Spend the Night

A day trip to Shenzhen is an amazing experience: It's power shopping to the max, and it will leave you exhausted but giggling. You'll sink into your hotel spa with a whimper and wake up the next day mad at yourself for not buying more. The experience is easier if you stay overnight. You can avoid rush-hour traffic, and you have a chance to get a grip on your mental health.

I used to do this excursion as a day trip but now sometimes take time out for an overnight, which I have done with several stays in downtown hotels: once at the Shangri La (the closest luxury hotel to the shopping) and, now, at the InterConti Shenzhen, which is about a half-hour drive from the shopping and is actually a resort next to a theme park. I found the major advantage of an overnight was the lack of pressure when shopping in the Mall. It was a far better adventure to spend the night, dine at a luxury hotel, have my feet rubbed, drink Great Wall wine, and pretend I knew something about the New China.

Getting There

BY TRAIN

From Hong Kong, take the KCR train from East Tsim Sha Tsui in Kowloon. The train costs HK$36 ($5) for regular service and HK$72 ($9.35) for first class, which consists of a plush, reserved seat. Rush hours are crowded; at other times, standard service is fine and you should get a seat. The train is easy to use and well marked. The place to stand while awaiting the first-class compartment is designated on the platform.

Trains leave so often that you don't need a schedule or a reservation—buy a ticket and wait for the next train. Get off at the last stop, Lo Wu, and follow the crowds. The ride is 34km (about 21 miles) and takes about a half-hour.

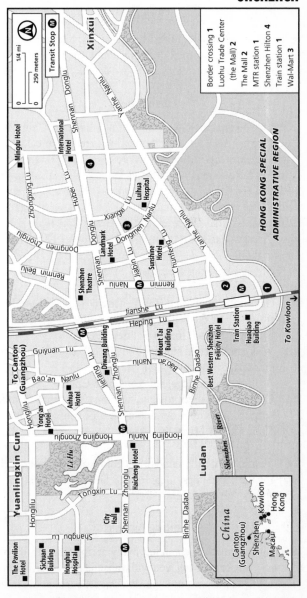

Shenzhen

Border crossing **1**
Luohu Trade Center
(the Mall) **2**
The Mall **2**
MTR station **1**
Shenzhen Hilton **4**
Train station **1**
Wal-Mart **3**

Transit Stop Ⓜ

HONG KONG SPECIAL
ADMINISTRATIVE REGION

1/4 mi
250 meters

Xinxui

Mingdu Hotel

International Hotel

Zhongxing Lu

Hubei Lu

Shennan Donglu

Yuhe Nanlu

Dongmen Zhonglu

Renmin Beilu

Xiangxi

Luihua Hospital

Xiangxi Lu

Dongmen Nanlu

Landmark Hotel

Shennan Donglu

Jiabin Lu

Sunshine Hotel

Chunfeng Lu

Shenzhen Theatre

Nanlu

Renmin

Yanhe Nanlu

Jianshe Lu

Heping Lu

Guiyuan Lu

Diwang Building

Jiefang Lu

Shennan Zhonglu

Mount Tai Building

Bao'an Nanlu

Binhe Dadao

Train Station

Best Western Shenzhen
Felicity Hotel

Huaqiao Building

To Kowloon →

To Canton
(Guangzhou)

Yuanlingxin Cun

Honglilu

Yong'an Hotel

Anhua Hotel

Hongling Zhonglu

Hongling Nanlu

Haicheng Hotel

Li Hu

Tongxin Lu

Binhe Dadao

Shenzhen River

Ludan

The Pavilion Hotel

Sichuan Building

Honghui Hospital

Shangbu Lu

Shennan Zhonglu

City Hall

Hongli Lu

China

Canton
(Guangzhou)

Shenzhen Kowloon

Hong
Kong

Macau

BY BUS

Citybus Express Coach offers bus service to Shenzhen; there is transfer service at the border. In Hong Kong, call © 852/2736-3888 for more information, or ask your hotel concierge.

Formalities

Because you are crossing the border into mainland China, it's not a breeze. Also note that due to the current political situation, the rules are in flux. As we go to press, U.K. and U.S. passport holders may not get visas at the border. You can get a visa in Hong Kong within 24 hours—your hotel concierge will charge approximately $150 for 24-hour service and a $50 service charge. There are less expensive ways to do it, but they aren't as easy. See "Getting a Visa," on p. 17 for more information.

Once you have the visa, this is the drill:

1. Get off the train at Lo Wu. You are now in the New Territories. Exit the Separate Administrative Region (SAR) by going through the formalities here.
2. Walk into a second building and officially enter China with more paperwork and your visa.
3. Walk across a bridge, and you are in China.
4. Change money, exit the immigration center, turn to your right, then go up the stairs in front of you, and you are 100m (328 ft.) from the Mall.

Going back, it's the same thing. Allow about 1 hour each way for the formalities; it can take 3 hours. It can also take 30 minutes, but that's rare.

Getting Around

Shenzhen is quite large and has many neighborhoods. If you are just going to the Mall, you will walk and never learn more. Those who are staying or exploring can get a taxi in the train station or hop into the new Metro: it is quite extensive.

The Mall shopping district is not downtown but in a commercial strip near the border crossing that is designated in addresses as Lo Wu district. Most of the international hotels are in this area also, although you may not want to walk if you have a lot of bags or luggage.

Note that streets and buildings are not usually marked in English, although this is changing and the big shopping buildings closest to the border now have signs you can read. Once you get oriented, so to speak, you will not need to read much—but you may find that my inability to give you more specific addresses is annoying until you get used to the lay of the land.

Taxis are cheap, but don't expect your driver to speak English. Have all destinations written in Chinese and in hand.

Calling Around

Shenzhen is in China and uses the 86 country code. The city code is 0755.

The Lay of the Land

The main drag, an enormous, wide highway with low-slung modern commercial centers in long strips, is called "Sino-British Street." It's technically in Shatoujiao, the area east of downtown—and leading right from the Shenzhen River and the Customs House. This street may be written as "Jia Dian" or "Jian She" in Pinyin. Most streets have a direction after the name—for example, Shennan Road East, Shennan Road Central, Renmin Road South, Renmin Road North.

This highway is lined with commercial centers and malls. Some have individual shops inside, and many just have stalls or tables or tiny selling areas. These malls have names like Shenzhen Commercial Center or Lo Wu Commercial Center and are hard to tell apart. They all offer four or five floors of selling space, with floors joined by escalators. There's usually a restaurant on each floor and toilets (have tissues on hand).

The more real part of Shenzhen is called East Gate, which also appears on some maps as East Gate Business Pedestrian street. This is one Metro stop away from the Mall, at the far edge of Lo Wu district.

Money Matters

In all other parts of Shenzhen, you now use Chinese currency, yuan (also called RMB). There are some 15 offices of major international banks in Shenzhen, as well as scads of ATMs.

The Mall

Luohu Trade Center, better known simply as the Mall, is five stories high, with escalators on each floor. There are restaurants and toilets on all floors. There are some vendors on the roof also, but you may want to avoid this as it's a bit scuzzy.

The Mall sells just about everything, although it is known for copyright violations. Do not buy fake DVDs as you could get in hot water for bringing them back into Hong Kong. There have been crackdowns on other fakes, especially with WTO (World Trade Organization) inspections and tall orders for upcoming Olympic perfection. Still, this building is amazing in terms of what's for sale, how low the prices are, and the sheer number of foot treatments you can enjoy.

I go mostly for gifts, and I do load up. The floors are more or less organized by categories of goods, but this is not a rule—so you will find jewelry on floors other than in the jewelry mart, and so forth.

The designer copy handbags are often in the ceiling hidden from police because there are constant crackdowns on fake merchandise. They cost $75 to $100 and rival the ones I bought in Hong Kong for $250.

Note that a "fake" has a logo on it, and an "inspiration" of a classic is a style without any attempt to fake the hardware or logo—such as bags inspired by the Birkin and Kelly styles. Inspirations are 100% legal. Some copies, especially in watches, are graded by quality. A triple-A (top)-rated Cartier-style watch can cost $150 after hard negotiating. A cheapie Chanel copy watch may cost $15. Expect $40 to be the going rate for a watch or decent handbag.

There is a fabric mart and a row of tailor shops, although it takes several visits to have garments made, making this impractical for the day-tripper. The better shops are on the fourth floor.

The merchandise available in the Mall very much depends on fashion trends and police crackdowns. On my last trip, the latest fad was Goyard handbags, which were selling for about $40 to $50 each. Prada merchandise was scarce. Franck Muller watches were "in"; Cartier watches are classics. Many stores had stacks of robin's egg blue boxes (fake Tiffany & Co.), though many of these boxes were actually the wrong color—too green. There were fake Hermès ties and scarves, some in fake orange boxes. Most of the fake stuff does not look or feel real.

East Gate

Not far from the Mall, perhaps a 20-minute walk or zippy subway ride (one stop), you are in East Gate, the part of Shenzhen where locals shop. There is a night market on a pedestrian street with a scene common to all major Chinese cities and fascinating for a first glimpse—the young people are out to spend their money and consume. Stores sell fashion, phones, DVDs, and electronics. The clothes won't fit you and the brands are possibly fake, but it's fabulous fun to observe the scene.

The Art Village

Perhaps you noticed this on your shopping stroll through Stanley Market, but there are vendors who sell copies of art masterpieces. They cost $10 to $30 depending on the artist and your bargaining skills. These paintings mostly come from Shenzhen, and you can indeed visit the Dafen Art Village.

I bought several "van Gogh" paintings on unstretched canvas, complete with white borders. I had them stretched onto frames, allowing the borders to show, then I took my paints, my glue gun, some stickers, and assorted tchotchkes and created my own statement over Mr. van Gogh's. This makes the work "original" (very original, that's for sure) and therefore more acceptable to me as a work of art and not a simple forgery. I mean, get real: Who am I to attempt to pull off a real masterpiece in my home?

But wait, it gets better—if you go to the Art Village, best with a photo of yourself, you can have yourself painted into a masterpiece. The most common is *The Last Supper*. Hey, don't ask me—I don't make up the news. I'm just the messenger.

Sleeping in Shenzhen

INTERCONTINENTAL SHENZHEN
9009 Shennan Road

Brand-new and modern, this is the latest guy to enter the fray of name-brand hotels fighting for a place in this Chinese border town of businessmen and shopping samurais. The hotel is located on the far side of downtown and has the usual pool, fitness center, and, of course, a 24-hour lounge, one of Interconti's specialties—and the reason you want to book a Club Floor room. Rates begin around $150 per night.

This hotel is not convenient for shoppers, but that is its beauty. You are forced to drive through town to get here, and that is an education in itself. The hotel itself is owned by the man who owns the theme park next door, Splendid China, so the hotel is also a theme, having to do with Spain and our friend Chris Columbus. I swear that outside the balcony of my spacious room was not only an exact replica of the Santa Maria but also the Eiffel Tower.

The hotel is gorgeous—truly a resort setting, it is perfect for romantic getaways or as somewhere to take the kids. It also offers that elusive magic we all travel to find. When I took a taxi out one evening (to a great mall for New Chinese Yuppies called MixC), I passed by Splendid China with its thousands of tiny red lanterns all lit up in the night.

Local © 755/3399-3388.

WELCOME TO CANTON

Canton is one of those famous names in trade and shopping that seems to stick, long after it has been replaced by the politically correct Guangzhou. Canton was one of the original 19th-century treaty ports and has been a center of commerce ever since. Now it stands midway between Shenzhen and Macau in the circular loop of the PRD. It is headquarters for those who are adopting a Chinese child (the U.S. consulate is here), home of the most famous trade fair in China, and one of the most exciting cities in the new China. I am not easily overwhelmed, but I admit it, Guangzhou intimidated me. This is not a day trip from Hong Kong (if you can help it) and can be a lot more raw than the other trips in this area that are suggested in this chapter.

Why Canton?

I asked myself this question the entire time I was there. I had a fabulous visit, my hotel was great, and I did buy some terrific items. But it's a hard trip—mostly because of the language difficulties, not because of the lack of Western lifestyle—and it's not for everyone. If you want a look into the New China, go to Shenzhen. If you want to want to explore a part of China that is almost gone—colonial roots—go to Guangzhou's Shamian Island. There is magic to be found, but you will have to look for it.

Getting There

BY TRAIN

From Hong Kong: KCR from Hung Hom. It's a 2-hour journey; Guangzhou is 75 miles north of Hong Kong. You will arrive at the East Railway Station in Guangzhou, which is the first of two train stations that are served.

By Ferry

From Hong Kong, there are four trips daily between Kowloon and Guangzhou, with departures from Hong Kong beginning at 7:30am and ending at 7:45pm. For the schedule from Guangzhou, call © 8620/8222-2555.

By Air

Guangzhou has a great airport, Baiyun International, that is meant to rival Hong Kong's. It has been created to handle some 80 million passengers a year in the upcoming years and will be the area's largest air hub. There are now nonstop flights from Paris on Air France, flights from the U.S. (often through Tokyo) on a variety of carriers (including Northwest), and a host of Chinese flights. Although you probably won't fly from Hong Kong, service is available.

By Bus

There was no train or ferry service from Macau to Guangzhou when I made this trip a few years ago so I took the bus, which was easy. You go to the Barrier Gate, cross into China, then cross the street and go down the escalator to the bus station. Buses leave every 15 minutes and cost about $5 one-way. The trip takes 2 hours unless traffic is bad. It's modern highway all the way. If your bus looks full or smoky, consider waiting for the next one. There is a bathroom stop after 1 hour, but there's no toilet on the bus.

Getting Around

Taxis are inexpensive; the flag falls at 7¥ (less than $1). I took taxis to far-flung areas that were over and under many freeways and way past where Grandma lives. The most I ever paid for a taxi was $5; you can go crosstown for $3.

If you take the bus from Macau, get off at the China Hotel (Marriott) and take a taxi to your chosen hotel. Taxis are easy to hail in the streets or at hotels.

Canton (Guangzhou)

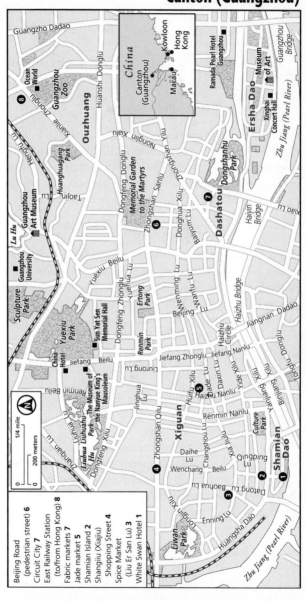

Guangzho Dadao

Ocean World

Guangzhou Zoo

Huanshi Donglu

Xianlie Zhonglu

Haiyin Lu

Huanghuagang Park

Taojin

OUZHUANG

Nonglin Xialu

Nonglin Nanlu

Ramada Pearl Hotel Guangzhou

Ersha Dao

Guangzhou Bridge

Museum of Art

Xinghai Concert Hall

Zhu Jiang (Pearl River)

Dongfeng Donglu

Memorial Garden to the Martyrs

Zhongshan Sanlu

Zhongshan Erlu

Lu Hu

Guangzhou Art Museum

Guangzhou University

Sculpture Park

Yuexiu Park

China Hotel

Sun Yat Sen Memorial Hall

Jiefang Beilu

Dongfeng Zhonglu

Renmin Beilu

Zhanqian Lu

The Museum of the Nanyue King's Mausoleum

Liuhua Park

Liuhua Hu

Dongfeng Xilu

Jinghua Lu

Zhongshan Qilu

Xiguan

Daihe Lu

Wenchang

Liwan Park

Enning Lu

Huangsha Dao

Longjin Xilu

Baohua Lu

Datong Lu

Qingping Lu

Shamian Dao

Zhu Jiang (Pearl River)

Yuexiu Beilu

Yuehua Lu

Ertong Park

Renmin Park

Beijing Lu

Jiefang Zhonglu

Jiefang Nanlu

Luorong Lu

Huifu Xilu

Haizhu Nanlu

Jade Lu

Daxin Lu

Yide Xilu

Renmin Nanlu

Culture Park

Xiajiu Lu

Changshou

Dongshanhu Park

Dashatou

Haiyin Bridge

Beijing Lu

Nyenming Lu

Wanfu Lu

Haizhu Bridge

Haizhu Circle

Jiangnan Dadao

Binjiang Donglu

Tonghu Donglu

Xianjiang Xilu

Binjiang Xilu

Xicun

Haijin Lu

Inset map (upper right)

China

Kowloon — Hong Kong

Canton (Guangzhou)

Macau

Legend

Beijing Road (pedestrian street) **6**
Circuit City **7**
East Railway Station (to/from Hong Kong) **8**
Fabric markets **7**
Jade market **5**
Shamian Island **2**
Shangjiu (Xiajiu) **2**
Shopping Street **4**
Spice Market (Liu Er San Lu) **3**
White Swan Hotel **1**

N

1/4 mile

0 · 200 meters

Private pickup and drop-off or shuttle transfers from the airport or train station can usually be arranged with your hotel.

There are two subway lines; both are relatively easy to use. But taxis are so cheap, why bother?

Calling Around

Guangzhou is in China, so you need the country code, 86, to call here. The area code for Canton is 020. If you have a new-fangled Chinese portable phone, it will automatically switch between Hong Kong and China zones. Otherwise, you will need to change SIM cards. SIM cards are sold on the trains.

The Lay of the Land

Guangzhou is a huge city and getting bigger as I type. For some reason, it reminded me of Caracas. I found it far more frightening than Beijing. Don't begin to think you can get a grasp on it in a day or two. Or in your lifetime. But then, you came to shop, and you won't be disappointed. Perhaps you should aim to just grasp your wallet and a few basics.

You can buy a book in Hong Kong called *Markets of Quangzhou* (available at Dymocks bookstores for $10) that has the addresses of all the wholesale buildings, but you can't possibly get to even a fraction of them. Time, energy, and ability to cope with a foreign environment will limit your explorations to just a few areas.

Note: Families who adopt babies seem to be plugged into a network of others who have already done so; they travel with their own shopping notes. Since adoption seems to mean 10 days in Guangzhou, there's a lot more time for exploration.

A Warning

Even old China hands are warned not to go into Canton's fresh-food markets. The stories I have heard still haunt me. Also, don't look too carefully at those cages in front of restaurants. Just high-tail it (excuse the expression) out of there. And while we're at it, in these days of epidemic and pandemic, stay away from bird markets.

Shopping Neighborhoods

You can get to Bar Street on your own. My list of shopping neighborhoods that are near the main hotels and easy to get to is below. And yes, I did travel into the Arab Quarter, and yes, I did track down various porcelain factories, and no, they are not listed below because I wasn't impressed.

Shamian Island: I haven't really figured out where the land ends and the island begins, but there's water all around once you get close to the White Swan Hotel. Behind the hotel is a strip of residential peace and quiet and greenery with sufficient tourist traps to keep you happy for a few hours. It's clean, safe, easy, and charming. There is a real Starbucks—as well as other coffee joints and cutie-pie restaurants. Don't ask me why, but many of the shops offer to do laundry. There are Internet cafes, crafts stores, and numerous TTs (tourist traps). A TT shop that I like a lot is **E-Gallery,** 61 Shamian Main St., which has a smaller branch around the corner closer to the White Swan in the strip of TTs there. My best find was the artist atelier **Ben's Gallery,** which sells many traditional prints and schlock-ola artworks but also features original work by Ben, which I consider a must-have. I bought two canvases from him, for $250 each. Ben's Gallery is located in the back end of the White Swan Hotel.

Shangiiu Shopping Street: Note that this Cantonese name is Xiajiu in Mandarin; same street, different dialect. This is one of the "new China" phenom streets and is especially fun in the evenings after people get off work. It's a pedestrian street where the locals go out for their promenade; many of the stores are malls and malls of tiny booths. My favorite building is **Liwan Plaza,** a mall with shops selling a jumble of fakes, new designers, and beauty services. There is a large (and somewhat legal) DVD shop in the front, facing the street. Legal DVDs cost 15¥ to 39¥ ($2–$6) and have holograms on them to signify they are legal, unless those are fake, too. Beauty treatments are good and cheap: I had a manicure ($8), hand-buffing treatment ($8), hand-hydrating and -whitening treatment ($10), and pedicure ($10).

Beijing Road: This is a different pedestrian street, not that different in feel from the Shangiiu/Xiajiu Shopping Street mentioned above, although farther from the White Swan Hotel. Here you'll find a famous local department store called Good Buy. I wasn't impressed by it because it is attempting to be a Western department store, but what do I know?

Jade Market: Adjoining some streets and alleys selling antiques, this market is a warren of fun and possible good buys. Prices are seriously lower than in Hong Kong. From the street, there is merely a modern arcade of shops selling jade, beads, and semiprecious stones. Head inward to discover an entire village of lanes, with antiques shops to the rear. There is construction nearby, so check the location before you head out. For do-it-yourselfers, this alone is worth the trip just to load up on beads and gewgaws.

Spice Market (Liu Er San Lu): There are no dead or live birds, snakes, or dogs in this market. It's just heaps of gorgeous spices and beautiful textures and colors, all within walking distance of the White Swan Hotel. This is not for those who can't walk up and down many stairs because you will take a walkway over a freeway. Don't fret: Street vendors sell illegal DVDs on the walkway.

Circuit City: There is an entire street of buildings called the Haiyin Electronics District. It is 1 block from the fabric markets, so you can do the whole thing in one swoop. The fabric markets feature home and fashion fabrics, although I was not particularly knocked out. The fabric market in Shanghai is far superior.

The electronics stores, however, are downright amazing. I spent hours here and feasted at McDonald's, which is conveniently located in the main shopping mall. Most of the DVD stores have video CDs on display. In most cases, you have to ask for English DVDs, then follow someone into a corridor. In some cases, the DVDs were right out in the open. The asking price was fairly good: about 7¥ (about $1) in most booths. (The *gweilo* price, for non-Asians, is 10¥/$1.20.)

Sleeping in Canton

GARDEN HOTEL
368 Huanshi Dong Lu.

This is the other top hotel in town; I have not stayed here. It's also modern and has over 1,000 rooms in a sky-high tower. As the name suggests, it is built around a garden.

Rates are slightly less than the White Swan Hotel, about $175 a night for a double room. Call © 8620/8333-8989 or visit www.thegardenhotel.com.cn.

WESTIN HOTEL
6 Lin H Zhong Road, Tian He District

This brand-new modern high rise, with designer shopping and all sorts of spiffy western-style amenities, is mainly geared toward business visitors. The hotel is actually walking distance from the East Station. Rooms begin around $200 per night.

Local phone © 8620/2886-6868. starwoodhotels.com.

WHITE SWAN HOTEL
Shamian Island.

This hotel is so famous that it doesn't have a real street address. Indeed, it's at the end of a street, on a dead end against the point where two rivers merge, so it affords incredible water views. This is a member of Leading Hotels of the World. It's a modern building with a shopping mall, many restaurants, and what locals consider the best dim sum in southern China, the home of dim sum.

The concierge team is great; they made all my train bookings for me and arranged the free shuttle to the train station when I was ready to return to Hong Kong. They hand out maps of the island as well as the city and have an extensive taxi card that lists the prime sites in town.

There is a Bank of China with an ATM out the back door of the hotel. The neighborhood behind the hotel is filled with tourist shops; they all sell pink baby clothes because of the high percentage of girls adopted here.

Aside from the immediate tourist shopping district behind the hotel, there is a nearby spice market (no dogs), and you are within walking distance (or a $2 taxi ride) of one of the main pedestrian shopping districts. There is shuttle bus service to the airport and the two train stations. For travel to Hong Kong, you want East Station.

Rates vary with room, view, and season; they begin at around $200 per night. Reservations through Leading Hotels of the World (© **800/223-6800** in the U.S.). Local © 020/8188-6968. www.whiteswanhotel.com.

WELCOME TO MACAU

The new Macau is even newer than the new Hong Kong, and the old, good, funky stuff has mostly been destroyed—except for the street where they make the antiques. The Chinese took possession in 1999, and the Las Vegas casinos arrived in 2004. Real estate is booming and architecture is looming, yet a resort feel prevails. Macau remains a luxury getaway destination where you can do a little shopping or gambling. The major furniture factories are on the Chinese side of Macau (Zhuhai) and are easy to shop as long as you have a visa.

Macau is a simple day trip from Hong Kong, or a weekend away. It has a new international airport, so you can also make it a main destination. This makes the most sense if you are going past the gates into the PRC and on to Guangzhou (Canton). On the other hand, shoppers who are shopping for pricey branded merchandise prefer Macau over Hong Kong because there is a $3 per $100 difference in the exchange rate. When you are spending $10,000 on an item, this adds up.

Why Macau?

As often as I go to Hong Kong, I rarely go to Macau—yet once I get to Macau, I kick myself for not having taken the time or trouble to visit. The colonial Portuguese architecture adjacent to modern high-rises gives you a glimpse of something very different from what you see in Hong Kong. The names on the shops and the Portuguese place names make the destination seem exotic. The atmosphere is laid-back; the casinos offer a little bit of Las Vegas.

Macau's shopping is not great, but it is less expensive than Hong Kong's. And if you need a Chanel fix, you need go no further than the **Wynn.**

If you are looking for furniture, waste no time in getting here. If you are interested in food, many come for the Portuguese-inspired home cooking. If you are in Hong Kong for only 3 days, don't burden your schedule, but if you have time, this trip expands your visual horizons.

Phoning Macau

If you're in Hong Kong and want to telephone or fax Macau for restaurant reservations, or whatever, the area code is 853. (The area code for Hong Kong is 852.)

The Lay of the Land

A 64km (40-mile) sea lane connects Macau to Hong Kong; it feels a million miles away. Macau itself is not an island but the tip of a peninsula attached to mainland China. You can walk to the gate. You cannot walk through the gate without a visa. On the other side is the economic free zone of Zhuhai.

The "downtown" shopping and gambling area is in the older part of town, or what is left of it. The main drag's official name is Avenida Almeida Ribiero, but it goes by its Chinese name: San Ma Lo. The really fun stuff to browse is up the hill toward St. Paul's cathedral, but the main drag has stores and banks and my new favorite, the Pawnshop Museum.

The area alongside the ferry terminal has become hot real estate. You pass two malls before you reach the nearby luxe Mandarin Oriental. If you arrive by ferry, you'll need a bus or taxi to get into town; you will also need a taxi to get to various destinations. Your hotel or casino may provide a free shuttle bus.

Getting There

Your choices are simple: one if by air and two if by sea. Assuming you're not flying into Macau's international airport or crossing the hills from China, you are most likely coming from Hong Kong (near Central) and through **Shun Tak Centre,** or from the Kowloon side, at **China Hongkong City.**

Shun Tak Centre is the name of the modern, two-tower ferry terminal in Hong Kong's Western District. The MTR stop is Sheung Wan, which is the end of the line. The building and terminals are several floors up in the never-ending lobby space; ride several escalators and read a lot of signs.

China Hongkong City is in Kowloon on Canton Road, almost part of the mall complexes Harbour City and Ocean Terminal.

Fares fluctuate; variables include the day of the week, the time of day (night costs more), and the class of service (first class costs more). First-class service on a weekday is HK$130 ($17) each way for an adult; departure tax adds another HK$25 ($3.25) or so. Weekends and holidays are about 10% more expensive; evenings after 6pm are also more costly. SuperClass, which costs HK$232 ($30) on weekdays and HK$247 ($32) on weekends, includes a meal.

Getting There Quickly

You can take a helicopter to the Ferry Terminal; it's a 16-minute journey. The fare is about $200, but it varies. For information, call © 852/2108-4838 in Hong Kong or visit http://api.air macau.com.mo/en.

Macau

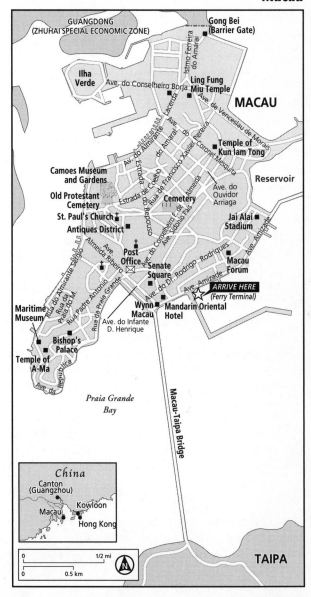

GUANGDONG
(ZHUHAI SPECIAL ECONOMIC ZONE)

Gong Bei
(Barrier Gate)

Ilha Verde

Ave. do Conselheiro Borja

Ling Fung Miu Temple

MACAU

Ave. de Venceslau de Morais

Istmo Ferreira do Amaral

Ave. do Almirante Lacerda

Temple of Kun Iam Tong

Camoes Museum and Gardens

Old Protestant Cemetery

St. Paul's Church

Antiques District

Ave. do Coronel Mesquita

Estrada de Coelho

Ave. do Francisco Xavier Pereira

Cemetery

Ave. do Ouvidor Arriaga

Reservoir

Estrada do Repouso

Ave. do Conselheiro F. de Almeida

Ave. Sidonio Pais

Jai Alai Stadium

Almeida Ribeiro

Ave. da

Post Office

Senate Square

Ave. do Dr. Rodrigo Rodrigues

Ave. Amizade

Macau Forum

Ave. do Almirante Sergio

Rua do Praia do M.

Rua da Praia Grande

Rua Padre Antonio

Wynn Macau

Mandarin Oriental Hotel

Ave. Amizade

ARRIVE HERE
(Ferry Terminal)

Maritime Museum

Bishop's Palace

Temple of A-Ma

Ave. da Republica

Ave. do Infante D. Henrique

Praia Grande Bay

Macau-Taipa Bridge

China

Canton (Guangzhou)

Macau

Kowloon

Hong Kong

TAIPA

0   1/2 mi
0   0.5 km

N

Travel Tips

Weekend prices are higher. Crowds are denser. And don't travel on Chinese holidays if you can help it.

If you plan to cross the border and go into China, there are a variety of visas available. Your options may also be based on what kind of passport you hold. There seems to be some prejudice against U.K. passport holders; they pay the most and have extreme limits put on their travels.

You can get your visa in Hong Kong before you leave, or in Macau. You can apply for a visa at the Barrier Gate (Gong Bei). For travel details, visit www.macautourism.gov.mo.

Arriving in Macau

You'll walk along a little gangway, enter a building, follow a walkway, and go through security. You are now in Portuguese Macau, and Portuguese is an official language. However, when I spoke Portuguese to our taxi driver, he thought I was nuts. Better luck to you and yours.

Once you're outside the terminal, you'll note that there are bus stops and many lanes for cars, taxis, and tourist buses. It's a little confusing, partly because so much is going on. Persevere—your shuttle bus is waiting for you. Mandarin Oriental guests can report to the hotel's service desk inside the terminal and will be escorted to the waiting shuttle.

Also note that you are next door to the New Yoahan Shopping Centre, which is actually a Western-style department store with a fairly good grocery store. It also has a food court and clean bathrooms. Perhaps leave time for this adventure as you depart.

Money Matters

Macau has its own currency, the pataca (symbol MP$). Storekeepers will accept Hong Kong dollars but will give change in local currency. The two currencies are more or less at parity:

HK$1 = MP$1.

US$1 = MP$8

1€ = MP$10
£1 = MP$15

Getting Around

The taxi flag falls at MP$10 ($1.35). Although taxi drivers have a destination chart in three languages, I promise you will not find a driver who speaks Portuguese. Use the Chinese chart or carry one from your hotel.

Shopping Macau

The main reason people come to Macau to shop is simple: The prices are lower than in Hong Kong, and the specialty is antiques and "antiques." Yes, they make 'em right here. These copies are so good that you will never buy another antique again, for fear that it just came out of the back room of a shop in Macau.

Every local from Hong Kong has his or her own private sources in Macau. Indeed, Macau is the kind of place where you need an inside track. There's no doubt that the really good stuff is hidden. And may be illegal.

The shopping must be considered fun shopping, unless you have brought along a curator from a museum or Sotheby's and really know your faux from your foo. If you give it the light touch, you're going to have a ball.

Note that designer shops such as Chanel are located within the new luxury hotels, such as The Wynn.

Sleeping in Macau

Metro Macau spreads over several islands, and most of the resort hotels are across a bridge. If you've come to shop, you probably want a central location and a luxury hotel. But understand that even in-town hotels specialize in a resort feel. Many are curious about the new Las Vegas–style hotels such as The Wynn, the Venetian, and others. I, however, am a traditionalist.

MANDARIN ORIENTAL
956 Av. da Amizade, Macau.

For 20 years the most famous and fancy hotel in town, the Mandarin Oriental has a country-club atmosphere and amenities in a location between the ferry station and the heart of town. There's big-name designer shopping and several great places to eat. My favorite is the Thai restaurant. Did I mention the spa?

Rooms begin at $300, but there are deals, especially during the week. Note that, naturally, a harbor-view room costs more than one with a city view.

U.S. reservations © 800/555-4288. Local © 853/567-888. www.mandarinoriental.com/macau.

Macau in a Day

Because addresses are hard to find in Macau, and many place names aren't clearly marked, the way for me to show you the best of central Macau's shopping area is to take you by the hand. If you are visiting Macau on a day trip, leave Hong Kong early so that you hit St. Paul's cathedral by 10am. Wander for a few hours and find lunch. Book the 4pm jetfoil back to Hong Kong.

- Tell your taxi driver *Igresia São Paolo* (St. Paul's Church), or be able to point to it on a map. A *Macau Mapa Turistica* is available free in Shun Tak Centre. This particular map has a picture of the church. St. Paul's was built in the early 1600s and burned to the ground in 1835, leaving only the facade, which is in more or less perfect condition. Not only is this quite a sight, but it's the leading tourist haunt in town and signals the beginning of the shopping and antiques district.
- The church is up a small hill, with two levels of stairs leading to a small square. If you go down both levels of the stairs, you will be at the major tourist-trap area and flea market heaven where dealers sell mostly new antiques . . . although you always hear stories of so-and-so who just bought a valuable teapot at one of these stalls.

- Before you go lickety-split down all the stairs to the stalls, note that at the bottom of the first staircase is a small alley to the right. Follow it for a block alongside the church until its end, just past the building: there you will find a tiny shrine.

- Not that it's well marked, but the name of this alley is **Rua da Ressureciao.** It's lined with tourist traps, porcelain shops, antiques stores, and even a ginseng parlor. Don't expect any bargains in these shops, and by all means know your stuff, but begin your shopping spree here. I must say that most of these stores are rather fetching: plates in the windows, red lanterns flapping in the breeze, maybe even a few carved dragons over the doorway. They all take credit cards, and you may have a ball.

- After you've done this alley, work your way around the vendors at the main "square" in front of the church steps. Film, soft drinks, and souvenirs are sold here; there are no particular bargains.

- Normally people head into town by walking down the hill to the market and shopping as they go. The way to do this is to head down the Rua de São Paolo to the Rua da Palha, passing shops as you go. This walkway leads directly to the marketplace and the Senate Square, which is the heart of downtown. There are a few cute shops this way, and I have even bought from some of them.

- But I'm sending you down the hill the sneaky, nontouristy way. If you have the time, you may want to go down my way and then walk back up the main way so you can see the whole hill (and shop, of course). Also note that if you're with people and decide to split up, you can always meet back at the church stairway flea-market area at an appointed time; this is a good place to get a taxi later on. Yes, I said flea market.

- The big red stall is not a toilet; it's a postal box. You can mail postcards here.

- If you are standing with the church to your back, a major tourist trap called **Nam Kwong Arts & Crafts** should be to your right, with the red postal box in front of it. (There are other branches of Nam Kwong in town.) Shop here if you are so inclined, then make a hard right (under the laundry from the balcony above) onto a small unmarked street. Once you have turned right, look to the left for an alley called **Calcada do Amparo.** Enter here and begin to walk downhill.

- It's not going to be charming for a block or so, and you'll wonder where the hell you are and why all the tourists went in the other direction. Trust me, you're headed into the back alleys of the furniture and antiques area, as you will soon discover. You are wearing good walking shoes, I hope. This is the Tercena neighborhood, by the way.

- The reason I haven't given you shop names and addresses should now be abundantly clear—there's no way of really even knowing where you are when you walk down this hill. In about 2 blocks, your alley will dead-end at a small street called **Rua Nossa Senhora do Amparo,** which may or may not be marked. These little alleys are called walkways or *travessas* and may have names (look for **Travessa do Fagao**).

- Get your bearings: You're now halfway to the main downtown square of Macau, on a small street that branches off from Rua do Mercadores, the main small shopping street that connects the main big shopping street to the area above at the top of the hill.

- This will make sense when you're standing there in the street, or if you look at a map. But don't look at a map too carefully because part of the fun of the whole experience is wandering around, getting lost and found, and feeling like what you have discovered is yours alone.

- When you are back on the Rua Nossa Senhora do Amparo, you'll find a ton of little dusty antiques shops. Some have names and some don't. They start opening around 11am; don't come too early. I wouldn't begin to vouch for the integrity of any of the shops here. I can only assure you that you'll have the time of your life.

- When you have finished shopping the antiques trade, work your way laterally across Rua das Estalagens to Rua do Mercadores. If you turn right, you will connect in a couple of short blocks to Avenida de Almeida Ribeiro, the main drag. I suggest instead that you keep moving laterally so that you run smack into the market.

- The market is called **Mercado de São Domingos;** it has an outdoor fruit-and-veggie portion tucked into various alleys, an indoor livestock portion, and a dry-goods portion. Wander through as much as you can take, and find yourself at the main fountain and a square (Senate Sq.), which instinct will tell you is the main square. *Note:* There are still garment factories in Macau, and you will sometimes find name-brand merchandise in the market and side street near here.

- If instinct isn't enough, look for the restored colonial buildings, the tourist office, the main post office, the deliciously dilapidated Apollo Theatre, and the Leal Senado, which is the Senate building. You have arrived in the heart of town.

- The address of the tourist office (in case you need help, a place to meet up with the people you came with, or someone who speaks English and can teach you how to use the phone or write something for you in Chinese) is 9 Largo do Senado.

- The huge post office across the square is where you buy stamps, but beware: Lines can be long. Now you're on your own for lunch, more strolling, some gambling, or the return to the ferry.

- If you've chosen to spend a weekend night, surely you're up for the Night Market, which is similar to the Temple Street Market in Kowloon—complete with Chinese opera singers. Head to the **Cinema Alegria** to find the market, or ask your concierge to write it out for you in Chinese. The market is not far from the harbor and can be reached directly by bus. Taxis are cheap, so I went by taxi. Prices on junk and clothes without labels tend to be less than in Hong Kong; there are amazing amounts of baby clothes.

Gong Bei

Gong Bei is the Barrier Gate. I won't bore you with what it used to be like. Let's go with what it is now: fascinating but neither charming nor old-fashioned. This is big business, with millions of souls in transit. From the Macau side, your taxi will drop you at what looks like a modern office tower. Follow the crowds. In two steps, you exit Macau and then enter China. You must have a visa to enter China.

In this case, do not follow the crowds. Look for the immigration gates marked FOREIGN PASSPORTS. They are usually at the far right, if your back is to the front door.

Once you enter China, you wander through a lobby and outside, where a million watch salesmen will descend upon you. Ignore them and cross the street. To get to the bus station, take the escalators right in front of you down one level. Buy your ticket, and then go down another level into the bus station.

If you want a taxi for exploring the area (and going to furniture warehouses), head to the far side of the plaza *before* you go down the escalators.

Fisherman's Wharf

I don't like Fisherman's Wharf in San Francisco, and now that there's one in Macau, I am amused and amazed. This new waterfront development in the outer harbor was designed by the venerable Stanley Ho, who must have had something other than casinos in mind until the boys from Vegas came calling. It is technically called the area's first theme park, with restaurants, a hotel on the way (with casino, of course), and family entertainment. And, oh yeah—did I mention the medley of architecture from all over the world, 150 stores, a volcano that erupts nightly, or the Roman amphitheater? I can just hear Tony Bennett now crooning about where he left his heart.

About Zhuhai

Okay, so I'm running from A to Z in one sentence—who could resist? Just so you know, Zhuhai is the city across the Barrier

Gate from Macau. It is one of those newfangled, fancy economic zones that are progressive and exciting for the Chinese while possibly unknown to the average tourist. This one has a fancy airport and Formula 1 racetrack, neither of which are much written about.

I like the idea of living here—I saw some gorgeous highrise luxury apartment buildings with sea views. But I digress. The reason most people come here to shop is the furniture warehouses. And yes, the warehouses will arrange international shipping.

If you are interested in only the furniture part (that is, Zhuhai) and don't really care abut Macau or the Barrier Gate, you can take a ferry directly from Hong Kong to Zhuhai and back. Rush hour ends at 5pm, and there are not too many ferries back to Hong Kong after that, so watch the hour or have a backup plan.

The furniture warehouses spread across their own district; you will need a taxi that waits for you. Make sure you have all the information written in Chinese (easily obtained at your hotel concierge desk in Hong Kong). Bring cash to pay in Hong Kong dollars.

A bridge between Hong Kong and Zhuhai is scheduled to open in 2009.

Dongguan

You think you were born to shop? Get a load of this one: It's one of the largest malls in the world, and it's not in Bloomington, Minnesota.

It's the **South China Mall**: it's a little bit country, it's a little bit rock 'n' roll, it's Las Vegas, it's Disneyland, it's amazing. Should you come here to shop? No! Should you come here to gawk? Yup! Is it worth the price of a visa? Only to an anthropologist.

Dongguan is between Shenzhen and Guangzhou.

Chapter Seven

....

WEEKENDS AWAY: HANOI, HO CHI MINH CITY & TAIPEI

HONG KONG GATEWAY

....

Some 60% of Americans visiting Vietnam get there through Hong Kong, so here is your guide to one of the most fun shopping destinations you will ever encounter. Worried about changing money again? You can use USD in Vietnam.

It's no secret that Vietnam is gorgeous and charming and has excellent shopping. So if you are looking for a destination that most of your friends haven't discovered, consider a trip to Taiwan, an island country 100 miles from China and yet totally different from every other nation in Asia.

That is perhaps the beauty of your trip to Hong Kong: You are so close to a bevy of Asian destinations that you can leave town for a few days with a simple connection from HKG. Don't forget that it's easy to get to the Hong Kong airport on the train, so you can check your big suitcases at your hotel when you depart, take a smaller rolly-roller on the train, check out a new destination, and then head back to Hong Kong.

Just Pick One

When I first began going to Vietnam, I had to choose which weekend away I wanted: Hanoi or Saigon. I went with Hanoi and have never been sorry. To me, it has more charm—and slightly better shopping—than HCMC (Ho Chi Minh City, the modern name for Saigon).

Financial Matters

The official currency is the dong, which trades at about 14,500 to $1. However, U.S. dollars are accepted almost every place and are often preferred. Few stores accept credit cards. I didn't see any ATMs except at the Hilton and an office building.

You can bargain in most stores. When the price is $2, it's hard to ask for a discount . . . but you can try.

Entering Vietnam

You will need a visa to enter Vietnam. The 1-day visa—mostly for those on cruise ships—is $65; the 30-day visa costs $130. **Zierer Visa Service** (p. 20) is the provider I use. You can also go online, download the paperwork, and submit it to the **Vietnamese Embassy** (© **202/861-2293**); or employ any number of "services," beginning at $40.

For details, go online or call the embassy.

Spelling Matters

Because Vietnamese is an Asian language (the language is Kihn), a Pinyin-like system (called Quoc Ngu) must be used to Romanize the sounds. As a result, there are various accepted spellings and writings for the same words. Your computer may not accept Vietnam as two words, and Hanoi will be written as two words when you are there. (The Sai Gon River is obviously where the city formerly named Saigon got its name.)

Renting a Car

You're kidding, right? You want a car and driver; your hotel will arrange it.

Calling Around

The country code for Vietnam is 84, and the city code for Hanoi is 4. The city code for Saigon is 8.

Best Buys

Ceramics: I went nuts buying ceramics—vases, place settings, everything. I even took an excursion to a village that sells only ceramics (p. 192). The problem is that shipping brings up the cost and packing adds to weight and worries. Still, I had no breakage, and I only regret that I had to give up two vases in Hong Kong when I couldn't carry them on the plane. Ceramics from northern Vietnam are superior to others because of the qualities of the local clay. Various villages specialize in different styles; you can also buy at the market in beautiful downtown Hanoi.

Chopsticks: I am not talking "with six you get egg roll" chopsticks—I am talking about an art form. Fancier stores sell chopsticks by the set ($2–$5 per set), but you can buy them in sets for 10 people for $6 at the market.

Contemporary art: I rarely report on art because taste is so personal. I was shocked and amazed by the number of art galleries, however, and the quality of the wares and diversity of styles. Many of the artists are highly collectible and have regular shows in Hong Kong and Europe.

Embroidery: What appears to be European-style embroidery is actually a local craft.

Ethnic Fashion: These items are fashionably ethnic and funky without being costumey. You can buy the traditional dress style, called an *ao dais*—what I call a Madame Nu dress, but that dates me. There are crinkle skirts and wraparound trousers, embroidered shoes, and all sorts of items that could turn up on the pages of *Vogue*.

Foodstuff: I always go to the grocery stores, although much foodstuff can be bought in the U.S. from Asian markets and specialty stores, either in person or online.

Horn: It's not tortoise shell, it's buffalo horn.

Lacquer: In most cases, this will be the most sophisticated, drop-dead-chic lacquer you have ever seen. Major home-style stores in Europe and the U.S. are already overcharging for it. **Beware:** Most stores have designs inspired by the likes of Monet and Hundterwasser, so you have to look past that to the likes of the eggshell crackle format.

Lanterns: Assorted lantern styles are available, but the most popular—and chic—is the style called Indochine, a sort of tulip-bulb shape in various sizes made of silk and usually finished off with a tassel. Prices begin at around $7.

Shoes: Believe it or not, shoes must be made here because there are tons of them. I actually even found a size 41 (American size 10)! I bought some embroidery raffia mules on a princess heel for $36.

Silk: Aside from the usual, you'll see silk duvet covers and hand-stitched silk quilts. I bought several shirts in silk and in linen; I liked the style so much that I then had the shirt made in English cotton (complete with monogram on the cuff) in Hong Kong. Vietnamese silk is thinner than that of other Asian countries and may not wear as well.

Tailoring: Many report that custom tailoring is a breeze. I didn't have the time or budget. My friends Karen and Toby were having Armani jackets copied for $65.

WELCOME TO HANOI

Although I had some emotional reservations at first, once I got going, I was able to overcome and shop Vietnam in style.

Over the years, I have come to appreciate Saigon more (and that Hyatt Hotel, oh my), but my heart belongs to Hanoi. Bring U.S. dollars. And again, don't be surprised if you see the city's name written out the proper Pinyin way as two words: Ha Noi.

Getting There

The flight from Hong Kong is about 2 hours. Hanoi is 1 hour behind Hong Kong, which may make you think the flight is 1 hour long or 3 hours long. Although various partners do code shares (Cathay, for example), all flights are operated by Vietnam Airlines (© 415/677 -8909; www.vietnamairlines.com).

Booking Hanoi

As a general rule, flights from Hong Kong to Vietnam are expensive. Air tickets bought in Hong Kong to Hanoi cost $750, so I buy tickets elsewhere. I've bought my tickets in Paris for $450 and through my regular Chinese travel agent in California (p. 24) for about the same amount.

My friends Peter and Louisa went with me one time—on the exact same flights—but bought a late-summer promotional package that included airfare, transfers, and 2 nights' hotel (as well as other perks) at the Sofitel Metropole for $650 each. They bought their package in Hong Kong. Obviously, it pays to shop around.

There's No Sense to It

Despite the fact that Bangkok is farther away from Hong Kong than Vietnam, flights between HKG and BKK are usually far less expensive. A handful of low-cost carriers operate from BKK, so you can even get to Vietnam from Bangkok for less than from Hong Kong.

Seasonally Yours

Prices and packages are related to the seasons, as in most destinations. Summers are hot and humid; you can get bargain prices in August. Fall and early winter are high season—Hanoi does a big Christmas and New Year's business. By January things slow down for Tet, the lunar new year, and then the rains start.

Arriving in Hanoi

The Noi Bai International Airport is brand-new, modern, and gorgeous; entry is as easy as chopsticks.

Your hotel can arrange a pickup for you; package tours probably include transfers. You can easily take a taxi into town. Travel time is about 45 minutes.

The Lay of the Land

The main "downtown" shopping area is called the "District of the 36 Guilds" and consists of small streets and alleys that make up a village of shopping ops. This area is just north of Lake Hoan Kiem, locally referred to simply as "the Lake."

The Opera House (called "the opera") is southeast of the lake, and most of the so-called luxury hotels are in the area between the opera and the southern shore of the lake. You can walk to the shopping district or take a taxi for very little money. The two best-known hotels here are the **Metropole** and the **Hilton.** Note that the latter is not called the Hanoi Hilton for obvious reasons but the Hanoi Opera Hilton Hotel.

Hotel Nikko Hanoi, representing a luxury Japanese chain of hotels, is closer to the southwestern section of the lake.

A third district for luxury hotels—but not that much shopping—lies on the far side of the lake in the opposite direction from the Nikko. The two anchors here are the **Sheraton Hotel Saigon** and the brand-new **InterContinental Hanoi,** which is more of a resort than a plain old hotel.

Although most hotels have some shopping in them, you'll want to shop downtown. You will need to use a map because

Hanoi

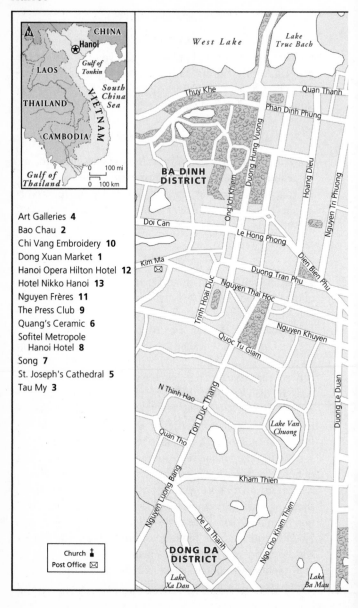

Art Galleries **4**
Bao Chau **2**
Chi Vang Embroidery **10**
Dong Xuan Market **1**
Hanoi Opera Hilton Hotel **12**
Hotel Nikko Hanoi **13**
Nguyen Frères **11**
The Press Club **9**
Quang's Ceramic **6**
Sofitel Metropole
  Hanoi Hotel **8**
Song **7**
St. Joseph's Cathedral **5**
Tau My **3**

Church ✠
Post Office ⊠

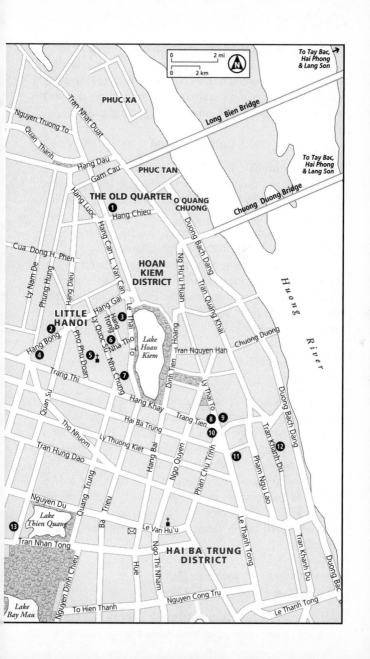

THE OLD QUARTER

❶ Hang Chieu

O QUANG CHUONG

PHUC XA

PHUC TAN

Long Bien Bridge

Chuong Duong Bridge

*To Tay Bac,
Hai Phong
& Lang Son*

*To Tay Bac,
Hai Phong
& Lang Son*

Tran Nhat Duat

Nguyen Truong To

Quan Thanh

Hang Dau

Gam Cau

Hang Luoc

Cua Dong H. Phen

Ly Nam De

Phung Hung

Hang Dieu

Hang Can

Ly Van Can

Hang Ma

Hang Chieu

Duong Bach Dang

Ng Hu'u Huan

Tran Quang Khai

**HOAN
KIEM
DISTRICT**

**LITTLE
HANOI**

❷

Hang Bong

❹

Hang Gai

Hang Trong

❸

❻

Pho Phu Doan

Ly Quoc Su

Nha Tho

Nha Chung

❺ ✝

❼

Trang Thi

Hang Khay

Hang Bai

Ngo Quyen

Quan Su

Tho Nhuom

Trang Thi

*Lake
Hoan
Kiem*

Le Thai To

Hang

Dinh Tien

Ly Thai To

Tran Nguyen Han

Chuong Duong

Huong

River

Duong Bach Dang

Tran Khanh Du

Hai Ba Trung

Ly Thuong Kiet

Tran Hung Dao

Phan Chu Trinh

Trang Tien

❽ ❾

❿

⓫

⓬

Pham Ngu Lao

Le Thanh Tong

Tran Khanh Du

Duong Bac

Nguyen Du

*Lake
Thien Quang*

⓭

Tran Nhan Tong

Quang Trung

Ba Trieu

Hue

Ngo Thi Nham

Le Van Hu'u ✝

⊠

**HAI BA TRUNG
DISTRICT**

Nguyen Dinh Chieu

*Lake
Bay Mau*

To Hien Thanh

Nguyen Cong Tru

Le Thanh Tong

0 ─── 2 mi
0 ─── 2 km

I can honestly report being lost several times. Good luck trying to find someone who speaks English . . . or French. In some cases, you may have to flag a taxi and go back to your hotel (or the Metropole) and start over. Have your hotel's taxi card with you at all times, and study the map in this chapter.

Getting Around

Only the downtown luxury hotels are within walking distance of the best shopping districts of Hanoi. Taxis are plentiful and inexpensive—a ride anywhere in the central shopping area costs $1. Pedicabs are cute but more expensive than taxis (and not air-conditioned)—expect to pay about $3 from your centrally located hotel to the shopping district.

Most luxury hotels have their own car service for transfers, day trips, and hourly rental. A car and driver costs about $30 an hour. We used a driver from the Hilton on the last trip; his English was great and he took us everywhere in an air-conditioned Benz.

HANOI OPERA HILTON
1 Le Thanh Tong St.

This relatively new hotel stands next door to the Opera House, at the edge of the shopping district. It offers Gold packages as well as the usual Hilton breaks and promotions. From the opera side, the hotel appears to have a colonial look to it; from the arrivals side, it's just modern and a bit ugly. Never mind. The restaurants are good, room service is efficient, the staff is great, and the location will serve you well. Rooms go for around $200. The adjacent ATM is a blessing. U.S. reservations ✆ **800/HILTONS.** Local phone ✆ 844/933-0500. www. hilton.com.

INTERCONTINENTAL WESTLAKE HANOI
1A Nghi Tam Village, Tay Ho District.

This is going to be the leading hotel in town, once it fully opens— it was in its soft opening as we went to press. The hotel is a five-star resort with 327 rooms and 36 apartments. Note that Westlake is becoming a destination unto itself, with shopping and fancy restaurants. The most notable restaurant to date is Bobby Chinn. The hotel is not downtown but near the Sheraton in an area called, duh, Westlake. Rooms have either city or lake views. There is a surcharge of $50 for the high season around Christmas. Otherwise, rooms begin around $220 and go up. Just to demonstrate how reasonable everything is, the airport transfer for a sedan is $18; for a van, $25. U.S. Reservations © **800/496-7621.** Local phone © 84-4/270-8888. ichotelsgroup.com.

SOFITEL METROPOLE HANOI
15 Ngo Guyen St.

This is the most historic hotel in town—the grande dame in a super location. The Sofitel Metropole prides itself on being a shopping headquarters and provides all guests with a local map and shopping resource list. Unfortunately, most of the great shops in the lobby are now gone, replaced by designer stores.

Promotional rates sometimes list two prices, for the modern wing of the hotel or for the older portion. Expect to pay about $200 for the newer part and $250 or more for the historic part, if you get a promotional rate. Otherwise prices are high and may seem too much so for what's on offer. Don't miss a meal at Spices, whether you stay here or not. You can take a special tour from this hotel in a vintage (1935) car that will really make your trip. U.S. reservations © **800/SOFITEL.** Local © 844/826-6919. www.accorhotels.asia.com.

Watch It!

Although there is a business in war souvenirs, I could not stomach the idea of shopping for them. Rumor has it that most are fakes anyway.

Watch It! 2

Stores come and go so rapidly that it's impossible for any guidebook to be totally accurate.

Shopping Hanoi

Hanoi has quickly grasped the concepts of the glam slam and the good deal. It has stores that would do Paris, New York, or Tokyo proud. The locally made merchandise is far more sophisticated than in Hong Kong and China; designer and brand business is just getting going. Obviously, you don't go to Vietnam to buy designer merchandise anyway.

I shopped nonstop for 3 full days and returned to Hong Kong kicking myself for not buying more. The raw authenticity of the setting is pure charm; the prices are heaven (few items cost more than $25; most cost $3) and you can truly shop 'til you drop. You'll also get a good giggle, perverse as it may be, in buying a size XXXXL.

Shopping Days & Hours

Stores are open 7 days a week. Some close for lunch. Hours are normally 9am to 6 or 7pm. Stores close during Tet, the new year's celebration, sometime in January or early February. (Tet is lunar, so the date changes every year.) On weekends some stores stay open until 9 or 10pm.

The Art Scene

Contemporary art from local artists is not only the rage of VN but also of Hong Kong and other parts of Asia. You may want to begin to educate your eye while still in Honkers and then hit the streets wide-eyed. Subject matter is split about fifty-fifty between local subjects and abstracts. Remember that shipping becomes an issue with a large picture under your arm.

The *New York Times* recently ran three full pages with lotsa color pictures on the gallery scene in Hanoi. Just search online for "The Awakening of Hanoi."

Markets

The **1912 Market** is named for a date in December, so you say "nineteen twelve." It sells everything. It's in a dark alley and, frankly, you can give it a miss. **Dong Xuan** is a series of street markets and market buildings not too far from the Cathedral—a tad rough, but very low cost. This is the market you want, just avoid the live-bird portion. **Pho Hang Dau** is a shoe market for those with VN-size feet.

Street Vendors

Street vendors abound. Most sell the same old stuff: postcards and guidebooks, along with a few Graham Greene titles (*The Quiet American* is the most popular). The "books," which appear to be photocopies of page proofs or computer printouts, are pretty hard on the eyes and have numerous typos.

International Brands

Brands are just discovering Vietnam and vice versa. Hanoi currently has a short string of brand-name stores ranging from **Pierre Cardin** (which looks nothing like anything you might guess was French) to **l'Occitane,** which is identical to its stores all over the world. The Sofitel Metropole has a very spiffy branch of **Louis Vuitton** and a small arcade of luxe stores. There are no bargains.

Western Merchandise

Most of the hotels have gift shops that sell American and European magazines. The **Press Club,** 59A Ly Thai To, behind the Metropole, sells cookbooks in English and in French. The Metropole has a grocery store that sells French foodstuffs.

Hanoi Overload

Please note that after a few hours of shopping, you may get a headache, have crossed eyes, or fall into that unfortunate state in which everything looks alike and you want to run away screaming. The merchandise is so abundant, so gorgeous, and so inexpensive that you can lose your mind. Apocalypse at any moment . . . let the shopper beware.

Best Shopping District in Hanoi

Thirty-six Pho Puong is the District of the 36 Guilds, the old quarter where each trade had its own little alley. The word *hang* tells the shopper that this is indeed a street of merchandise, and the word that comes next says what kind of merchandise. Hang Gai is one of the leading streets for silks and embroideries. It's in the center of town near the Cathedral.

Hanoi's Best Shopping Street

You'll find the best stores, but not necessarily the best prices, on **Nha Tho,** a short street in the heart of the shopping district, on the side of Nha Chung, a more mainstream shopping street. Nha Chung means Church Street; the street runs alongside St. Joseph's Cathedral. The good stores include **Mosaique, Kien Boutique,** and **LaCasa.**

The Best Stores in Hanoi

BAO CHAU
48 Hang Bong St.

In including this on my best-of list, I am advising that part of what is so wonderful about this store is its location on a street filled with great stores laden with lacquerware. This store is unusual in that it has a mix—real and fake antiques, crafts, gift items, and so on. I saw many items here that I did not see elsewhere. The store also had the best price on raffia embroidered handbags, which elsewhere are about $30 and here were $16.

CHI VANG EMBROIDERY
17 Trang Tien.

This large store is close to the Hilton and the Metropole, but slightly out of the mainstream downtown shopping district. It's worth the walk for the architecture of the building and the merchandise—more chic embroidery than you can imagine, at prices that will make your palms sweat. I saw an entire bed set for $150. Don't forget to go upstairs. © 844/936-0027. chivang@fpt.vn.

COCOON
30 Nha Chung.

I went downright nuts my first time in this store—everything whispered my name, from the shawls to the bathrobes. I bought handbags, tote bags, drawstring silk pouches, and then more bathrobes. I bought so much that I got a 15% discount. I tried to charge it, but the sales clerk was not adept at using Visa and kept saying my card had expired. A few years later, the store was still good, but not as good. You never know until you try. © 844/928-6922.

HANDICRAFTS
23 Trang Tien St.

This is a tiny shop, near the Hilton, where I bought tons of lacquer. It's not hard to find lacquer stores all over town, but the selection here seemed to be more sophisticated than most other stores we looked at. © 844/936-2508. hoanglananh 1903@yahoo.com.

KHAI SILK
121 Nguyen Thai Hoc St.

This is the single-best-known name in local silks throughout the country. A few other branches are dotted around town, with another store in HCMC. This is somewhat of a TT (tourist trap) but is nonetheless a good source for everything silk from bathrobes to umbrellas. © 844/747-0583.

MOSAIQUE DECORATION
12 Hoa Ma St.

Furniture, tabletop, some fashion—the gamut of locally made chic. Mosaique has other stores around town and a bar. It's a lifestyle thing. © 844/971-3797.

NGUYEN FRÈRES
3 Phan Chu Trinh St.

Study your copy of the movie *Indochine* and get ready to shop: the style here is pure colonial chic. This is not in the regular downtown shopping area but is within walking distance of the Metropole. It is a house turned into a store that sells home decor—of the glam Indochine variety. Remember that lamps are 220-volt and must be converted for the U.S.; furniture has to be shipped. Small items are great for table accessorizing and gift-giving. One of the most chic stores in the city.

NIA-NIA
63 Hang Bong.

This is a tiny art gallery that also sells lacquer, a somewhat strange mix of product. It is not a knock-your-socks-off store, yet the selection impressed me, and, yes, I did buy a painting here. In fact, I considered buying everything here.

QUANG'S CERAMIC
63 Hang Trong.

This is not a cutie-pie shop and may not really even be a consumer shop—it sort of feels like a hotel supply showroom. Not all of the ceramics are attractive (to my taste), but some of the wares are both stunning and inexpensive. A teapot with six cups was sold as a set only, for $12. I bought many things that I swear were twins of items I saw at Armani Casa in Milan.

The company takes credit cards and even shows in Germany. © **844/928-6349.** www.quangceramic.com.

Song
27 Pho Nha Tho.

Be still my heart; stop breaking. What was once one of the best stores in the world is now sort of ho-hum. While the merch is nice, you won't rate this as a life-changing experience. The brain-child of an Australian designer, Song sells home style, women's fashion, and accessories. Prices are high for the locale, and you can find similar merchandise for less. © **844/928-8733.** www. asiasongdesign.com.

Tau My
16 Hang Trong.

There is no question that this is one of the best embroidery stores in town; it is also expensive. Of course, expensive by local standards is not necessarily expensive in the real world.

Tours

TOUR 1: 1 PERFECT DAY IN HANOI

- Begin with a good breakfast—you may want to hit a buffet and load up on carbs. Don't forget to drink lots of liquids, especially if it's hot and humid. Grab a bottle of water for your tote bag: You want to last the day.
- Now is a good time to try a pedicab. Your destination is technically Saint Joseph's but locally referred to as just "the Cathedral." Make sure you have agreed on the price before you set off on the journey—you could be cheated otherwise. If the fee is more than $3, something is wrong . . . or you have pedaled in from the airport.
- The Cathedral is on a little square that abuts **Church Street** (Nha Chung)—this is an excellent shopping thoroughfare and good place to start the day. Use the Cathedral as your home base; it's always easy to get a taxi or a pedicab here.

- Work both sides of the street rather than up and down—you will not be returning this way on this tour. Do it all in one visit if you can, at least getting your bearings, learning the merchandise and the prices. The street looks a tad funky, but there are many fancy stores here. There is good shopping up 1 block and then to your left (west) from the Cathedral, so don't miss anything.
- Walk west (away from the Sofitel) on Nha Chung for 1 shopping block and then turn right on **Nha Tho** Street. This street is only 1 block long but has fabulous stores.
- You should work Nha Tho Street up one side and down the other. But don't forget the turnaround spot at Hang Trong. You might not see the street sign, but never mind—you will see two or three stalls dead ahead of you that sell silk lanterns and lacquerware. Don't hesitate to buy.
- So now you are headed south on Nha Tho, essentially on the other side of the street from Song, where there are more great stores, such as **Caprice** and **Mosaique.** This short meander onto Nha Tho will bring you back to Church Street and you will turn right, with Song to your rear. Do note that Nha Chung (Church St.) has become Ly Quoc Su; this is still the same main thoroughfare that is home base.
- Continue shopping another block, and then turn left onto **Hang Gai,** which is the art gallery street.
- Follow Hang Gai until you come to a crooked crossroads—you can actually take any of these streets and get lost and found as you shop them all. For tour purposes, choose Hang Bong and continue to shop.
- From the main street, Pho Trang Thi, take a taxi back to your hotel or to the Sofitel Metropole for a cold drink.

TOUR 2: BACK-STREET HANOI

- This tour begins at the Sofitel Metropole, where you will want to look at the gift shops. You may not need the Louis Vuitton shop, but a few shops sell some great stuff. Poke around the hotel property if you are not staying here.

- Walk out of the old building of the hotel, past the pool and into the new part of the hotel, and then right out onto the back street, Ly Thai To. You are shopping your way to the **Opera House,** just a block or two away. Several enjoyable cafes and restaurants are on this block.
- The Opera House stands at a crossroads. Here you turn right onto Trang Tien and shop your way south (toward the Cathedral). This is not totally developed as we go to press, but this is Back-Street Hanoi; the whole thing is worth it just to stop at a shop named **Broderie,** 36 Trang Tien.
- When you get back to Pho Hang Bai, essentially the front of the Sofitel (you have walked around a big block), take a taxi to the Dong Xian market. The market is more of a neighborhood of buildings and alleys and street action, so work it to your heart's content.
- Take a taxi directly to **Quang's Ceramic,** 63 Hang Trong, but only if you are interested in dishes, dishes, dishes.
- An alternate: Should your idea of a dish be edible and should you not want to visit the ceramics, instead take a taxi to **Hoa Qua Kinh Do,** 33 Bang Boum. The tiny shop sells fresh fruits, confits, and jams—all local and quite unusual.
- When you are done with the markets, take a taxi to **Nguyen Frères,** 3 Phan Chu Trinh, one of the fanciest interior-design shops in town.
- Now you are just a few blocks from the Opera House and more or less where you started. Walk the streets around the Metropole—there's even a **street of booksellers.**
- Continue walking toward the Cathedral on the book street or one street over—Pho Trang Thi—for another block until you get to a modern, Art Deco–style building across the street from Vietnam Airlines. This is a modern mall with rather boring shops, except for the supermarket—be sure to load up on noodles and fish sauce.

Excursion to Bat Trang

Once I found out that there was an entire village of ceramics shops, I hired a taxi for the half-day excursion (about $40). The drive took almost an hour.

The town is larger than you think, and shopping it all takes a good eye and a strong back. In no time at all, everything starts to look alike. I have heard of people who hated it here, mostly because there is a lot of junk and they don't care if the vases cost $3. I had the time of my life, although I bought little and was exhausted afterward.

Sarah Lahey, *BTS* Editorial Director, made the trip—she went with a car and driver, saw the town, and even signed up for the local ox-cart tour, which was one of her favorite parts of the entire journey.

Excursion to Van Phuc

I am mentioning this because it may be offered to you and you may shrug and say, "Why not?" Van Phuc is a so-called silk village right outside of town—maybe a 20-minute drive. I found it very, very touristy, and prices are the same as in town. You can tour the factories, and you'll find a little bit of rural charm. But I'd go with the ox carts in Bat Trang (see above).

Departing Hanoi

Remember that you are most likely flying to another Asian or European city, so you'll be governed by the kilo weight system, not the piece system. Show an onward-bound ticket for the USA for leniency. If you just came with weekend gear and left everything else in Hong Kong, you can buy inexpensive luggage at a series of shops and stalls on the far side of the Lake. You are allowed two valises of 22 kilos (49 lb.) each.

Departure tax is paid after you check your luggage. Note that because Chinese airports now charge their departure tax in a ticket, you may not be used to the concept of "departure tax" or the need to stand in a different line to pay it.

WELCOME TO HO CHI MINH CITY

While it is written HCMC in newspapers and magazine articles, most people still say Saigon when they refer to the southern and former capital of Vietnam.

I am often asked which of the two cities—Hanoi or Saigon—has the better shopping. I invariably say Hanoi, but I think it's just because I have been to Hanoi more often and know it better. Not only is there nothing wrong with the shopping in Saigon, but you do pretty much find the same merchandise as up north and you have the delight of strolling a lovely lantern-lit night market.

You'll find more rebuilt colonial architecture in Saigon than in Hanoi; a bit of a funky, down-home feeling pervades the city and the old airport. But, oh my, do I see a hammer-and-sickle flag flying from yonder flag post?

Getting There

You can actually fly into HCMC nonstop from some European capitals or from the U.S. United has inaugurated its first flight since the end of the war. You can also get here from most Asian hub cities such as Hong Kong and Bangkok. In fact, you are little more than an hour or two in flight from everywhere in Asia. (Mind the 1-hr. time change.) Note that in travel, the name of the city will always be HCMC, never Saigon.

Arriving in HCMC

The old airport was/is charming and adorable, but it is being replaced by a big, modern, 21st-century job, similar to the one in Hanoi. A date for completion has not been announced.

The "old" airport is about 5 miles from downtown. I loved arriving there because it was so small and simple and thrust you right into the middle of the fantasy. We were met by a hotel representative and whisked right on our way. It was all very Graham Greene.

Ho Chi Minh City (Saigon)

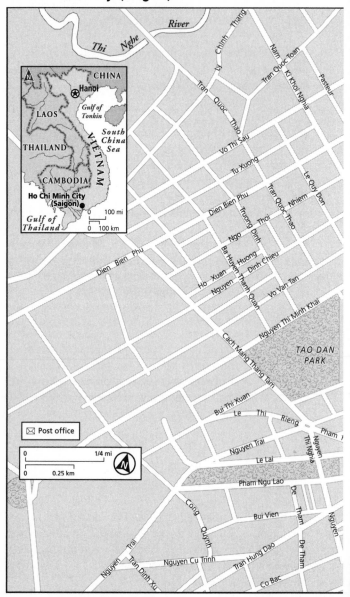

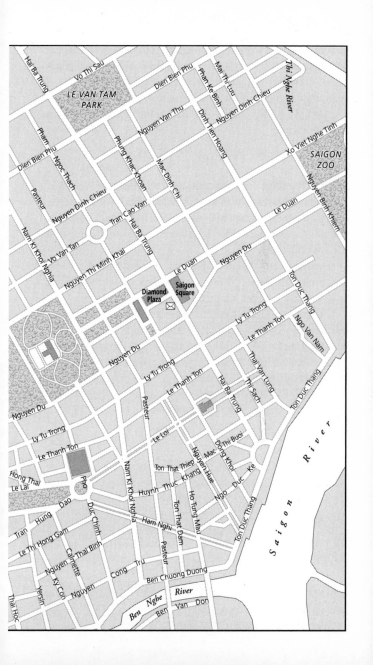

I must say that driving through the city streets and seeing the banners written in local script, all I could say inside my head was "Dien Bien Phu: Rest in peace." Dien Bien Phu is where the French fell and lost Indochine, and—while I'm not a colonialist by any means—the loss of life here on both sides still upsets me.

Lay of the Land

HCMC is a large city (population around seven million) and is divided into districts, sort of like French arrondissements. The district system may make sense to a local, but you'll find it a tad disjointed. District 3 is adjacent to District 1; District 10 abuts Districts 3, 1, and 5.

District 1 is the main downtown area and the most likely place to stay and shop. The market, and most of the shopping, is in District 1, which may be written as D1 on maps.

Just go up and down each street—this is easier than Hanoi, that's for sure. The main shopping thoroughfares are Dong Khoi, HaiBa Trug, Le Thank Ton, and Le Loi. For those in a hurry, Kong Khoi has just about everything you might want, from silks to lacquer.

Shopping Hours

Stores are open from 10am to 10pm, 7/7. The Night Market, in District 1 right near the Ben Thanh Market, is a visually thrilling adventure because of the atmosphere—it's almost like a movie set. The shopping becomes secondary to the outdoor dining, the families on motorbikes, and the softly lit lanterns.

Sleeping in Saigon

CARAVELLE
19 Lom Son, District 1.

Before the Park Hyatt opened, this was the best hotel in town and the most sought-after. And for good reason: The location is great (it's across the street from the Park Hyatt), and the hotel not only offers everything you want and need (good eats, nice bar scene, pool, gym), but the rates are a little lower, from $175 to $250. © 848/8243-4999. www.caravellehotel.com.

PARK HYATT SAIGON
2 Lam Son Sq., District 1.

Saigon has other hotels, but forget about them: This hotel is a simple miracle. If you can't get a room here, change your dates of travel or save your dong until you can spring for the best. This is a modern European-style luxury hotel set into the middle of Asian history.

Walking distance to everything, the hotel is drop-dead chic, gorgeous, wonderful, heavenly, and is a welcome respite from the buzz of motorcycles outside. Every detail of the hotel is sublime from the room decor to the jazzy little free map of the city they give you to the low-cost dry cleaning. (Send out all your clothes.) The food is great, too; I suggest you eat here at least once a day.

They've got a pool, spa, and all the amenities and services you would expect from a five-star property. The hotel is also situated right smack in the middle of everything. U.S. reservations © 800/492-8804. Local © 824-1234. www.saigon.park. hyatt.com.

Shopping Saigon

Aside from the magic of Saigon's Night Market, the city is simply not as cute as Hanoi in terms of the shopping atmosphere. The goods are very much the same, but I prefer the ambience of Hanoi.

Several of the best stores in Hanoi also have branches in Saigon. I don't think **Song** here is nearly as good as in Hanoi, but I could have hit it on a bad day—and Song in Hanoi has changed a lot lately so it's not as exciting as it once was either. **Nguyen Frères,** one of the best furniture and home-style shops in Hanoi, also has a branch.

The main market building (this is an indoor market), **Ben Thanh Market,** is filled with stalls selling clothes, souvenirs, silk tops for $5, wigs, makeup, and sunglasses (Ray Bans, $3). Illegal DVDs tend to be hidden but can be found. There are rows of shoe and handbag dealers. The foodstuffs are to the rear and left—avoid the fish department perhaps.

The scene is great fun and very interactive—more fun than the similar market in Hanoi. When Sarah and I sat down at a stall, tried on wigs, and took turns holding the mirror for the other, a crowd of locals drew around us and cheered the wigs they preferred. Yes, gentlemen do prefer blondes, even in Vietnam.

As you walk the alleys and stalls, shop girls pop up to talk to you. "You my best friend, lady? I like-a you. You good luck. You see my shop?"

Nearby, a few streets are lined with stores. For me, I'll take the string of shops on Le Loi that sells silk clothing by the designer line Dosa; I'd swear it came from Bergdorf's. Try **Orchids,** 84-86 Le Loi St.

TOURS

This plan is more simple than my suggestions for Hanoi—so you don't really need hard-core directions.

1. Go to the market at **Ben Thanh** and walk around, looking at everything. Price things you may be interested in, but don't get into serious price negotiations or you will have to surrender.
2. Walk 2 blocks back toward Lam Son Square, stopping at **Orchids** (see above) if you want silk clothes.
3. Now you are on Dong Khoi street: Turn to the right and shop the stores there, then double back and shop the side of the street you didn't choose when you turned right.
4. Return to Ben Thanh Market for those items you didn't buy in the shops.

WELCOME TO TAIPEI

Since you may not be as up on this as you think you are, let's have a quick review:

- Taiwan is the country; it's an island.
- Taipei is the capital city; it's to the north.
- If you remember back to your fifth-grade geography class and are now confused, yes, the island was once called Formosa.
- The Tai symbol is repeated in the name of the country and the capital; if you are reading Chinese, it can be confusing.
- Most importantly, as we go to press, Taiwan is an independent democracy and is not part of China. Referring to the people as Chinese is offensive to them: They are Taiwanese. However, to the Chinese politicos, this island is a part of greater China, and this is a very sore subject

When I was a girl, in the oversimplified version of real life that I was taught in school, Chiang Kai-shek was a good guy because he fought communists. Taiwan was founded as a refuge for his beaten-back army while he tried to retake China and reestablish the Republic of China. I also learned the tuck-and-duck method of putting my head under my wooden desk in case of a nuclear attack.

As it turns out, CKS (as it is written everywhere in Taiwan) did fight communists, but was not particularly more freedom-loving than Mao. In fact, he was a real S-O-B. His army wasn't very welcome in Taiwan, which in fact had been a Japanese colony for 50 years before the end of World War II. (This will be on the quiz because there is much more affinity for Japan here than in the PRC, and the Japanese association explains the architecture, the street-numbering system, and many other oddities.) Things didn't really get booming in Taiwan until recently.

Nonetheless, until a few weeks ago, the tallest building in the world was located in Taipei. One of the world's fanciest

Taipei

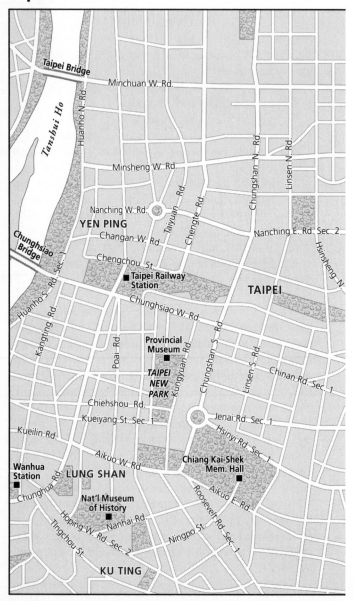

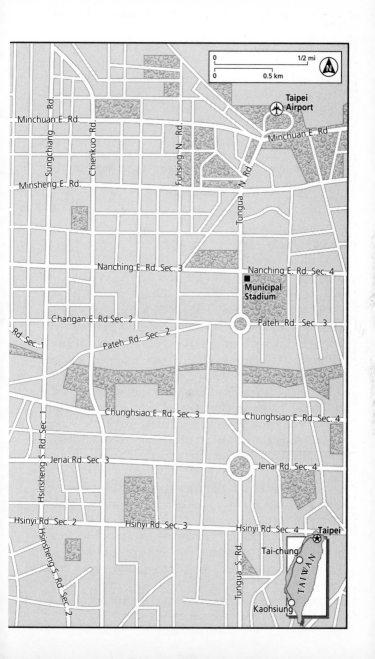

and chicest designers (Shiatzy Chen) is based in Taipei. Taiwan has one of the fastest and most sound economies in Asia. "Made in Taiwan" is not nearly as frightening as "Made in China" can be, although many Taiwanese products are indeed made in China, too.

Why Taipei?

You may wonder how I even got interested in Taipei or why I would send you here for a weekend or even a week. So here goes:

- United Airlines
- EVA Airlines
- Museums
- Shiatzy Chen

And if you don't think I would fly halfway around the world for either of the last two, then you don't know me very well. In fact, when United Airlines began the first nonstop flight (from a U.S. carrier) to Taipei, I knew something was up. Although I have known about EVA Airlines since their start-up, I wanted to learn about Taipei as a hub city rather than, say, Narita . . . or even Hong Kong. Finally, I had heard that the National Palace Museum is one of the best in the world, truly astonishing, and then learned that Taipei has many, many museums and is the leading destination for those interested in Chinese art.

Another important fact in exploring Taipei is that there are very few tourists. It's a cozy place—a big city without traffic and with plenty of luxury hotels . . . and branches of Starbucks. The destination is also very complete—you are an hour from the sea, from the hot springs, from the mountains and from various tea plantations. There's a lot more going on here than you ever imagined.

You can buy goods from a selection of brands known in Hong Kong and/or Japan; prices may be slightly higher than in Hong Kong but the ease in shopping may be greater in Taipei. Taipei is not overwhelming like many other big Asian cities and it is nothing like the People's Republic of China.

A Short History of Taiwan & Its Wonders

This is a short and oversimplified history, although I have already given you the lowdown on our old buddy CKS. The most basic of Taiwan history is new because although inhabited by aborigines (good museum), the island didn't really get quacking until the mid-1800s. As colonies go, that's pretty late.

Chinese Qing dynasty only established Taipei Prefecture in 1875; 20 years later the Japanese had taken over. (Watch the movie *The Last Emperor* for details on the end of the Qing dynasty.) They lasted for 50 years and then came CSK. He ruled for 25 years. What you're looking at, to put this into an Anglo historical perspective—is a Victorian state.

Things are booming now, but that slow start is what makes things here so cozy and the capital city so easy to deal with.

Meanwhile, we have to take geography into account—as this is the single biggest unmutable factor that any country must deal with. Taiwan is a small island, close to mainland China, but it is subtropical and ideal for growing tea. It also has mountains, many rivers, and natural hot springs.

Finally, lets talk about, uh, looting—only that's not what we're going to call it. Back in 1945, as World War II ended, the Japanese gave up China, and Chinese factions—mostly led by CSK and Mao—were fighting it out. The Nationalist government, led by General CSK, found itself in charge of the royal art treasures stored in the Forbidden City. Because the Communists threatened to smash this heritage to shards, the Nationalists dutifully packed it all up and shipped it here, there, and yonder. Truly, the crates traveled for years.

They ended up in Taipei with the general and the remains of the day. Although China has tried to get this stuff back, the truth is that the treasures are staying put and that's why we all have to go to Taipei to see them. Class dismissed.

About Language

The level of English spoken or understood is not what you might think it is . . . or want it to be. Far and away, Hong Kong has better overall English-language skills in its people, its hospitality industry, and its infrastructure. Signs in Taipei may be in Pinyin, but you will be hard-pressed to find English easily spoken. Also, there are two different forms of Pinyin for official use, so you may find some differences in spelling. Please also note that there are several ways of writing the place name for Taipei, as one or two words, with or without a hyphen. For simplicity sake, we are going with one word.

Getting There

Since Taipei is about 100 miles off the coast of mainland China, we're not talking about saving any time off the long-haul flying time. We could be talking about convenience, or sheer pleasure . . . and making the best of your connections if you must change airplanes.

As mentioned, both **United Airlines** and **EVA** fly nonstop. As we go to press, I have not tested the United service, although I often fly United throughout Asia. They have a strong hub in San Francisco.

EVA Airlines is one of the best secrets I know. They offer four classes of services, which means they have first, business, extended economy, and economy. Their extended economy costs less than business class and is wonderfully comfortable for a long-haul flight. They also fly various craft. In the 747 the business class is no nicer than extended economy. In Airbus planes and in 777s, everything is new and plush. EVA has also won awards for their airport lounges. For fans of transatlantic flights, EVA flies from Paris to Taipei.

Note that connecting through Taipei is a fabulous trick, as the airport is new and modern and gorgeous but not as congested as other Southeast Asian airports and certainly a better place to make a connection than Narita. Seoul has a lovely new airport also, but is much farther north, which means your final flight to the destination city is longer. If you make your connections in Taipei, you are 1 hour from Hong Kong and 3 hours from Bangkok.

With EVA there's also a price issue—even full business class is about $1,500 less than other airlines—and their extended economy is well worth the money. Check out www.evaair.com.

Arriving in Taipei

This one is tricky, but not very important. The international airport was once named CKS. (C'mon, you've already learned this, see p. 199.) The airport is not named CKS any more, but may be referred to as such because old habits don't die easily. Technically, the proper name for the airport is now Taiwan Taoyuan International Airport; it is written TPE.

Taipei does have a second airport that is only for domestic flights, named Songshan Airport.

The new airport is one of the nicest you'll see anywhere and has fabulous shopping concourses with not only the usual designer and duty-free stores, but stores from many of the local museums.

All manner of transportation awaits you at this airport. We called ahead and arranged car service with our hotel; while waiting for the car to arrive, I noticed there were several booths selling SIM cards on promotional deals. Should you take a taxi, don't be alarmed to learn that there is a 50% surcharge for airport-to-city runs.

Also note that if you fly EVA from the U.S. West Coast (they have five West Coast gateway cities, four in the U.S. and one in Vancouver), you will leave past midnight—in the wee hours, which will make you wonder what day you actually go to the airport—and you will arrive around 6am, which may mean booking your hotel for the night before.

U.S. passport holders do not need a visa for visits of 14 days or less.

Hubba-Hubba from Taipei

While this chapter is written to support a weekend away from your stay in Hong Kong, don't forget that you can take good advantage of the TPE airport and EVA Air and get from Taipei to either of the Vietnam cities in this chapter in about 2 hours. You can easily create your own circle tour by starting in HKG, going on to TPE, and then choosing another destination before ending up back on HKG for your return home or more adventures there.

Money Matters

You will need the local currency, which is called the New Taiwanese Dollar, written NT$. The exchange rate is US$1 = NT$30, so US$10 = NT$300.

There are banks and ATMs everywhere; getting money from a wall is not hard.

As for prices, Taipei's per diem is less than Hong Kong (hotel, taxi, dim sum)—in fact, if you get lucky, you can book a very swank hotel room for about $150. The most expensive rooms are around $300, half the price of those in Hong Kong.

Prices on shopping tend to be the same or higher. There are no bargains on either designer brands or even Hong Kong brands . . . or even on electronics.

Note that at the end of July 2007, old NT$500 and $1,000 notes went out of circulation. New notes have a vertical stripe on the right-hand edge of the note. Do not let anyone give you any old notes from under the cash drawer.

Shopping Hours

This is a serious shopping culture filled with very busy people, meaning that some stores are open 24 hours a day, every day. Regular shopping hours tend to be 10am to 10pm, but there are night markets in every district and neighborhood, so people can shop 'til dawn.

But wait: In some neighborhoods, stores do not open until 2pm because they stay open so late at night. Such stores and areas are discussed later in the text.

Taipei is known for its nightlife and in many cases, shopping and partying are synonymous. That's my motto.

Tax Refunds

There is a system for getting VAT refunds, which in Taiwan is called a TRS refund. If you spend over NT$3,000 (about US$100), you qualify for about 5% back. As usual, you fill in the forms and show the goods at the airport.

The Lay of the Land

As a relatively new city, Taipei works on a simple grid system. That was the good news. The bad news is that because of the 50 years of Japanese occupation, the numbering system is done in the Japanese fashion—which is odd at best.

You *must* know the section number of the street in order to get somewhere. Main streets have an east and west pattern; there are alleys and lanes. The single most important part of the address, again, is the section number.

Getting Around

This is a large city that is somewhat confusing. As an Old China Hand, I was happy to see familiar names for streets, but confused as to which city I was remembering. Since taxis are cheap, it's easy to get around without totally understanding the landscape.

Always have your destination written in Chinese and keep a hotel card with you. Do not count on your taxi driver being able to understand one word of English.

There is a good MRT/underground system that works best for a non-Chinese reading/speaking tourist on short-haul hops in downtown shopping areas. Tickets cost less than $1, or you can get a 1-day unlimited-use pass for about $7.

Sleeping in Taipei

GRAND FORMOSA REGENT
Lane 39, Zhongshan N. Rd., Sec. 2.

This hotel does have Four Seasons management and may be the best located for those who want to be smack-dab in the center of the designer and big-name shopping. If you go online looking for deals, you can get this room for about $250 a night. The hotel is large, it is local HQ for weddings and bar mitzvahs (well, you know what I mean), and it has some good restaurants for a shopper's break at lunchtime. It is a large hotel, modern and sleek. Rooftop pool and swanky two-story wellness spa. © 02/2523-8000. www.grandformosa-taipei.com.tw.

GRAND HYATT
2 Songshou Rd.

Adjacent to both the convention center and Taipei 101, the famous bamboo-shaped-tower-cum-fancy-pants mall, the Hyatt keeps with its international image of very modern, very chic, and very easy on the senses. The lobby has a lot of open space . . . and some nice shops. Rooms have every modern amenity. Expect to pay $250 and up. U.S. reservations ©800/492-8804. Local© 02/2729-1234. www.taipei.hyatt.com.

LANDIS TAIPEI
41 Minguan E. Rd., Sec 2.

This hotel has a slightly odd location but is otherwise so wonderful that it's probably my favorite. It's a member of Leading Hotels of the World, very fancy with Art Deco design and the best French kitchen in town, but it's also intimate, and much of the world I've come to know and love in Taipei is right out the front door. Better still, if you get an off-season deal, you can book a room for about $160. There's no pool, but there's a spa, a hot tub on the roof, and a large gym. Across the street is one of the most famous dim sum restaurants in town, Dian Shui Lou, which is open from 11am to 10pm.

About the Grand

The Grand Hotel is one of the most famous buildings in Taipei and the best-known international hotel. It stands on its own, on a hill, outside of downtown—meaning you must take a taxi to get there. You can take the MRT but it's not easy. How you get there is not the point.

The hotel was created by Mme. Chiang Kai-shek as the hotel for official guests who were visiting her husband and her country. It is, according to its name, very grand if you take the French reference: big. It might have been drop-dead impressive in the early 1950s, but by now most of us have been to Epcot Center, which is more impressive. The hotel is very old and getting worn—it is not your best choice for anything more than a photo op or two. Furthermore, any insider can confirm that neither the restaurants nor the stores are worth tipping the doorman. In fact, this is one landmark you can miss.

Also note that the Landis has a sister hotel at the hot springs and can arrange a visit and treatment for you. See p. 216. U.S. reservations through Leading Hotels of the World © 800/223-1230. Local © 02/2597-1234. www.landistpe.com.tw.

SHERWOOD
111 Minsheng E. Rd., Sec 3.

This is possibly the fanciest, most stunning, and most European of the Taipei luxury hotels. Everything about this hotel is a dream, including the gym where you are handed a towel and a cold bottle of water and lead to a pool, treadmills, and training machines. The restaurants are all good; there is a Starbucks half a block away. If you get lucky, you can book a room for about $225. Member of Leading Hotels of the World. The hotel is in the main business district—you can walk or taxi to some shopping. U.S. reservations through Leading Hotels

Beware When Booking

Since most tourists come to Taipei for the wonderful museums, note that most of them are closed on Monday. If you are planning a long weekend, come earlier in the week and make Monday your travel day or save the National Palace Museum for Monday since it is open 7/7. Stores are open on Monday but most museums are closed.

of the World ☏ 800/223-1230. Local ☏ 02/2718-1188. www. sherwood.com.

The Shopping Scene

I was daft, dumb, and stupid in assuming that Taipei would be a miniature Hong Kong. The 50 years of Japanese rule cannot be ignored. There are a lot of Japanese department stores in town; many of them anchor malls. Malls are as popular as in Hong Kong; the most Western in terms of style and tenants is the four floors of mall located within the Taipei 101 tower.

There are the usual crafts and souvenirs; all the museums have gift shops. There are also markets galore—for everything from electronics to teen fashions. Most importantly there are food courts and markets where the food stalls are considered a raison d'être. I don't eat street food, but foodies tell me I am nuts—Taipei is the place to do it.

It isn't so much that you will find merchandise here that you can't find elsewhere, it's that this is a 24/7 economy—many stores never close. There are about a dozen night markets; coffee is more popular than tea so everyone is on a caffeine high and the young population leans toward youth-oriented, fast fad fashions.

Taiwan is a relatively young country; Taipei is filled with young, working people who want fashion at a price, so there are many opportunities for those who are small enough to wear a Chinese size or wriggle into what's called Asian fit.

SHOPPING NEIGHBORHOODS

As is my wont, I make up the names to most of my shopping districts so that you can know what I am talking about and get some clues as to what they are. No local person uses these nicknames. Check with your hotel concierge for the proper names and the Chinese written forms before you head out.

Dihua Wholesale Street Bulk sales in Chinese medicine, dried foodstuffs, and textiles have been taking place in this area for about a century. The area is close to the river, which is how goods were originally transported into town.

Downtown Sogo Since there are several branches of the Japanese department store Sogo, note that I am sending you to a specific one and to the area that surrounds it. You want Zhongxiao East Road, sometimes called Eastern District. You start your exploration at the Sogo on Fuxing Road (and you know how I pronounce this street name), which is also the name of the MRT stop you can use. See below for info about the mall that stretches underneath this shopping district. Note that you are also next to the Dinghao Market.

Convention Center Located in the Xinyi District, the Convention Center is a modern complex that is orbited by several malls and a few hotels. The famous 24-hour Eslite bookstore is on one corner; the tallest tower in town, Taipei 101, is a sneeze away, connected by a walkway.

Ex-Pat Because of the large number of multinational firms in Taipei, there is a large expat community that tends to live in the same district, in the north of the city, around Tienmu International Circle. Things are more Western in this part of town, although businesses cater more to expats than to tourists. There are two large Japanese department stores in this district, although not at the circle itself.

Fortuneteller Alley You'll need a translator to go with you, or a friend, and then you shop for a fortuneteller, a method of telling fortunes, and a future you like.

Old Town In the district originally known as Manka, where Taipei was first colonized by the Chinese, there are numerous old storefronts and other old businesses, some of which are over 100 years old, which for Taiwan is old.

Grand Formosa The streets surrounding this hotel host all the fancy big-name designer boutiques as well as some local heroes, including Shiatzy Chen (p. 208).

Teahouses & Plantations The subtropical weather is perfect for growing tea; various oolong teas are the local specialty. Thanks to the Japanese influence, tea ceremonies are in the Japanese style; there are various old-timey teahouses throughout the city. Further to the southeast lie the tea plantations as well as the Museum of Tea, where you can learn the complete process and then enjoy a cuppa. The tea district is named Maokong. I can't help but think if tea is king, then this is King Kong.

Ximending The key to finding this area is California Fitness. There are six California Fitness gyms downtown but the one located on 52 Han Chung Street *(MRT: Ximen)* is where you want to go to explore the back streets and check out the kids, their clothes, and their cool. Note that stores don't open until 2pm, and the scene really happens from early evening and into the night.

MARKETS & MALLS

ELECTRONICS   God, I wish I were a geek! I wish I even knew what all those cords were for. There are many buildings filled with phones, gadgets, computers, and all sorts of electronics. Knowing what you are talking about—most of these guys speak English—is helpful in bargaining, although I don't think there is a lot of bargaining going on here. I bought my son a KRZR phone for $200. I decided this was a fair price because I had recently flushed my LG down the toilet and been forced to buy a RZR at Verizon for $289. The booklet was in Chinese, but what's a little thing like language between friends? The market is named **Guanghua Market;** it's at an underpass of the freeway, beneath the Guanghua Bridge, in a series of hut-like tube buildings that are thankfully air-conditioned.

FLOWER MARKET   Since I know you aren't shopping for flowers, I only mention this because the market is held only on weekends—like the Jade Market—and it's down the street (actually, across the parking lost) from the Jade Market. This area is very close to the East Metro Mall in one direction and the Linjiang Tourist Night Market in another.

HERB ALLEY   Alongside the Longshan Temple; also called Grass Alley by some. They do not sell weed.

JADE MARKET   One of the reasons I have sent you here for the weekend is so you can visit this market, similar to the one in Hong Kong. There's far more than jade at stake and fashionistas and those who like to play with beads will be impressed with the choice. Expect many of the stones and ropes of semiprecious gems to be fake, but if the price is right, who cares? *Insider's tip:* Near the Jade Market are many antiques shops. Check out Chienkou South Road as well as Hsini Road Section 3.

SHILLIN NIGHT MARKET   This is really putting my rep for honesty to the test. Okay, I love night markets; I love junky night markets. I did not like this market very much. If I did street food, I would have been impressed by the food court and the international reputation of this market's food vendors. I did like the many (many) reflexology salons, but by chance, I had already had one foot treatment that day. Like many Hong Kong night markets, this one has vendors in the street and shops behind them. There are herds of people. There aren't even any good fake handbags. It just doesn't touch my soul, that's all I can say.

SNAKE ALLEY   Official name is Huaxi Tourist Night Market and the snake feature is just part of the market. I frankly don't like anything or anyone who messes with animals, even snakes. I don't like tourist markets much either.

TAIPEI 101   This building held on to the world record as tallest building for a year or two, but has been forced to give up the title. The building is designed to resemble a stalk of bamboo; four floors are an upmarket international shopping mall where all sorts of big-name stores and brands are located.

EAST METRO UNDERGROUND MALL Stretching beneath Zhongxiao East Road Section 4 from Fuxing to the Dunha MRT station is a giant underground mall that provides everything you need in real life. The main Taipei rail station is aboveground, so if you are taking a train somewhere, you can shop your way right to the platform. This mall stretches about 6.5km (4 miles) in length.

WUFENPU This market area is across from the Songshan Railway Station and has developed as an area with young Taiwanese, Korean, and Japanese designers who sell street fashion to teens, tweens, and 20-somethings. The market is comprised of small stores in rows, not stalls in the street. You do bargain here.

YONGLE FABRIC MARKET Stalls, vendors in storefronts, fabrics on the bolt; not impressive compared to Shanghai.

WANHUA This is the formal correct name for the district but I call it "Down by the Riverside." You may also want to peg this neighborhood to the Longshan Temple, the most famous of the local temples and the one that anchors several markets, including **Herb Alley** (p. 213) and **Snake Alley** (p. 213). Snake Alley is part of the **Huaxi Night Market,** which is the most touristy of the night markets. In this neighborhood you'll also find the **Guangzhou Night Market.** I have repeatedly mentioned this as the most touristy district in town—to wit, there's the aptly named **Taipei Longshan Temple Tourism Mall.**

BEST BUYS & CURIOSITIES

BOOKSTORES For a small nation, Taiwan breeds a lot of education and therefore interest in multilanguage bookstores. My favorite bookstore is **PageOne** (p. 96), which, aside from a large selection of books in English, has an excellent office-supply department. You also have to be impressed with **Eslite,** which is open 24/7 complete with cafe and culture. There are a few branches but the one not to miss is right near the Convention Center and Taipei 101. **Caves** is another popular bookseller. Naturally all museum stores sell books; there are also specialty bookstores throughout town. Bookstore Street, as is known, is Chongqing South Road, Section 1—there are used books in various languages, but mostly Chinese.

BUBBLE TEA   While mainland China is still a tea-drinking culture, Taipei is much more coffee-oriented. There are scads of coffee chains; Starbucks is just one of a dozen. The only tea that seems to compete is novelty tea, and the newest novelty is called Bubble Tea or Pearl Tea—it's made with a type of tapioca so it has large balls inside it and you therefore drink it from a special, large straw. Bubble tea is just making it to the U.S. as a novelty also. You can order the tea and the special straws online and have bubble-tea parties at home in the States, much to the amusement of your family and friends. I like it served both hot and cold.

CHARCOAL FAN   The charcoal removes impurities from the air. Buy it from the store on the ground floor of the paper museum; about $12.

COFFEE   The Chinese drink tea; the Taiwanese prefer coffee. There are zillions of chains of coffee shops that are much like Starbucks.

CONTEMPORARY ART   There is a museum of contemporary art, of course, and then there's the Apollo Building with about 30 different art galleries in the one building. The contemporary art scene is almost as hot as in Beijing with several of the local museums featuring the work of those artists.

COTTON PAPER   Taiwan, like many parts of Asia, has had a paper trade for hundreds of years. Paper can be made with any number of fibers; in Taiwan it is made with cotton. There is a paper museum as well as museum store for papers and paper-made products (see "Charcoal Fan," above). You can also take classes in papermaking.

CRAFTS   This is a small island with not that much individually developed craftsmanship, but Japanese, Korean, and

Chinese crafts are sold. There are a few big stores, something like the old version of the Friendship Stores in China, that sell a good selection

D-CUP MASCARA   Stop laughing, this is a serious product that I am so in love with that I have to share it, with the hopes that when you visit and go to Watson's you can find the way to fuller, plumper lashes. Not in Watson's in Hong Kong. Go figure.

GEL DRINKS   In an economy driven by young people and with a heavy Japanese influence on style, it's easy to understand why gel drinks are so popular. The Japanese have gel snacks; here you buy your gels in any 7-Eleven or at a night market or even gourmet grocery store. They are sometimes passed out in tastings in tiny paper cups; some flavors have added vitamins, minerals, or are for energy. You may also see them referred to as 'jelly drinks'.

HOT SPRINGS   Hot springs are especially valued in Japanese culture, so the 50 years of Japanese rule developed this area in the north of the city. The Yangmingshan National Park houses the Landis Resort, where you can go for treatment. From Beitou (you can take the MRT) to the park, there are various resorts (Landis is the most resorty) and treatment centers, as well as a museum and, of course, treatments and salts to buy.

MOVIES   When the shopping gets to be too much, or you just need a break but want some local culture, head to the movies. Sure, the malls have movie theaters, but movies are a big deal in Taiwan so there are entire streets and neighborhoods known for their movie theaters. If you want to really catch the vibe, wait until after-work hours to observe the natives. **Warner Village** has Hollywood blockbusters; there's a museum of cinema and plenty of art-house movie theaters. **Wuchang Street** is called Movie Street; 2 blocks are packed with theaters and attract the young crowd.

MUSEUM STORES   Since Taipei has some of the most famous museums in the world, it makes sense that there are also plenty of museum stores. A few of the museums even have stores at the airport. The best museum store in town is in the National History Museum; the most disappointing is the National Palace Museum where the merchandise is divided between animated bok choys (could I make this up?) and 3-D graphics. Haven't any of these folks been to the Shanghai museum store?

NIGHT MARKETS   Night markets are mentioned throughout this text but must also be taken as not only a cultural phenom but a celebratory one. If your visit coincides with a Chinese holiday, ask which market is most likely to be celebrating so you can join the fete. Often the markets have grown up next to or surrounding temples.

OLD STOREFRONTS   Hong Kong, China, and, of course, Taiwan have done a good job in tearing down the old to make room for the new. Old-fashioned storefronts are therefore a curiosity. You can find old shops dotted all over, especially in the western portions of the city. Don't miss **Lin Tian Barrel Store,** which makes handcrafted wooden tubs, now a luxury item because the wood is nearly impossible to find nowadays.

REPRODUCTIONS (MUSEUM & ANTIQUE)   All of the museums have museum stores. Aside from the dancing bok choy and fridge magnets, they sell reproductions of the masterpieces held within the glass cases. These come in all flavors—scrolls, porcelain, and so on. Expect to pay about $200 for a small vase.

TOUR OF TAIPEI

I was recently asked to do a presentation for a group of women who were in Taipei for a tour group and very interested in museums. I love the trip I designed for them so much that I am providing a modified version of it for you here. It's meant to fit into a 3- to 4-day visit. If you're just here for a weekend, you'll want to speed up the pace and cut per your personal interests. Remember that the Jade Market just takes place on Saturday and Sunday.

DAY 1

- National Palace Museum
- National Museum of History & Botanical Gardens with coffee break at cafe there
- Taipei 101 mall, then New York New York Mall (next door) and Eslite (across the street)
- Dim Sum Dinner & A Foot (reflexology treatment)—across from Landis Hotel

DAY 2

- Paper Museum and Papermaking class (if not interested in paper, go to Longshan Temple and explore Old City and Herb Alley)
- Lunch at Regent Grand Formosa hotel and visit to local design diva Shiatzy Chen and nearby designer stores
- Apollo Building with contemporary art galleries
- Shop Sogo Downtown area or go to Contemporary Art Museum
- After-dinner adventure to Avenue of the Fortunetellers with translator or to a night market

DAY 3

- Jade Market
- Electronics Market
- Optional lunch and Starbucks Taipei or Bubble Tea Tasting, Tea & Cha.
- Tea Plantation and museum (1-hr. drive each way) with tea ceremony and tasting . . . or tour to Hot Springs with optional treatment (also 1 hr. each way)

Chapter Eight

....

SHANGHAI

WELCOME TO SHANGHAI

....

If you have an older version of this book, you know that I found
an apartment to buy in Shanghai and was planning to live there
for at least a few months of each year. I was very excited with
the whole notion and was telling some friends in Hong Kong
about the apartment I had chosen, in one of the luxury towers of the city. I told them how sad I was that you were not
allowed to cook in the building, what with all the gorgeous
produce readily available in Chinese street markets.

My friends listened patiently, exchanged looks, and the
husband, Phil, cleared his throat. He explained that one of his
jobs for the British army had been to test those foodstuffs for
possible use for the army: None of them had passed quality
controls or been deemed safe to eat.

I tell you this story now because even back then, a few years
ago, people knew that the foods and products in China were
not up to Western standards. These days, newspapers are filled
with reports on unsafe toys and goods. You must stop and
remind yourself that nothing is new; China has always been
this way; sit back and enjoy the wonders.

And there are many wonders: lovers dancing on rooftops
overlooking the river, a veritable *bong*-uette at the Cupola of

Three on the Bund, big-name French chefs popping up every-where, and top Australian tastemaker David Laris doing spicy chocolates on the side when not cooking at one of the town's snazziest new restaurants: Shanghai has it all, and the produce is now flown in fresh. (Phew.)

Shanghai was once the Paris of the West, the Whore of Asia . . . you should see the old girl now. She is, without doubt, one of the most exciting cities in the world. Sure, we all know about the 2008 Olympics in Beijing, but in 2010 Shang-hai hosts its own big show: World Expo, so the beat goes on . . . and on.

Westerners are welcome. The new Shanghai seduces you with the delicious state of euphoria generated by luxury hotels, fine restaurants, clean streets, and fabulous shopping. All those antiques and DVDs can't possibly be fake, can they?

There's dinner for two at about $50 a head at a restaurant that would cost four times that in London or New York; there's the world's largest Louis Vuitton store; there's a brand-new circular train station (South Station) that required the inven-tion of the world's first circular crane for construction to be completed . . . it looks like a sports stadium ready for the World Series. Oh, and I forgot the most important metaphor of them all: the Formula 1 racecourse. Gentlemen, start your engines. Next stop: Shanghai. Who needs *Survivor: China* when you can fast-track it here?

If you're expecting a honky-tonk scene or the sing-song girls pictured on cigarette cards and calendars, forget it, pal. Twenty-five new malls opened last year alone. Ten Carrefour hyper-markets are open as we go to press, with who knows how many by the time you read this. Over 150 hypermarkets from vari-ous brands dot the landscape—Wal-Mart is opening up less than a mile from Lotus Centre. Gap is coming, H&M is here, the Spanish retailers have landed (Loewe, Zara, and so on), and—get this—Saks Fifth Avenue opens on the Bund in 2008. "*It's a new world, Goldie,*" as the Fiddler once said.

ABOUT WORLD EXPO

Sure, you know all about the Beijing Olympics . . . You might not know that Shanghai has its own version, a world fair called World Expo, which will be held in 2010 to the tune of 70 million expected visitors. It has been reason to spruce up the city, tear down slums, and destroy many historical buildings. This is a disease that seems to be going around the eastern seaboard of China. Somehow a few Shanghai architectural landmarks are still standing. Everything else is new and very impressive.

GETTING THERE

See chapter 2 for information about carriers and Asian travel details; the information here is more city specific.

Arrival by Air

Shanghai has two international airports; most international flights serve the newer one, Pudong. The other airport, Hong Qiao, was being renovated at press time. In the next few years, the two airports are expected to welcome some 80 million people a year—each.

You can fly nonstop to Shanghai on transpacific routes from the U.S., transcontinental routes from Europe, transpolar routing from the U.K., and from down under via Dubai or Australia. I frequently go to Shanghai from Hong Kong; there is a **Dragonair** (www.dragonair.com) flight just about every hour. You can also get there through Taipei, on **EVA Air** (www.eva air.com). **American Airlines** has nonstops from Chicago and L.A.; **United** flies from Chicago.

If you arrive in Shanghai from an international destination (including Hong Kong), you will be asked to fill in a landing card and will, of course, already have a visa. You may also have to fill in a health card. The lines move quickly; you will be through Immigration in no time, waiting at carousels for your luggage. Luggage carts are available.

About that visa: Don't panic. Under some circumstances, you don't need a visa—if you are in the country less than 48 hours with a group (possibly on a cruise) or you hold a passport from 1 of the 17 countries that have recently relaxed their relationship with China and waived the visa requirement. Normally, of course, Americans and Brits do need visas. For more on how to obtain a visa as an American citizen, see p. 17.

The Pudong Airport is one of Shanghai's new architectural highlights, with lots of glass and light, reflecting the latest trend in airports that resemble museums. This airport is so well hidden in the middle of nowhere that you may be shocked at how far out it is. Don't worry about the distance, or about the fact that you may have to stand in line for 30 to 50 minutes if you want a legal taxi. You sure don't want an illegal one, so ignore those bozos who ask to ferry you about town.

After clearing formalities, you go to the hotel desk for your transfer—or outside for a taxi. Driving time from the Pudong International Airport to the InterContinental Hotel in Pudong is about 45 minutes, so figure at least an hour to a hotel on the other side of the Bund or in Shanghai proper.

The big news is that there is a fast train—one of those fancy maglev jobs—from the Pudong Airport right to Pudong. The bad news: This train doesn't go directly to downtown Pudong. It stops at Long Yang Road; you can change there for a train to downtown Pudong or deeper into Shanghai. Besides, you may not arrive with much luggage, but I promise you will leave with more than you can handle.

The maglev train also serves Hong Qiao Airport, a stop on the green line, which was under construction as we went to press. *Important:* Do not confuse the airport stop with the Hongqiao Road stop on the blue line.

About Your Luggage

More and more airlines are going by weight rather than piece, but several international carriers have recently created new rules that combine the two. For example, most U.S. flag carriers allow you two pieces of checked luggage, each weighing 50 pounds, no matter what class of service you travel. If you travel business class, first, or have premium status, you may get additional perks, weight allowance, or pieces. It goes downhill from there. If you are a shopper, you're going to be sick over this. As you research airfares, also check out the luggage allowances and charges for additional pieces of luggage.

Low-Cost Carriers

Most of the Asian low-cost carriers are based in Bangkok, but local **Shanghai Airlines** (021/6255-0550 in Shanghai, 800/820-1018 elsewhere in China; www.shanghai-air.com) may or may not meet your needs for travel in China. Of course, if you want to go to Bangkok, you're all set with many choices. Uh-oh, one of them just had a nasty crash. Try Air Asia (**8659/2516-7777**; www.airasia.com) instead.

Arrival by Cruise Ship

Shanghai's importance to China has always been its port; today many cruise ships call here at a number of berths on the Huangpu River; the fancier ships usually get berths near the Bund. A new cruise terminal is being built in what's called the North Bund district; it should be open by the time you read this book. The new building will be the largest terminal in China and will be able to welcome up to three cruise ships at once.

Fast Train, Going So Fast

The bullet train to connect Beijing and Shanghai (by 2008) never came about, but may still someday be built. This also means no fast train service is available to Hangzhou; see page 272. But I remain hopeful because the Chinese can do anything once they set their minds to it.

Train Travel

You may want to travel within China by train—I regularly use the overnight service between Shanghai and Beijing. Whether you are coming or going, your biggest problem will be luggage. I shop, therefore I schlep.

If you are arriving in Shanghai, don't plan to meet up with friends for a ride—with four exits, it can be very confusing. (I fear Peter and Louisa are still waiting for me.)

If you are departing Shanghai by train, don't rush to the station, because you will not be allowed out of the lounge area until 30 minutes before the train leaves. The lounge area is quite nice (for China), but you are a long way from done with the journey—you may have to go up an escalator, trek down a hall, climb down sets of stairs, and walk a mile along the platform before you find your car. You may find this a rather tense adventure . . . until you are onboard and marveling at how chic the train is (complete with video screens).

Porters are not plentiful and are normally banned from taking you directly to the platform or from actually loading the luggage onto the train for you. This can be overcome with an extra ticket—I usually buy all four of the beds in a compartment, even if there aren't four of us traveling. Those who can easily manage their luggage were not born to shop.

Various Metro lines serve the city's new South Station, which is considered a revolutionary architectural project. It will probably change the face of travel in and out of Shanghai.

Money on Arrival

If you have not arranged a hotel pickup, which will be charged to your room, you will need yuan for paying your taxi fare. If you don't have any on you, expect a nice long line at the exchange booth. The ATM is at the departure gate.

THE LAY OF THE LAND

If you're familiar with Hong Kong, you'll quickly understand my Hong Kong parallels. Pudong is the equivalent of Kowloon— the boomtown on the far side of the river. Today it has an impressive array of towers and tenants, all with breathtaking views of the waterfront promenade known as the Bund. In 10 years (maybe in 10 min.), Pudong could rival "downtown."

But Pudong is far more than a contained space on the "other side of the river"—it is an enormous metro area and includes much, much more than what we have been led to believe is the sum total of the city. The "new territories" of Pudong are also very convenient to the airport and downtown.

If you've never been to Hong Kong, don't fret. You can still find your way around simply by realizing that a river separates the two parts of town and that the giant Pearl Tower is in Pudong, on the far side of the river.

The city of Shanghai (Pu Xi) lies on the west bank of the Huangpu River. The neighborhoods bear the traces of the original Chinese city (though the walls are long gone) and the foreign concessions, or territories, of the 19th century (the French concession is still the nicest). Despite its size, there actually is a system, especially for the streets in "downtown": North-south streets are named after Chinese provinces, and east-west streets after Chinese cities. Of course, you need to learn your provinces in order to use this information—or keep a map on you at all times.

Shanghai Orientation

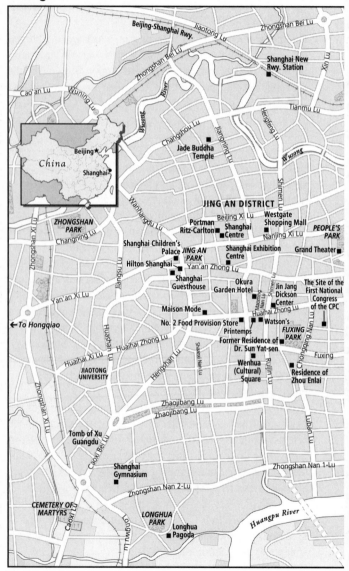

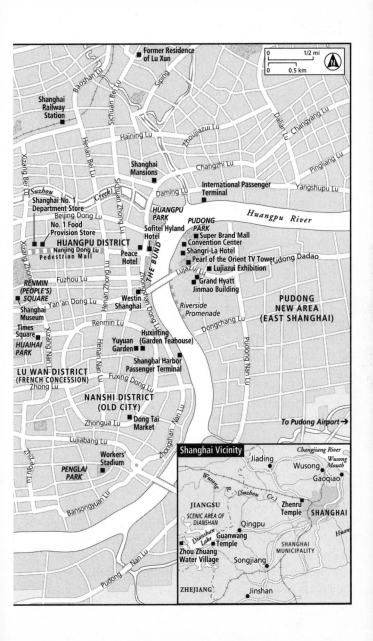

GETTING AROUND

....

This is an enormous city that is getting bigger as I type. Oops, another high-rise just went up.

Traffic is bad and will only get worse. I recently suffered a shopping adventure outside of town that took over an hour to reach—yet only 20 minutes on the return to my hotel. Traffic increases in certain directions at certain times of day—ask.

Even the leap from Pudong into "town" can take time if you get stuck in traffic, so plan ahead.

Taxis

Taxis are inexpensive and, especially at hotels, plentiful. There are new, clean cars and fleets that can be identified by their livery colors, such as metallic soft green or bordeaux lacquer. The good taxi companies give you a receipt (keep it) and promise that if you were cheated, you will get your money back, plus some. Drivers don't expect to be tipped. You can hail a taxi on the street or find one at any hotel. White gloves are optional but are indicative of a higher level of service.

I stumbled upon a taxi driver with a van I loved, had some Chinese friends make a deal with him, and used him as my private car and driver for $10 an hour.

Private Cars

Most luxury hotels do a good business in private cars; this pays if you have lots of stops to make or need to be dressed up for appointments. Fees are based on the type of car and length of time; there are also flat fees for airport transfers and for day trips. Half a day in a Lexus costs about $125; a car to Suzhou for the day (and back) is about $300. A private taxi company can also provide a car and driver, but it is unlikely that the driver will speak English.

Metro

Shanghai has a great Metro system, and it's growing constantly (see map, p. 230). It now has five lines, it's busy, it's pushy, it's not as clean as Beijing's Metro, and it's not a summer sport. If you ride during non–rush hours, you should be fine. A different color designates each line. Note that all station names are written in Pinyin and that the Renmin Guangchang station is also called People's Square.

Line 2 serves Pudong and connects the two international airports; in so doing, it connects the two sides of the city. Metro Line 3 is an east-west sort of transverse, all on the Shanghai side of the river and crossing the Suchow Creek.

About Addresses & Guidebooks

A guidebook to China is a good starting point, but no guidebook can keep up with the changes in China, especially in Shanghai. Buildings and stores are being torn down in Shanghai so fast that they can disappear overnight.

This problem doesn't exist just with guides; many (maybe most) concierges don't know what's going on either. No one in Shanghai can keep up with the changes. Hearsay—even concierge hearsay—is cheap and cannot be trusted. Sometimes you just have to get out there and see for yourself.

Important Announcement

No matter where you go or how you get around town, make sure you have one of the hotel cards on you that says "My hotel is. . . ." Hotels give them out by the zillion. Most hotels also have short charts of addresses in English and Chinese and often also in Pinyin so you can point to where you want to go and show it to the driver. Take it from me: No Chinese person will understand your Pinyin pronunciation of anything more extravagant than hello: *nihau* ("knee-*how*").

Shanghai Metro

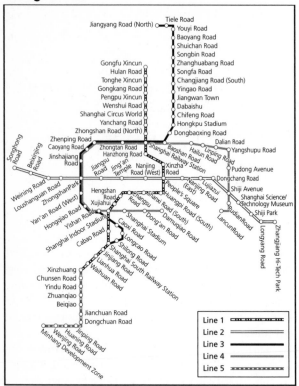

SLEEPING IN SHANGHAI

The new Shanghai has attracted enough business travelers over the last decade to ensure that there are plenty of suitable hotels with Western-style amenities. Just about every big, four-star chain already has at least one hotel here, and it is not unusual for a chain to have a hotel on each side of the river.

Because Shanghai is so spread out, where you stay can be important to how you feel about the city; on the other hand, where you stay doesn't matter that much because little in Shanghai is within walking distance and taxis are cheap.

Do note that hotels always have promotional rates, depending on their occupancy rate or whims. Ask.

When the **Shangri-La**—the first really razzmatazz luxury hotel in Pudong—opened, rates began at $138. **Ritz-Carlton** had a summer special for Visa cardholders of $130 per night on the weekend and $150 per night on weekdays. Also remember that the **Westin, Sheraton,** and **St. Regis** chains are all part of the **Starwood** group. As a member of AAA (American Automobile Association), I get a coupon for a discount at Starwood Hotels if I book 14 days in advance. The Westin had a winter rate of about $200, while the St. Regis—in a far corner of Pudong—was about $180. Ask!

Various neighborhoods are taking off as luxury hotels move to anchor them and bring in the traffic—for the Expo and for history. **Conrad** is opening a new hotel right near the new **Landis;** these are both near the Expo Center. **Hyatt on the Bund** is already open and the **Peninsula,** at the corner of The Bund right at Suchow Creek, will open in 2009. As we go to press, the only one of these hotels that is open is Hyatt on the Bund, so get in line for promotional deals and be the first in your group to check out the parade.

When a hotel comes to town, they often feature attractive rates. Two new luxury hotels are **Peninsula** and the **Landis,** both in excellent locations. If you've never heard of Landis, step this way; it's one of my new discoveries (p. 233).

Be sure to ask about upgrades, and don't grab the least expensive room. Because the better hotels court business travelers, they all have executive floors with many perks that often make paying more an actual bargain.

If you aren't a business traveler and prefer a boutique hotel, double happiness to you and yours. Several boutique hotels have opened—most notably **Jia,** 931 West Nanjing Rd., Shanghai (© **8621/6217-9000; www.jiahongkong.com**), successfully launched in Hong Kong and now open in Shanghai. This hotel chain was designed by Philippe Starck.

Shanghai Central (Pu Xi)

HILTON SHANGHAI
250 Hua Shan Rd. (Metro: Jing An Temple or Chang Shu Rd.).

This was one of the first Western hotels in town and is somewhat famous for providing comforts. If you think, "Oh Hilton, ho-hum," you are totally off base. This hotel keeps up with all the amenities, offers excellent service, specializes in business travel, and—while not as luxurious as some of the deluxe properties—should not be counted out of the game.

The hotel has a small mall, several restaurants, and that old-fashioned newly restored Hilton style. The location is a little off-center, but taxis are cheap and rates are reasonable. You'll get good concierge service and free shuttle buses. The fabu bar on the top floor of the hotel boasts lovely decor, comfy chairs, and a view of Shanghai. Also good: the Szechuan restaurant alongside the bar. *Note:* You have a choice of nearby Metro.

On a promotional deal, you can get this hotel at $129. Otherwise expect to pay $250 to $450. U.S. reservations © 800/ HILTONS. Local © 021/6248-0000. www.shanghai.hilton.com.

LE ROYAL MERIDIAN
789 Nanjing Rd. E. (Metro: Peoples Square).

This relatively new hotel is right smack-dab in the heart of downtown, only 2 blocks from shopping, museums, malls, and everything else. If you like to walk, this is perhaps the best location in town.

The hotel is part of a larger tower (66 stories), so you may be slowed down as you attempt to check in. Once upstairs, you are in total luxury and high enough to have a view seemingly all the way across China from your floor-to-ceiling glass window. Among the several good restaurants, one specializes exclusively in dim sum. An excellent gift shop is on the lobby floor, but don't let that stop you from visiting the bar on the top floor: The views are incredible. Great location and stunning choice.

Rooms are about $350 per night. U.S. reservations © 800/223-6800. Local © 021/6361-6688. www.starwood.com.

PENINSULA SHANGHAI
32 the Bund; 32 Zhongshan Dang Yi Rd.

Located right off the Bund where the British Embassy once stood, the Peninsula brings all of its charms and wonders to one of the best locations in town—the northern part of the Bund, just south of the creek. The hotel is not open as we go to press, but should open in 2009. www.peninsula.com.

PORTMAN RITZ-CARLTON
Shanghai Centre, 1376 Nanjing Xi Lu (Metro: Jing An Temple).

The fanciest and possibly best hotel in Shanghai—even as the new ones bring on the competition—this is the standard by which all others must measure themselves. The executive floors offer lounge privileges that really make a difference in the comfort of your stay and more than balance out the price of the upgrade with the perks you gain. There is also an excellent business center and what many expats say is the best hairdresser in town.

The hotel is large, and I think the concierge staff downstairs is overworked, which is one reason it pays to upgrade to a room that has use of the lounge and its private concierge service—which is fabulous.

Regular rooms cost under $200 a night but can go to $400; it's usually about $50 more per night for the club rooms, which pay for themselves in extras. U.S. reservations © 800/241-3333. Local © 021/6279-8888. Fax 021/6279-8887. www.ritzcarlton.com/hotels/shanghai.

SKYWAY LANDIS HOTEL
15 Da Pu Rd. (Metro: Remin Square).

I lucked into this find right as the hotel was opening; this is a chain of luxury hotels that many Americans do not know about. The chain may be small but many of the hotels are not—especially this flagship, which is in one of the tallest new buildings in town and is *the* five-star hotel closest to the site of World Expo 2010. The location is convenient for shopping in Puxi. You're also very close to Xintiandi, and—because it's near the freeway—most of the city is accessible from here.

The hotel also has a residence program if you want to extend your stay. There are 654 rooms in the hotel portion with the usual deluxe amenities—health club, pool, spa, and so on. Look for numerous promotional deals because the hotel is so new, but expect to pay about $175 for a weekend rate, or $250 with airport transfers included. Local © **8621/3318-9988.** www.skywaylandis.com.

SOFITEL HYLAND HOTEL
505 Nanjing Rd. E. (Metro: Renmin Guangchang or He Nan Rd.).

This is one of my secret finds, although since it has just been renovated, the secret could be out and the rates may be on the way up. The hotel is small and in one of the most fabulous locations in town—smack-dab in the middle of the shopping district right on Nanjing Road.

Prices are less than at other luxury hotels ($105 on a winter special); I paid $200 for my room on the club floor, which offers many, many perks, making it worth the splurge. Prices are higher in market weeks, during fairs and events. U.S. reservations © **800/SOFITEL.** Local © 021/6351-5888. www.accor hotels.com/asia.

Sleeping in Pudong

INTERCONTINENTAL HOTEL SHANGHAI
777 Zhangyang Rd., Pudong (Metro: Dong Fang).

This hotel looks average from the outside, so step inside for the atrium, the chic Chinese style, and a hidden destination you might not otherwise discover. The hotel is not on the waterfront in Pudong, like the Shangri-La, but it's not inconvenient and the Metro is nearby.

Rooms are good, decor is Chinese modern, and the lounge floor and facilities are excellent. The hotel has a wonderful spa, and good eats are available on the ground floor. It's also far more cozy than most Shanghai hotels, partly because it's not as huge as many of them, with a mere 400 rooms and 78 suites. It pays to upgrade to a club lounge room for all the extras. Best buy: spa packages with four treatments often go for about $130 for 2½ hours of bliss—try to book ahead to help cure jet lag.

Rates on a standard room are about $175 per night; a king-size-bed business suite is $250. U.S. reservations ✆ **800/496-7621.** Local phone ✆ **8621/5835-6666.** www.ihg.com.

SOFITEL JIN JIANG ORIENTAL (AKA J. J. ORIENTAL)
889 Yangga Na Lu (Metro: Expo Center).

This very tony hotel is in the middle of a still-developing area. But by 2010 this is expected to be the heart of Pudong. You do have to take taxis everywhere, but if you're mindful of traffic, a ride to Yuyuan Gardens is a mere $5. It's also easier to get to the airport from here than from the other side of town. Furthermore, prices were low (I got a winter promotional rate of $105), there's a shopping mall in the basement, and the club floor was luxe personified. My personal butler was a nice touch, and sitting in my bathtub next to a wall of windows overlooking Pudong wasn't bad either. I'm hopeful there will soon be a shuttle bus to the nearby Lotus Centre.

This is a great hotel to know about when prices are crazy in town, which happens during big conventions and special events (such as Formula 1 racing). U.S. reservations ✆ **800-SOFITEL.** Local ✆ **021/5050-4888.** www.accorhotels.com.

DINING IN SHANGHAI

Shanghai is famous for its own style of cuisine (rather bland, actually), its **crabs** (in season in Nov), and its **pan-fried brown noodles.** I have not only become addicted to these noodles but have now tasted them in enough places around town that I know where the best ones are. They are also one of those things that you can hardly ever go wrong with—good for kids, picky eaters, and the travel-weary.

Should you happen to be a street-food person, there are a few streets for wandering and eating your way to heaven . . . or somewhere. Check out **Wujiang Lu,** near the Shi Men Road Metro station. This is a strolling street—the first part is devoted to Western-style fast food, and the second part is for local diners who prefer the real thing. Chef Jean-Georges says his street food of choice comes from **Xiang Yang Road,** between Julu and Changle roads.

Shanghai has a growing reputation as the swinging spot in the Pacific Rim, and a lot of this is related to European-style dining. Shanghai could be in London, New York, or Paris.

Restaurant Concepts

THREE ON THE BUND
No. 3 the Bund, 3 Zhong Shan Dong Yi Rd., at Guangdong Rd. (Metro: Renmin Guangchang).

About the address: The building is on the Bund, but the door is on Guangdong Road. About the concept: Until recently, the Bund was best seen in the opening scenes of *Empire of the Sun.* About 10 years ago, an Australian chef by way of Hong Kong opened M on the Bund, the first of the Western-style fusion-chic restaurants—and with a spectacular view. Now the concept has gone further, with the first Western-owned landmark building on the Bund, across the street from M on the Bund in a building that was once "the club" to local foreigners. It's been totally redone—the decor is stunning—with a handful of designer restaurants and the only Evian health and beauty spa this side of France. This is also home to a few stores, including two Armani shops and 3, a designer store on two levels that carries many Euro big names. Online: www.threeonthe bund.com.

Make a reservation for all of the restaurants:

THE CUPOLA: Dinner à deux? This is marriage-proposal central. The private dining room in the building's cupola has a view to die for. You ring for the waiter; otherwise, it's private. It is amazingly gorgeous and dreamy. ✆ 021/6321-1101.

JEAN-GEORGES: I visited for lunch, which was a good insight into the fashion scene, but dinner is probably better—for the view and the dress-up version of the fashion scene. The food at either meal is sublime; the bar is a re-creation of the famed Long Bar of Shanghai's storied past—where each man had a position at the bar based on his status in the business world. ✆ 021/6321-7733.

LARIS: Perhaps this was the most exciting of my meals at Three on the Bund because I already knew the Jean-Georges concept so well from Market in Paris, one of my favorite restaurants. The chef here came from Paris, so there is some crossover in the fusion. Laris is David Laris's first name restaurant; heralding from Conran's big-name places in London, he does Australian and Pacific Rim fusion contemporary, then serves you his homemade chocolates after dinner. ✆ 021/6321-9922.

NEW HEIGHTS: This is the bar, the cafe, the casual restaurant that includes the terrace—the "in" spot to see the view of the Bund and the river. ✆ 021/6321-0909.

WHAMPOA CLUB: This is the Chinese restaurant of the group; I am over the moon for the private rooms for tea service. My lunch here was a tad too Chinese for me, but the place was full, and the locals loved it. The decor is gorgeous, the view sublime, and the food creative Shanghainese, by a chef who made his name in Singapore. With six you do *not* get egg roll. ✆ 021/6321-3737.

XINTIANDI
Huai Hai Rd. E. (Metro: Huang Pi Nan Rd.).

This is a destination, not a restaurant—it's sort of a theme park of great architecture, some stores, and many bars and restaurants. Surely a must for seeing what's hot. I'd suggest just wandering and picking a restaurant that appeals to you. Or you may prefer to barhop. If you're looking for addresses to check out, there's **Nooch,** 123 Xinye Lu (© 021/6386-1281), and **TMSK,** 11 Beili Lu (© 021/6326-2227), which is best as a bar or a lesson in design. The prices in all the restaurants are more in keeping with New York than China.

Museum Concepts

First things first. I screwed up on this, so there's a chance you will, too: Most museums have cafes, but the Shanghai Museum and the Shanghai Art Museum are two different places.

Kathleen5 is the talk of the town—a restaurant at the Shanghai Art Museum. The chef is American-raised Chinese, and this is her fifth restaurant since returning to Shanghai. For off-the-Bund dining, this is the place for taste, view, and new style, complete with a large terrace. Even when the museum is closed, lunch is served; just take the elevator upstairs. *Be warned:* I happened to go here one day and almost left due to language problems, despite a luncheon reservation. A Western menu is available. Shanghai Art Museum, 325 Nanjing Rd. W., fifth floor (© 021/6327-2221; Metro: Renmin Guangchang or Shi Men Rd.).

Nearby is the **Shanghai Museum Café.** The modern cafe is on the ground floor and serves Western-style snacks. It's chic, clean, and convenient. Good bathrooms, too. Figure $15 per head without drinks. Shanghai Museum, 201 Renmin Da Dao (© 021/6372-3500; Metro: Renmin Guangchang).

Snack & Shop

If you're out sightseeing or shopping and want a simple lunch or a quick bite, here are a few of my regular choices. When in doubt, I test a luxury hotel's coffee shop.

LAKE PAVILION TEAHOUSE
257 Yuyuan Lu, Yuyuan Gardens (no nearby Metro).

When you go to Yuyuan Gardens and see the teahouse in the center, you will invariably want to dine there. I can't tell you the whole deal because we went on a Sunday and were trying to beat crowds, so we were there at an odd hour and almost everything was odd. However, here goes: The type of tea you are served and the price are related to your location in the teahouse. Upstairs is better. There are set tea menus, but you get no cucumber sandwiches, just tiny eggs and bits of local nibbles. We saw people eating dim sum downstairs—they seemed to have brought in their dim sum from a nearby takeout place. About $10 per person without serious food. We were not amused. ✆ 021/6355-8270.

OLD CHINA HAND READING ROOM
27 Shaoxing Rd. (no nearby Metro).

This will probably require a taxi ride and some effort. But it's really fun and possibly worth doing, especially for the ladies. The place is right out of a novel or a movie—a true English tearoom with chinoiserie edges for those wearing whalebone and toting stiff upper lips. Britannia rules the waves. Assam, m'dear? About $5 for a cuppa. ✆ 021/6473-2526.

SUPER BRAND MALL FOOD COURT
Pudong (Metro: Lu Jia Zui).

Don't confuse the food court on the fifth floor of the Super Brand Mall with the mini–food court in the basement at the entrance to Lotus Centre. The food court has many of the usual

Western suspects as well as a cute fast-food Thai place, which will set you back less than $10 per head, with beer.

SHOPPING SHANGHAI

Stores in Shanghai are an incredible jumble of styles; few were what I was expecting. In short, there's plenty of Western style while communist-era shops are disappearing. Shanghai has a far greater rep for trendiness than Beijing—there's lots of fashion, from Euro name brands to Chinese no-names. This is the place to shop for clothing, especially for teens, tweens, and others in need of the latest thing.

The flea markets (there are several) are pure heaven; the museum stores are also good—especially the one at the Shanghai Museum. Most hotels have shops; prices in hotel gift shops are always higher than elsewhere, but at least you don't have to deal with crazy salespeople or bargaining techniques.

Shanghai Home Style

Ah, Shanghai style, that design category in home furnishings—and a little bit in fashion—that conjures up the 1930s and the days of drugs and jazz and decadence in the foreign concessions of old Shanghai. David Tang capitalized on this style enormously when he created his **Shanghai Tang** stores, but the look is the stuff of movies and hotel lobbies and dreams of pearl-shaped silk lampshades and overstuffed easy chairs and girls in tight, tight dresses selling cigarettes.

There was romance in 1930s Shanghai style, which David Tang has used in his Shanghai Tang stores and private China Clubs. **Xintiandi** (p. 250), created from ancient stone buildings, reflects an entirely different kind of urban reclamation and old-fashioned Shanghai style. There is a Shanghai Tang store in Xintiandi.

Brand Awareness

Duties on foreign-made merchandise are incredibly high, so brand-name goods sold in China have never offered any value. Although all brands are now available in Shanghai, even Hong Kong is cheaper for such items. In fact, many say that Hong Kong has survived the latest financial downturn because the wealthy Chinese go there to shop.

We all know that China is expected to be the world's largest consumer market. With Shanghai considered a more fashion-motivated city than Beijing, most brands have tried to break into the Shanghai market. The brands already established in both cities often say they have better customers in Beijing and that Shanghai shoppers are too picky.

More and more luxe malls have opened in Shanghai. I think we should all be learning the Chinese brands, but the shopping ops are more and more oriented toward Western brands. The world's largest Louis Vuitton store has arrived. Phew. Cartier has just opened on the Bund, thankfully next door to a bank, which you can rob before shopping.

Bund Awareness

The Bund is still *the* place to be, to see, and even to dance (ask your concierge about the dance lessons). The big-name stores (Saks) and hotels (the Pen) continue to move into historical buildings and sites, further enriching the scene. If you do nothing else, stroll the Bund and shop at **Shiatzy Chen** (p. 244), and you will understand the new China in a blink.

Money Matters

See the "Money Matters" section in chapter 2 for a complete discussion of money in China. ATMs are readily available. You should bargain in all markets.

Aaron's Turn

One of the things that makes shopping in China so unbelievably great is the all-out, excessive bargaining. Honestly, you will buy things you didn't even want just because you got caught up in the bargaining process.

I became the King of Bargaining because of my take-no-prisoners attitude. I was cheated on my first shopping adventures and terribly upset because I was dumb. After that, I felt compelled to make up all that I had overpaid. At the time of my first shopping/bargaining foray, I was convinced that I was making out like a bandit. It wasn't until later that I added up all the prices and realized that I could have bought the same stuff for the same price at Wal-Mart. After that, I honed my skills and managed to buy twice the amount of merchandise for half the price.

I try to be polite, I don't criticize the merchandise, but I like to pay 12% to 25% of the asking price. I tell the vendors I'm poor, I'm a student, I don't have that kind of money, and I know they are offering tourist prices.

The important thing is to not let them know that you are too interested. In fact, it works better if there are two of you to play good cop–bad cop—or, in this case, good shop–bad shop. For instance, you examine the item and get an initial price from the vendor. The bad cop friend says, "No way, man. You don't really want that, and it's *waaaay* too expensive."

The vendor jumps in and lowers the price. It's very important at this point that you express genuine interest. Once they know you will buy, all they have to do is close the sale, which is a matter of price.

The biggest problem is that the prices you are quoted at first are good prices compared to those we are used to in America. It's just that these are very high prices for China and for the quality of the merchandise.

Tipping Tips

As you all remember from Communism 101, which we were taught in high school near our bomb shelters, Communists do not believe in tipping. At one point, tipping was almost illegal; then it was merely frowned upon. Now it seems to be frowned upon by expats who don't want you to ruin the system because they have been getting by without tipping. Tourists do indeed tip. In fact, the best way to teach capitalism is to prove that it works; that is not done with a lecture, but with a tip. I tip everyone, and I tip big-time for work well done. *Note:* You can tip in U.S. dollars.

Shipping Tips

DHL: The company has a comprehensive shipping network throughout China and Hong Kong. For Express Centre locations, call ✆ **021/6536-2900** or search www.cn.dhl.com.
UPS Shanghai: To find shipping locations or to arrange for pickup, call ✆ **021/6391-5555**.

Best Market in Shanghai

SOFT SPINNING FABRIC MARKET
Shanghai Soft Spinning South Bund Material Market, 399 Lujiabang Rd., at Nancang St. (no nearby Metro).

You may be frightened when you arrive and think I've done you wrong, but step inside and join the party. The main market is in what looks like a warehouse of wholesale showrooms; two similar buildings stand across the street from each other. Follow the crowds in search of yardage.

This is an indoor market, with open stalls, tables laden with fabrics, and merchandise hanging from the ceilings. Tailors lurk in the side shops, and some of the fabric vendors have goods already made up. You can also find handbags and totes. There are several floors to explore, but I happen to find the main floor the best (although everyone knows prices are higher on the ground floor and closer to the doorways, right?).

The market is open 7/7, 9am to 6pm. Have your taxi wait for you. *Buyer beware:* Word is that this market will be moved north of Suchow Creek in the near future. Ask your hotel concierge before you set out.

Best Stores in Shanghai

Each of these stores is described in the Resources portion of this chapter. But if you're in a hurry, consider these your must-sees. They all take plastic.

HU & HU
8, Lane 1886, Caobao Lu (no nearby Metro).

Out in the boonies a bit (have your taxi wait), but worth it if you are looking for antiques, mostly restored. This large ware-house has incredible home style. A limited selection of origi-nal ancestor scrolls is available, too. An extra shed or two houses stock that you can buy and restore yourself or have restored to your color and finishing choices. They will arrange ship-ping and even send you e-mail photos of pieces that may come in after you've left town. The owner speaks American English; she is wonderful.

SHANGHAI MUSEUM ANTIQUES SHOP
201 Renmin Da Dao, People's Sq. (Metro: Renmin Guangchang).

You can get into the shop without going into the museum, although why you would do that is something only I under-stand. There's everything from books to gift wrap to repro-ductions of items from the museum collections. Silk scarves, porcelain, postcards, calligraphy. You get the gist.

SHIATZY CHEN
This is simply one of the most incredible stores you will ever see in your life. Shiatzy Chen is from Taiwan, and her husband is a wealthy garmento. Her work is more sublime than Armani

and encompasses men's and women's clothing—both work and dress-up clothes—home style, and women's accessories.

SUZHOU COBBLERS
17 Fuchow Rd. (Metro: He Nan Rd.).

The world's tiniest store, right off the Bund, sells embroidered slippers in Chinese styles that have been Westernized to the point of high chic. Don't miss it! *Note:* This store is just around the corner from Shiatzy Chen, described above.

W. W. CHAN & SONS TAILOR LTD.
129A Mao Ming Rd. (Metro: Shi Men Rd.).

The best tailors in Hong Kong have traditionally been from Shanghai families who fled in 1949. Now they are beginning to come back to serve the New China. W. W. Chan is one such tailor—one of the big two in Hong Kong.

This free-standing store across the street from the Okura Garden Hotel off Huai Hai Road is swank and western and all you need. They offer men's suits, shirts, ties, and such. Prices are about 20% less than in Hong Kong. You will pay about $600 for a custom-tailored suit.Company representatives visit the U.S. twice a year. For an appointment write sales@wwchan.com.

Shanghai Shopping Neighborhoods

PUDONG

Pudong isn't really a neighborhood, it's a city—a big city with many neighborhoods. It is sometimes written as "Putong."

To further confuse you, the business district of Pudong is called Lu Jia Zui; the Stock Exchange is here, as are many main offices of the big banks, the Jin Mao Tower, the Shangri-La Hotel, and, of course, the Pearl TV Tower. In short, tourists call it Pudong and some business guys call it Lu Jia Zui.

Pudong has changed so much that it's hard to keep up. Whether you stay in this part of town or not, you must, must,

must come over and get a view of the Bund at night. And don't forget the brown noodles. Or the **Lotus Centre,** which is in the Super Brand Mall.

To see what's happening, you want the area nestled between the river and the Pearl TV Tower. This can be done in a drive-by, and then you can explore the mall on foot.

THE BUND

Located on a bend in the Huangpu River, the Bund is enhanced by the river's natural curve. It is called *Waitan* in Chinese. There are buildings on one side of the waterfront, then comes the part for cars (some call this a street), and then, right along the quay-side, there's a large boardwalk so that one can promenade along the river. Yes, there are guys with cameras who will take your picture for a small fee; it's just like Atlantic City. This is not a great shopping street, but it is changing. Armani has arrived, and so has **Shiatzy Chen** (see above). And **Saks Fifth Avenue** is coming, I swear it. The side streets jutting away from the river right off the Bund are the ones to watch, starting with Fuchow Street.

SUCHOW CREEK

Back in the old days, the international concessions ended at the Suchow River at Henan Road, just north of the Bund. That area is now being turned into a hot new enclave for artists, and warehouses are filled with ateliers.

Note: Do not get the area known as Suchow Creek mixed up with the city named Suchow, aka Suzhou (p. 269), even though the creek once was a river that connected the two.

A fairly good market (lotsa fakes and junk) is in this area; it's called **QiPu Market** because, yup, it's on QiPu Road. Take Henan Road north from the Bund, cross the creek, and turn left on QiPu Road. *Shishi.*

Nanjing Road

Perhaps the most famous street in Shanghai after the Bund, Nanjing Road (p. 249) is also the city's main shopping drag, despite its enormous length (over 10km/6¼ miles). Much of the main shopping district is a pedestrian mall. Don't miss this at night—stores are open until 9 or 10pm. If you plan to have a stroll to see a good bit of this famous street, begin at the Bund and the Peace Hotel. After a few banks and hotels and after you cross Shanxi Road, you'll be in the heart of the pedestrian mall and shopping greats. This is the eastern part of Nanjing Road. It is not really within walking distance of the western portion of Nanjing Road.

In the eastern district, you'll find everything from silk shops to TTs (tourist traps), to pearl shops, to stores that specialize in gadgets and others for sports equipment to wannabe Jing Maos. There's Western style, Eastern style, and no style whatsoever. But plenty of McDonald's and lotsa bright lights. *Note:* In between the neon and the teenagers are some old-fashioned Chinese stores, just like the ones they don't have back home.

Huai Hai Road

If you care about your sanity, avoid Huai Hai Road (formerly Ave. Joffre to the French, and also written Weihai Rd.) on Saturday. This is the main drag of the fashionable French concession and the high street for local fashionistas ages 20 to 30. Most of the stores are either big-name global brands or Chinese inspirations—copies of European trends selling at low Chinese prices, with equally low quality. In no time at all, you can have a Huai Hai headache.

But wait—did I tell you that **H&M** has opened? Their first Chinese store opened last year at 645-659 Middle Huai Hai Rd. But the clothes are cut to what's called "Asian fit." That means small.

Note: Do a drive-by in a taxi first to find the areas you want to explore on foot. Not only is the street very long, but it also has east and west portions. The western portion has the shops

Jenny's Turn: Introducing Changle Road

While staying at the Okura Garden Hotel, I decided to take advantage of the fact that the famed **Huai Hai Road** was a block away. This bustling street of consumerism has the reputation of being the "it" road for shopping in Shanghai. What I found was the same old Western and global stores you find at home . . . and way too many people.

There were crowds, bad attitudes, and much shoving and pushing—and that was just in Starbucks. I was quickly losing my sanity. Luckily, on the way back to the hotel, I discovered **Changle Road,** a street that anyone could fall in love with. This smaller, less busy street not only runs east-west, but it sells East and West style-wise. It parallels Huai Hai Road on a map, but it is much more than a parallel universe.

The atmosphere and merchandise in half the shops was funky and trendy—think Greenwich Village in New York or Melrose Avenue in L.A. The rest of the stores have high-quality, traditional Chinese merchandise—both fashion and accessories. This street is perfect for both the young and the hip or the older and more sophisticated.

More important, Changle Road has it all, without lines, crowds, or pushy people. The street is as long as Huai Hai Road, and the best shopping parts are near the Okura Garden Hotel. There's no bargaining, but prices are more than fair.

you will be most interested in; the eastern portion is just now getting it together.

TAIKANG ROAD

Just when you thought you'd run out of shopping options, you discover the lanes. Sure, you know about the lanes in Hong Kong, that *soi* in Bangkok are lanes, and that Taipei is overrun with lane addresses—but several lanes are beginning to blossom off Taikang Road in the southern end of the French concession. A few stores are actually located on Taikang Road

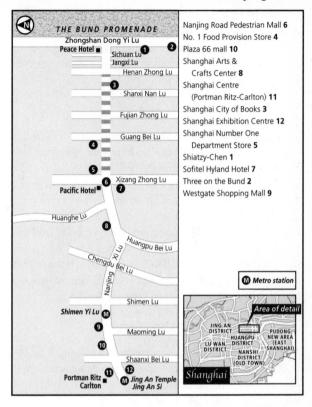

THE BUND PROMENADE

Zhongshan Dong Yi Lu

Peace Hotel ■

Sichuan Lu ❶ ❷
Jangxi Lu

Henan Zhong Lu

❸
Shanxi Nan Lu

Fujian Zhong Lu

Guang Bei Lu

❹

❺
Xizang Zhong Lu

❻
❼
Pacific Hotel ■

Huanghe Lu ❽

Huangpu Bei Lu

Chengdu Bei Lu

Nanjing Xi Lu

Shimen Lu

Shimen Yi Lu Ⓜ
❾

❿

Shaanxi Bei Lu
⓬
Portman Ritz ⓫ Ⓜ Jing An Temple
Carlton ■ Jing An Si

Nanjing Road Pedestrian Mall **6**
No. 1 Food Provision Store **4**
Plaza 66 mall **10**
Shanghai Arts &
Crafts Center **8**
Shanghai Centre
(Portman Ritz-Carlton) **11**
Shanghai City of Books **3**
Shanghai Exhibition Centre **12**
Shanghai Number One
Department Store **5**
Shiatzy-Chen **1**
Sofitel Hyland Hotel **7**
Three on the Bund **2**
Westgate Shopping Mall **9**

Ⓜ **Metro station**

Area of detail

JING AN
DISTRICT
HUANGPU
DISTRICT
PUDONG
NEW AREA
(EAST
SHANGHAI)
LU WAN
DISTRICT
NANSHI
DISTRICT
(OLD TOWN)
Shanghai

itself, but you will be sorely disappointed if you don't go into the little lanes: The shops, many of them in restored buildings, are chockablock cute.

The lanes, like all proper Asian lanes, have numbers, not names. You'll want to pay attention to several of them. Lane 248 is indeed an alley—mostly pedestrian traffic, although a car can catch you off guard. I like Lane 210 the best.

There are cafes as well as shops for novelties, art, and fashion. Ask the taxi driver to drop you at the main road where it intersects with this series of lanes; if you want an exact starting point, head to **Suzaar,** room 108, Building 5, Lane 210,

Taikang Road (© **8621/6473-4388**), or **ShirtFlag**, 7 Lane 210, room 8 (© **8621/6466-7009**).

Note: Stores typically open around 11am and stay open until 8 or 9pm. You can easily hail taxis on this main street when you are ready to depart.

JING AN

The Portman Ritz-Carlton, the Four Seasons, the JC Mandarin, and many, many other hotels—and a few shopping malls—are in this part of town. It includes West Nanjing Road and the Shanghai Exhibition Centre, which is across the street from the Portman Ritz-Carlton. This is not much of a funky shopping district, although it has a big mall, **Westgate;** several other malls are building up around here, such as **Plaza 66.**

This part of town is also called Nanjing Road West because the far-reaching Nanjing Road comes up here, but it is not the same animal as the Nanjing Road you will learn to love in the center of town near the Sofitel Hyland Hotel.

XINTIANDI

Xintiandi is in the French concession and resembles a film set or an American festival marketplace, although it was built with Hong Kong money. It is said to be a restoration of old houses, converted to stores and restaurants. The feel is nothing like Colonial Williamsburg or even Disney but is wall-to-wall charm with tons of hot design looks in the use of tiles, inventive seating, and unusual light fixtures. In short, this is a village of cutting-edge chic.

This complex—a true must-do—is at the eastern end of Huai Hai Road, a part of town where redevelopment began only recently. Office buildings have arrived; luxury housing is expected soon. The bars are downright inspirational, from a design point of view. In a not-so-obvious part of the complex, you'll find the design atelier of **Xavier** (p. 259), one of the leading style mavens of the city. Just taxi on over here at least once, and surely for a meal—it's especially nice at night, and the stores are open 'til about 10pm.

Also note that several new hotels are springing up here, such as Conrad and Landis.

OLD CITY

This is the name most often given to the oldest part of town, which is also known as **Nanshi.** This was the Chinese city in the days of the foreign concessions. It was walled many years ago. It is quickly being torn down and replaced with the New China, but some quaint winding roads, alleys, and tin shanties remain to fill you with glee.

Also here are the **Yuyuan Gardens,** a Disney-meets-Chinatown parcel of land with buildings and gardens, a teahouse, a temple, a market, and antiques stores. It's the city's number-one tourist attraction—and for good reason, although I am sick at just how touristy this area has become.

The Old City is home to the **Dong Tai Antiques Market,** which feels a lot more authentic than just about any other part of town. Nearby is the **soft fabrics market** (p. 243)—which may be my favorite shopping space in Shanghai.

HONG QIAO

This area includes the Hong Qiao International Airport, many furniture and antiques warehouses, a mall or two, and huge gated communities where wealthy expats live in either modern high-rises or town houses organized as village developments. Even though traffic can be fierce, if you have any interest in furniture, you won't want to miss this district. This is an area in transition, going from funky to fab on a daily basis. It requires a lot of coming-and-going shopping, which must be done with car and driver; you'll need a list written in Chinese and the ability to be organized, flexible, and a little bold.

Get a taxi to stay with you and wait as you shop.

Note to old China hands: If you lament the passing of the fakes market that used to be right in the heart of French concession shopping, it has moved out to this area. The word *xiangyang* seems to mean fake, so several markets have this word in the name. You want the one in Hong Qiao: **Xiangyan Hong Qiao.**

SHANGHAI RESOURCES A TO Z

Note: If you don't find listings here that are mentioned in other guidebooks, there could be a good reason. Maybe they are gone, or maybe I didn't think them worth your time, or maybe something else happened. . . .

Antique Furniture

See "Furniture" section, p. 261.

Antiques

MINGYUAN ANTIQUES STORE
Cui Xiu Hall at Big Rockery, Shanghai Yu, Yuyuan Gardens (no nearby Metro).

This store is expensive, but it has excellent stuff. Note that it is inside the garden part of Yuyuan Gardens, which you must pay to enter.

SHANGHAI MUSEUM ANTIQUES SHOP
Shanghai Museum, 16 Henan Lu (Metro: Renmin Guangchang).

Not to be confused with the downstairs gift shop, this is an upstairs shop, maybe 72 sq. m. (775 sq. ft.), of expensive but government-approved antiques. Everything is behind glass, and it looks much like an exhibition. Lots of little teapots, lots of high prices.

Antiques Markets

If you go to Shanghai for one shopping experience, it has to be for buying antiques, both small decorative pieces and furniture. The antiques markets are heaven, and the prices are so low you will want to weep. There are also good markets in Beijing, so don't blow your wad. Remember, most of this stuff is fake; trust no one. But if you see any more of those pewter and ceramic bowls, get me a few, please.

DONG TAI MARKET
Dong Tai Lu (no nearby Metro).

This is one of my favorite addresses in Shanghai, where I want to buy out all of the stalls. An outdoorsy type of thing, the market is not particularly large and takes place on just two perpendicular streets. The vendors sell from wagons or little trailers; there are a few shops. Not too many dealers speak English, but I didn't find that to be a problem.

Whatever you do, the first time you fall in love with an item, price it but don't buy. You tend to see a lot of similar things, and prices can vary dramatically—even without bargaining. I almost bought a set of three blue-and-white ceramic men for $100. I figured I could get them for $50 and liked the idea a whole lot. I didn't do it because they were hard to pack. Days later I found them, priced at $50 for the set of three, at a fancy hotel gift shop. The market price should have been $30!

FANG BANG MARKET/SHANGHAI OLD STREET
Henan Nan Lu and Fuxing Zhong Lu/Fang Bang Zhong Lu (no nearby Metro).

Shanghai Old Street is a very commercial section that looks almost like a festival marketplace from a bad American mall, with carts in the street and vendors selling baskets and kites. The closer you get to Henan Lu (and the farther from Yuyuan), the more it turns into something that feels like an authentic neighborhood. Finally you get to a dumpy little building that will surely be condemned soon. This is the home of the Fang

Bang Market. On weekends there are antiques in the street and more dealers sitting on the curbs bearing tote bags crammed with hot or fake (or both) Ming vases that they will try to entice you to buy.

The market takes place every day. *But* it's not very good on weekdays, when only about 30% of the vendors show up. On weekends, especially Sunday, it is crammed and quite the scene.

To get here, I'd suggest a taxi to the Henan Nan Lu side (after 11am on weekdays, 9am on weekends). Or walk from the Haobao Building (see below). Look for rather touristy torii gates and a pedestrian shopping street. Before your eye can figure out which part is real and which is stagecraft, you see the dealers and spy the heaps of delicious junk, on the curbs and falling out of stalls and tiny shops. They're to your left if your back is to the torii gate and Henan Road.

HAOBAO BUILDING
Yuyuan Gardens.

Many people don't even know that there is an antiques mart within the "village" of the gardens, or another one a few blocks away. This market has changed in recent years and now leans toward the Tibetan. The prices on antique silk garments and other items here are so low that I became giddy on my first trip; I touched and tried everything from padded silk jackets in dusty mauve to small embroidered pockets (popular because Chinese clothes do not come with pockets). Bargain like mad. Many dealers speak English.

Art (Contemporary)

Contemporary art is popping up all over Asia, especially in China. The area just north of the Bund on the far side of Suchow Creek (p. 246) has become the new art-and-gallery district. Find 50 **Monganshan Rd.**, and then browse the various buildings for galleries and ateliers. The most famous name—and probably the dealer to begin with—is **Shanghart,** Building 16 (© **8621/ 6359-3923**). You can get a bite inside the complex at the cafe, **Guolu Fang Kafee Guan.**

Arts & Crafts

LIFESTYLE FURNITURE
17 Fuzhou Rd. (Metro: Renmin Guangchang).

This furniture store has mostly ceramics, including many pieces created with photos of Old Shanghai. Most stunning: the coffee mugs with silk tassels. Suzhou Cobblers (see below) is at the same address but up a different stoop.

SHANGHAI ARTS & CRAFTS CENTER
190-208 Nanjing Rd. E. (Metro: He Nan Rd.).

Four floors of fun—every type of crafts product you can imagine is sold here, including silk by the bolt and all sorts of silk products. I bought printed silk scarves and cut-velvet silk scarves. The pajamas were rather expensive; no one at home would ever believe you paid that much ($85–$100) for them.

SUZHOU COBBLERS
17 Fuzhou Rd. (Metro: Renmin Guangchang).

Right off the Bund near Jardin de le Sens, this is the cutest little store in Shanghai. It sells amazing embroidered shoes of a quality far above souvenir slippers, and the designs employ modern motifs. My favorites were green satin with bok choy dancing across the toes. Prices are about $50 per pair. Horribly chic; an undeniable must-have.

Books

If you stroll the midsection of Fuzhou Lu, on what was once called Culture Street, you will find an entire street of Chinese booksellers. I also like a small chain called **Shanghai City of Books;** there's one on Nanjing Road near the entrance to the Hyland Sofitel and another on the above-mentioned Fuzhou

Lu (no. 465). You can find legal CDs and DVDs here at low prices.

Booze

Look in the "Foodstuffs" listings later in this chapter for large food emporiums; the ones that have liquor departments usually sell specialty wines that incorporate dead mice, snakes, and so on, or are made with parts of animal bodies. I bought superchef Alain Ducasse seal-penis wine for his birthday.

You will pay top yuan for international brands of booze, but local brands are inexpensive.

Ceramics

HAICHEN CERAMICS
No 17 Fuzhou Rd. (Metro: East Nanjing Rd.).

This tiny store is next-door to Suzhou Cobblers, a few meters off the Bund, so you have no excuse to miss it. I realize that packing and schlepping breakables is annoying, but several items here are not only stunning but well worth the trouble. Check out the mugs with Chinese tassels attached. © **8621/6323-0856.** haichenceramics@hotmail.com.

SPIN
758 Julu Lu, Building 3 (Metro: Changshu Lu).

Japanese restaurateurs began to have their simple and classic styles made locally, and *voilà,* now a shop. If you don't feel comfortable sending home a set of dishes, look at the platters or the teapots. For about $100, you can get an eat-your-heartout Martha Stewart teapot with teacups. © **8621/6279-2545.**

Chinese Style

SHANGHAI TANG
Jin Jang Hotel, 59 Mao Ming Rd. (Metro: Shi Men Rd.);
Xintiandi, 15 North Block, 181 Tai Cang Rd. (no nearby
Metro).

The selection here is not as good as in Hong Kong. The style
is fabulous, but the prices are high. Check out the cashmere
Mao sweaters.

SHIATZY CHEN
9 the Bund, 9 Zhongshan Dong Yi Road (Metro: Henan).

The first time I visited this store I was so profoundly moved
that I booked air tickets to Taiwan to see the mother store
(p. 244). As it turns out, the flagship is nowhere near as glam
as this temple to men's, women's, home, and accessory styles.
No stroll on the Bund is complete without a stop here. Classic Chinese styles are whipped together with couture and high
fashion to create timeless beauty. Figure on prices in the
$1,000-and-up range (although I did buy a blazer for $450 on
sale in Taipei). There is also a small branch on Mao Ming Nan
Lu near Changle. Open 10am to 10pm. © 8621/6321-9155.
www.shiatzychen.com.

ZHANG'S TEXTILES
Shanghai Centre, Nanjing Xi Lu (Metro: Jiang An Temple).

Antique textiles for collectors. The most famous dealer in
China, Zhang's also does business in Beijing.

Department Stores

ISETAN
1038 Nanjing Xi Lu W. (Metro: Jing An Temple).

This branch of Isetan is about 1 block from the Portman Ritz-
Carlton in a modern, Western-style mall that was recently
remodeled and filled with big-name stores. Isetan is a Japanese

department store known for younger brands, kickier fashions, and lower prices than some of the other Japanese department stores. Not only does it carry an international lineup of brands, but many names (such as Michel Klein) do specialty lines, and there are many super brands you just haven't ever seen before. Large sizes need not apply.

SAKS FIFTH AVENUE
Coming soon to a Bund near you.

This news is too big to ignore. Saks says they will have a store *in situ* by 2009. I have to assume this is for local money and will feature clothes in Asian fit. Still, this is such remarkable news that I had to report it. www.saks.com.

SHANGHAI NUMBER ONE DEPARTMENT STORE
830 Nanjing Rd. (Metro: Renmin Guangchang).

Number One is one of the most famous, old-timey communist-era Chinese department stores. It's at the beginning (or end) of the commercial part of Nanjing Road, right near Renmin Park where Nanjing Road changes from eastern direction to western. Now it sells Chanel makeup; how the world changes.

YUYUAN DEPARTMENT STORE
Yuyuan Gardens (no nearby Metro).

I discovered this department store by accident while shopping at the downstairs flea market. This is sort of a smaller and classier version of Number One (see above). It not only has a good fabric department, but the staff actually bargained with me while the salesgirls fought each other for my business. I paid $12 per meter for silk *dévoré* (cut velvet).

Designers

European and international designer stores are popping up everywhere, especially in hotel lobbies and big, fat malls. Prices are at least 20% more than in Hong Kong and may be even higher compared to your local mall in Hometown, USA. And did you really come to China to see Louis Vuitton?

But wait! There are a few hidden resources. You might not know about **Xavier.** As an important design fixture in Shanghai for 20 years, Xavier's British designer Anthony was well positioned to become one of the best-known and most influential designers in town. Then all the new money showed up, hungry for feathers, Art Deco, and high style, and . . . *vavavavroom*! Anthony designs ready-to-wear, accessories, bridal, some furs, and, of course, bespoke. Boutique: Unit 2, Number 15, 181 Taicang Rd. © **8621/6328-7111.** Studio: Unit 603, 119 Madang Rd. © **8621/6385-1155.** www.xavier.cn.

I also like **Annabel Lee,** who does a very different kind of look—less edgy, more soft, and very chic—in both home style and accessories. Put this address on the top of your must-do list. She's right on the Bund, slightly after no. 3 on the Bund, but before the Peace Hotel. No. 1, Lane 8, Zhongshun Dong Yi Lu. © **8621/6445-8218.**

Drugstores

WATSON'S, THE CHEMIST
Huai Hai Rd. W. (no nearby Metro).

One of my favorite stores in Hong Kong, it's no surprise that I love Watson's in Shanghai. I spend a few minutes each day loading up on candy bars and soft drinks, health and beauty products, medicines, and gadgets. Avoid U.S.- and European-brand makeup and fragrances, which are stunningly expensive. I've bought many marvelous gifts here for my $3 friends; the gifts look like they're worth at least $5, maybe more.

DVDs

Most locals buy pirated DVDs from favorite sources that come and go like the wind—for good reason. The action is mostly at night. You will be approached if you promenade on Nanjing Road after dark. I like legal DVDs from **Shanghai City of Books,** 345 Nanjing Rd. There is usually someone on staff who speaks enough English to tell you if the disc you favor is in English.

Fabrics

SILK KING
819 Nanjing Xi Lu (Metro: He Nan Rd.), and other locations.

The stores in this chain vary with the location. They are easy to shop; usually at least one salesperson speaks English. Prices are higher than in the fabric market, but the store is almost Western in style.

SHANGHAI SOUTH BUND SOFT SPINNING MATERIAL MARKET
399 Lujiabang Lu (no nearby Metro).

I've rarely had so much fun in my life. It's not very funky, but there are floors and floors of vendors, and you can bargain a little bit. My favorites are the totes, handbags, and gift items.

ZHANG YAN JUAN
*Wife Ding Cloth Store, 438 Fang Bang Zhong Lu
(no nearby Metro).*

This store is part of a development called Old Shanghai Street, which I adore. The store features only fabric and items made of the fabric in the homespun blue cloth of the Henan region of China. For blue-and-white freaks, this is really a find.

Fakes

The fakes market in Shanghai isn't nearly as good—or as much fun—as Beijing's. Both are drying up quickly due to Olympic, WTO, and governmental concerns. If you insist, this is the kind of merchandise that is now under the table. The best-known market was just torn down; ask your hotel concierge about new ones.

Foodstuffs

LOTUS CENTRE
Super Brand Mall, Pudong (Metro: Lu Jia Zui).

This is my hypermarché and grocery of choice; it was created in partnership with the U.K.'s TESCO and that's exactly what it shops like. It has one floor of groceries and one floor of dry goods. I won't get into the story of the day I went to buy a bra and the saleswoman decided to help fit me—over my clothes.

NO. 1 FOOD PROVISION STORE
720 Nanjing Rd. E. (Metro: Renmin Guangchang).

This just might be my favorite store in Shanghai. It is on the pedestrian mall part of Nanjing Road and is open in the evening, so you can go here on a nighttime stroll. The store is large, in the colonial European architectural style, but only two stories high. The ground floor sells fresh produce, dried fruit, liquor, and gift baskets. It's Harrods Food Hall come to Shanghai. All signs are in Chinese (no Pinyin, even). Upstairs there's a supermarket.

NO. 2 FOOD PROVISION STORE
887 Huai Hai Rd. W. (Metro: Shan Xi Nan Rd.).

This store is smaller than No. 1, not nearly as much fun, and somewhat ruined by the enormous KFC sign out front. It's worth a visit if you are strolling this part of Huai Hai Road and haven't been spoiled by No. 1.

Furniture

There are so many furniture warehouses in Shanghai that you will go nuts with greed and desire (at least, I did). In terms of bargaining on final price and making shipping arrangements, it's easiest to give all your business to one dealer.

You'll pass many furniture warehouses as you drive into town from the Hong Qiao Airport—Hong Qiao is the main district for antique furniture warehouses, but not the only one.

Note that many an expat has taken the furniture back to a different climate in the United States, only to have it crack during the first winter. Consider buying a humidifier once in the U.S.

Also, a true story: I bought a piece of rustic-style chinoiserie at Galeries Lafayette in Paris (for my Paris apartment) for $600, delivery and taxes included. It turned out to be a better deal than shipping from Shanghai, although the piece bought in China would have cost only $200 to $250.

If you plan to ship your purchases, consider several factors: Prices on shipping are not that high, and you will be impressed. However, prices on clearing goods through a Customs broker and trucking from the port of entry may be obscene. I paid $125 to ship a piece and an additional $425 to have it delivered, a mere 161km (100 miles) from the port.

And speaking of money: While I found prices in Shanghai laughably inexpensive, dealers say that outside of town there are warehouses that are even cheaper, such as **Nineteen Town,** 19 Jin Xin Lu, Jiu Ting. Needless to say, the farther off the beaten path you wander, the more you need a translator.

G-E TANG ANTIQUES
7 Hu Qing Ping Hwy. (no nearby Metro).

This establishment is extremely tourist-oriented; it has a website (www.getang.com), advertises in the city's freebie tourist map, and has a reputation among visitors and expats. There's even a most impressive English-language brochure.

The shop is very chic and sleek; the young men who work here could have stepped out of an Armani showroom. Many speak English. The goods are gorgeous. Too gorgeous (and too expensive) for my taste.

I asked the staff to show me the junk and was led to a warehouse of unrestored furniture in the rear. This was much more fun. I was quoted various prices for the same piece—as is, cleaned up, or restored. Shipping usually doubles the cost, and—having seen the quality of the pieces before they were restored—I simply didn't think they were worth it.

The place is very seductive—and a good starting point as you learn what you want and what you want to spend.

HENRY ANTIQUE WAREHOUSE
359 Hongzhong Lu (Metro: Xujiahui).

This is an enormous warehouse with excellent salespeople. There are more than 2,000 pieces of furniture on hand. They have been restored and, yes, you will want them all. Due to the incoming, ongoing Metro construction, the warehouse moved since we were here last. Open 9am to 6pm 7/7. All major credit cards. ℂ 8621/6401-0831. henryantique@eastday.com.

HU & HU ANTIQUES
8, Lane 1886, Caobao Lu (no nearby Metro).

First off, one of the Hus is a young woman named Marybelle Hu, who is an American-educated Chinese who attended Smith College and has since come back to China. I hope she gets into politics and becomes president, or whatever they have— empress? Needless to say, her English is flawless, her organizational skills are amazing, and the store functions like a professional New York showroom. I haven't ever seen anything like this in China. She's warm, she's wonderful, she makes you feel at home, and—most importantly—she's honest.

The warehouse is modern, not crammed or dirty and dusty. There's an open-air shed with not-yet-restored furniture; you can negotiate a price. ℂ 8621/3431-1212.

Malls

BUND 18
18 the Bund (Metro: Renmin Guangchang).

This isn't really a mall any more than Three on the Bund is a mall—it's a similar restaurant-and-retail complex that houses the restaurant created by the Pourcel twins (three-star French chefs) and the snazzy new **Cartier** shop, as well as other designer shops.

JING JANG DICKSON CENTRE
400 Changle Rd. (Metro: Shi Men Rd.).

The fanciest and most upscale Western mall in Shanghai is owned by the same businessman who owns Harvey Nichols in London. The mall is so chic it doesn't open until 11am (but it stays open until 9pm). Most of the really big-name shops, including Ralph Lauren, Lalique, and so on, are in this mall, which is the kingpin of the Huai Hai Road shopping district. The building is new but done up like redbrick-goes–Art Deco. Remember, there are no bargains on designer goods in China because the import taxes are outrageously high. The stores are mostly empty and the help is very cool, probably terrified you will require them to speak English.

MAO MING CENTRE
Mao Ming Rd. at Changle Rd. (Metro: Shi Men Rd.).

This luxury mall is right near the Dickson Centre and across the street from the Okura Garden Hotel. It boasts the usual Western suspects.

PLAZA 66
1266 Nanjing Xi Lu (Metro: Jing An Temple).

Yawn, another fancy mall with big, big, big Euro names. Here's the largest Louis Vuitton store in the world, along with brands like Chanel, Dior, and Escada. You get the picture.

SHANGHAI CENTRE
Nanjing Xi Lu (Metro: Jing An Temple).

This is not a traditional mall but a multiuse center with a hotel, an apartment block, and various stores. It has a brand-new Gucci, a Ferragamo, a Starbucks, and so on.

SUPER BRAND MALL
Pudong (Metro: Lu Jia Zui).

The mall was not quite ready for prime time on my recent visits, but the **Lotus Centre** was bustling, and I had a ball. We also had good fun in the food court on the seventh floor; try the Thai fast-food place. The best way to get here is to walk from the Shangri-La Hotel next door, or take the Metro or a ferry to Pudong.

Lotus is part-owned by TESCO, the British hypermarché—a two-level store that is supermarket on one level and sells dry goods on the other. Can you believe I didn't buy a down coat for $10? This is a great place to buy telephones and small electronics. You may also have fun with foodstuffs—aside from the inscrutable, you will find brands you know in flavors created for the local market, like Lays Beijing duck–flavor potato chips—one of my faves.

TIMES SQUARE
93-99 Huai Hai Rd. E. (Metro: Renmin Guangchang).

The first mainland China branch of the mall that changed a portion of Hong Kong's shopping style. It's a youth-oriented mall with name brands and attitude—but wait, it has a branch of my favorite supermarket, City Super.

WESTGATE SHOPPING MALL
1038 Nanjing Xi Lu (Metro: Jing An Temple).

I like this mall because it's 1 block from the Portman Ritz-Carlton, across the street from the JC Mandarin, and near the Four Seasons hotel. It's very Western, and it has a branch of Isetan, the Japanese department store—and a branch of everything else, too.

Pearls

If you are going on to Beijing, I suggest you wait for the Pearl Market there. Otherwise, have a look at **Pearl City**, 558 Nanjing Rd. E., a minimall of dealers.

Aaron's Turn: Sneak Me Some Feet

I saw some amazing shoes in China. I'm big on Puma and the Adidas-Kick brand. In China I saw lots of cool designs that aren't available in the States. One pair of blue Adidas will forever be the pair that got away; it was pure love. Alas, I have size 13 (American) feet, and the largest pair of shoes I saw in China was size 10. And these were considered something of a novelty.

I was so depressed about having to leave stores without shoes that I actually started taking pictures of the shoes I couldn't have. Talk about desperation. I would have been totally depressed except I kept thinking about Houston Rockets center Yao Ming. If I couldn't find a fit, where does he get his shoes?

Spas

BANYAN TREE SPA
Westin Hotel, 88 Henan Central Rd., Level 3. (Metro: Henan Zhong Lu).

Billed as a sanctuary for the senses, this is the only feng shui spa in town, offering very unique treatments to create balance in your life. © 8621/6335-1888, ext. 7271. www.banyantree spa.com.

EVIAN SPA
Three on the Bund, 3 Zhongshan Dong Yi Lu (Metro: Remin Square).

This is perhaps the most glorious spa you have ever seen in your life, or in Shanghai. The multilevel spa is almost like a grotto: You step over stones and running water, go up and down stairs, and nestle into heated beds for heavenly treatments. Since this is not part of a hotel, anyone can book. The spa is for women guests, but Barbers Three does designer shaves and treatments for men. Hours: daily 10:30am to 10:30pm. © 8621/6321-6622.

TANG DYNASTY HEALTH CARE CENTRE
339 Shang Cheng Rd., upstairs (Metro: Pudong).

This is around the corner from the InterConti Shanghai, which is how I found it. It's a clinical kind of place where you go for reflexology. I've been here several times and referred many people. I wouldn't taxi all the way over here, but if you're in the hood, don't miss it. Treatments are $10 to $25. © 8621/5882-0653.

Supermarkets

NO. 1 FOOD PROVISION STORE
720 Nanjing Rd. E. (Metro: Renmin Guangchang).

There's a supermarket upstairs. See p. 265.

PARK 'N SHOP
Westgate Mall (Metro: Jing An Temple), and other locations.

Another Hong Kong supermarket chain; this branch is near the Portman Ritz-Carlton.

WELLCOME
Shanghai Centre, Portman Ritz-Carlton hotel, Nanjing Rd. (Metro: Jing An Temple).

I'm not certain if you would make a special trip here just for the Wellcome, but boy, was I excited to find it. Its Hong Kong–style supermarket luxury was a welcome comfort after too many dog days on the streets, and I was happy to load up on snacks and my favorite fiber cereal.

Tailors

Before the communist takeover, Shanghai was famous for its community of tailors. Most of them left in the late 1940s and reestablished themselves in Hong Kong. Now the trend is reversing.

W. W. CHAN & SONS TAILOR LTD.
129A-2 Mao Ming Rd. (Metro: Shi Men Rd.).

Peter Chan's family is from Shanghai; he was born in Hong Kong and was the first Hong Kong tailor to return to Shanghai. His Shanghai shop is directly across from the Okura Garden Hotel right off Huai Hai Road. He specializes in men's clothing. Prices are approximately 20% less than in Hong Kong. To make an appointment prior to arrival, e-mail sales@wwchan.com or call © **8621/6248-2768.**

Tea

There are a few tea markets for locals, but they are far out and you will need a local guide or interpreter. The best-known market, **Tian San ChaCha,** is in Hongqiao. (*Cha* is "tea" in Chinese.) All grocery stores and Chinese herbal shops sell tea.

For a more upmarket experience, begin your quest at Three on the Bund, which has a tea sommelier and 80 different kinds of tea.

Not to be outdone, try your hand at the teeny-weeny stall of **Yun Tian Tea Shop,** 347 Fang Bang Zhong Rd., located between the flea market and Yuyuan Gardens. The teas here are in flower-bud format, and they will be happy to demonstrate for you or do a tasting. The buds open in hot water, providing a performance that is great at dinner parties. You'll pay $8 to $10 per box of tea; jasmine is always a popular one. © **8621/6330-2906.**

Teens

A walk along Huai Hai Road is all you need to see more shops of young fashions than your brain can compute. Also see Jenny's report on p. 248. Remember that western brands such as H&M have arrived, too.

UNIQLO
333 Nanjing Rd. E. (Metro: Han Zhong Rd.).

This is a Japanese fashion supermarket, something like Gap with simple and classic must-haves, such as T-shirts in good colors and other basics. To get here, you go up a tube-enclosed escalator. This store is near the Sofitel Hyland Hotel.

Wedding Photos

Although there are wedding-photo salons in Beijing, the ones in Shanghai are better and much more fun. I will not name specific addresses, but I'll point you in the right direction so you can stare, or dare. Head to Huai Hai Road, in the thick of the French concession.

With China evolving into a Western consumer market, nothing is more valuable than a Western-style wedding or wedding photo. Because few can afford the real thing, there are zillions of salons where the bride and groom go for the day to be made over and photographed. Hair, makeup, and clothes are provided; you just say "cheese."

I was tempted to do this many times but figured that no wedding dress would ever fit me . . . and I didn't want to have to be the groom. Aaron and Jenny were going to do it, but the least expensive package was still several hundred dollars.

DAY TRIPS & OVERNIGHT EXCURSIONS

Suzhou

I am thinking of changing my name to Suzhou Gershman; I mean, I'd still be Suzy, right? And then I could share the glory of the new Suzhou, because, baby, has this place perked up.

I once dreamed of Suzhou as one of those destinations on my list of places I had to see before I died; it was part of my Shanghai fantasies. The Venice of China, a city of canals, home of the old silk factories, pearl-bargain heaven. What's not to like?

Well, then I got there. Oy vay, as my Grandma Jessie used to say. What a bore. I was crushed. For years I have used these pages to advise people to skip Suzhou and to try something more rewarding, like Zhouzhang (p. 271).

Now, everything's up-to-date in Suzhou. Business is booming because real estate in Shanghai is so dear that many companies are relocating here. Meet the new Silicon Valley. So what if it's not the Venice of China; you come here for the I. M. Pei–designed Suzhou Museum, not for the shopping. (Local boy makes good.) The gardens are excellent; there are things to see . . . and, of course, things to buy.

The silk factories are a joke. The unattractive main shopping street is amusing only in that a) you're a long way from Shanghai architecturally, and b) it looks like news footage of Hanoi in 1969. Sure, the pearls are cheap; they're cheap everywhere. You'll have more fun buying pearls in Beijing—I promise.

GETTING THERE

Most people take tours to Suzhou, enjoy its delights as part of their China package, or take a hotel car and driver. You can get there and back by train—it's about an hour-long ride. My hotel concierge quoted a flat fee of $300 for a Mercedes with driver for the day trip. Express buses from the Hong Qiao Airport operate between 10am and 4pm. The bus ride is about an hour and a half.

SHOPPING SUZHOU

Not the main thrill. I hate the so-called silk factories because they are TTs to me. But wait, you may find a selection of silk duvets here—a far better selection than in Shanghai or other big cities—and this could be reason enough to shop. The duvets are not inexpensive ($200 and up), the sizes are by Chinese standards (figure a Chinese king is a U.S. queen), and they are bulky to carry home. Though the factory will air-pack the quilt so it's smaller and easier to pack. Silk-factories also sell the usual suspects in clothes, robes, scarves, and the like.

STAYING IN SUZHOU

Many international hotels have branches in Suzhou, most of them being modern, business-oriented hotels. The priciest and fanciest is **Shangri-La,** but the **Holiday Inn** (the Holiday Inn Jasmine) is very, very nice. The number of brand-new hotels increases steadily.

If you spend a night, you can explore the area and get a much better feel for the real China than just big-city Shanghai. You can also take an overnight boat trip to Hangzhou from Suzhou.

HOTEL ONE
379 Chang Jiang Rd., New District, Suzhou.

Hotel One is a division of the Landis Hotel Group, a group I have only recently met, but have already come to trust. This is a contemporary hotel with minimal design and maximum amenities, including Wi-Fi, a variety of dining choices, and any other features the business traveler could want. Rooms cost about $100. ✆ 86-512/6878-1111. www.hotelone.com.cn.

The Magic City of Zhouzhang

I am reluctant to tell you about this because it is so fabulous that you will rush there immediately and then it will be overrun with tourists and ruined. But because you've just read my rip on Suzhou, and you're thinking I'm as bad as any theater or restaurant critic, and you're mumbling that it's easy to find what's wrong without finding what's right—well, I have found the real Shangri-La. Zhouzhang is everything that I wanted Suzhou to be.

Zhouzhang is an ancient city, southeast of Suzhou and about 2 hours from Shanghai, in the "Water Country." The city consists of two parts, modern town and old city, which is across a series of bridges from modern town and is closed to vehicular traffic. You can walk or take a pedicab to the old city and then stroll the landmarks at your leisure. Because it's so scenic, it might be the most romantic place on earth at night, but taking advantage of it would entail an overnight in a hotel that does not compete with Four Seasons or Shangri-La.

You can get here by private car, by taxi, or by express bus from Shanghai Stadium. The bus fare includes the ride and the entrance fee to the village. About four buses make the run per day (the last bus departs Shanghai at 2pm); check with your concierge.

Hangzhou

Hangzhou is a Chinese resort city and has been for eons, but it is also known for tea and silk. The best hotel in town is Shangri-La, which was just totally renovated. The hotel is close to West Lake, which is what tourists have been coming to see for centuries: The scenery really does look like virtual calligraphy. You should have been able to get here by the new fast train; but, alas, all resources are dedicated in Beijing, and this route is not yet finished. With a current travel time of 3 hours each way, this is not a great day trip. Wait for the fast train or plan to spend at least 1 night. A rep from your hotel will meet you at the train station.

Chapter Nine

·····················

BEIJING

WELCOME TO BEIJING

··

I don't care if you are reading this book before 08-08-08 or after: Put it down and write a letter to the Olympics people to request that shopping become an official event.

As you probably know, 888 is a very highly regarded and lucky number to the Chinese. You are in luck if you get to visit the new Beijing, cleaned up and reinvented. The push is on to make a spectacular Olympics venue, clean the air and streets, and get the sewers working better. Be sure to see some of the new architecture and take advantage of the changes in the air. Just don't breathe *too* deeply.

Because so much is changing so quickly, I can only do the best I can do in these pages. All listings have been verified as we go to press but new stores and opportunities are springing up like wildflowers.

GETTING THERE

··

Note: See chapter 2 for information on air carriers that serve all parts of China, including Beijing.

There are often airfare promotions to Beijing—**Air France** recently offered two attractive possibilities: 1) buy one

Electronically Yours: Beijing

Please note that these sites are specific to Beijing; see chapter 2 for more resources.

- **www.beijing-2008.org** is the official website for the 2008 Beijing Olympics. There's also information about Beijing in English, along with a vocabulary lesson.
- **www.thebeijingguide.com** is an English-language resource that covers everything from the Olympics and culture to dining and, yes, shopping.
- **www.beijingpage.com** features similar information but also has links to additional resources, such as Beijing photos and traveler blogs and advice on touring the city.

business-class ticket and get a second free, and 2) buy one business-class ticket and get an automatic round-trip upgrade to first class. This offer was good between Paris and Beijing or Paris and Shanghai.

More and more U.S. flag carriers are serving Beijing with direct and even nonstop flights. **Northwest** was a leader in this, and **American Airlines** is trying to gain a Chicago–Beijing flight. If you want to hub in Asia, take a good look at a map before you choose the carrier, as Beijing may be farther north than you imagine—easier to get to from Seoul or Narita than Taipei or Hong Kong. If you are looking to do something interesting, consider the American Airlines flight from Dallas–Forth Worth to Osaka and then take a local flight the extra hop.

Arrival by Air

The new Terminal Three at Beijing Capital Airport has been created to impress. Taxi service from Capital Airport to central Beijing runs about $15. All major hotels have transfer packages that cost about $40 to $50. There is a long line for taxis, but it is orderly.

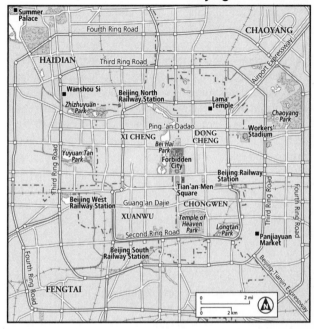

About Departures

As the main airport for China, Beijing is busy. Flights book up quickly, and it may be hard to change tickets.

On departure from Beijing's Capital Airport, your driver will drop you off at the curb and possibly even load your luggage onto a cart. For security purposes, you aren't allowed to take the cart into the airport terminal. You must transfer to another cart, piloted by a bellboy (flat fee), who will take you to the airline check-in desk. For a little extra, he may even take you right through immigration and get you to the lounge.

Other Arrival Possibilities

TRAIN

Beijing has five train stations, so if you arrive or depart by train, know which is where.

Travelers from Shanghai arrive at the new South Station. The train station is blocked off to taxis and hotel cars, so you have to walk quite a distance. If you have a lot of luggage, it pays to arrange a hotel transfer (ask to be met at the tracks).

If you want train tickets departing from Beijing, call and fax your hotel concierge as soon as you choose your dates. Tickets are sold only a certain number of days before travel and go quickly. The overnight train is very Western; ask for a "soft seat." We usually book all four bunks in a sleeping cabin for privacy and space for the luggage.

You can now travel to Beijing or Shanghai by train from Hong Kong (actually Kowloon). Travel time is 27 hours. Book through the KCR (p. 58) or your hotel concierge. FYI, I have friends who just did it and they said it was fun.

CRUISE SHIP

Beijing is landlocked; however, it is not terribly far from the sea, and many cruise ships use Beijing as a "turnaround city" and transfer passengers by bus to Tianjin. Tianjin has rebuilt its consumer portion of the port and has a new cruise terminal. See p. 308 for what to buy in Tianjin.

THE LAY OF THE LAND
....

Beijing has purposefully been built in a series of circles, starting with the Forbidden City as the core, and has added ring roads: "First Ring Road," and so on. There is a clear north-south axis as well as a modern east-west main drag, making it easy to divide central Beijing into four quadrants for directional purposes. Even if your hotel is located on an outer ring road, you will be able to get around relatively easily.

GETTING AROUND

Taxis

Taxis are plentiful and cheap, with three different fares posted in the window: 1.20 yuan (15¢), 1.60 yuan (20¢), or 2 yuan (25¢) per kilometer. Few 1.20-yuan taxis have air-conditioning, which you will care about in spring and summer.

Before you leave your hotel, ask for its standard preprinted taxi checklist of popular destinations, already written out for you in English and Chinese. Taxis are fairly easy to hail in busy shopping districts, but not in out-of-the-way districts or at some tourist sights. If you take a taxi to the Summer Palace, have your driver wait for you.

Taxi cheats are rampant. I have noticed an unrelenting talent for taking the long way or for choosing the most trafficked route in order to run up the meter. Make sure the meter is turned on; if there is no meter, get out.

Pedicabs

I am a little embarrassed to say this—it must be quite socially incorrect—but I love the pedicabs in Beijing and I will be sorry when they disappear, as invariably they must.

The drivers range in age, which I always take into account, depending on the difficulty of the journey. A few speak some words of English, but don't count on it. Always determine price before you get in. A tip is not expected, but I tip if extra effort has been made. I love capitalism.

The Metro

The Metro (also called "the subway") is marked in Pinyin. You can easily connect to "downtown" (Tiananmen) on your own. This subway is far nicer than the one in Shanghai. With traffic as bad as it is, consider using the Metro.

The subway opens around 5:30am and runs until 10:30 or 11:30pm, depending on the line. The fare is about 25¢. The

Beijing

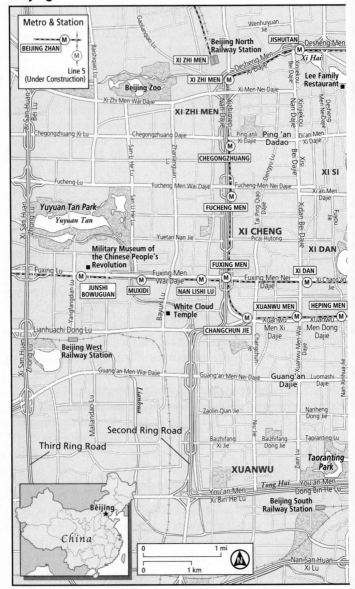

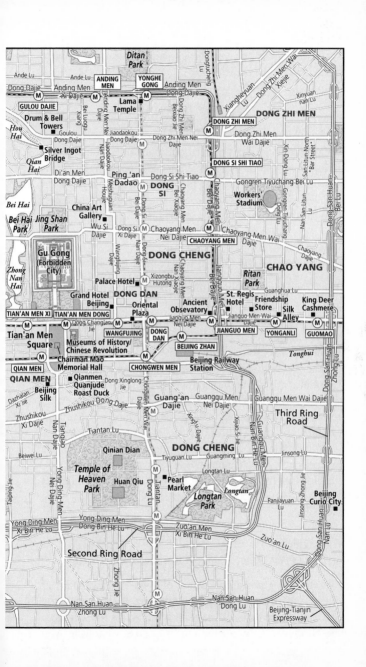

Ditan Park

Ande Lu · Ande Lu · **ANDING MEN** · **YONGHE GONG**

Dong Dajie · Anding Men · Xi Dajie · Anding Men · Dong-Dajie

GULOU DAJIE

Drum & Bell Towers

Hou Hai · Goulou · Dong Dajie

Silver Ingot Bridge

Qian Hai · Di'an Men · Dong Dajie

Bei Hai

China Art Gallery

Wu Si Dajie

Bei Hai Park · *Jing Shan Park*

Gu Gong (Forbidden City)

Zhong Nan Hai

Palace Hotel

Grand Hotel Beijing · **DONG DAN**

TIAN'AN MEN XI · **TIAN'AN MEN DONG** · Dong Changan Jie

Tian'an Men Square

QIAN MEN

Museums of History / Chinese Revolution

Chairman Mao Memorial Hall · **CHONGWEN MEN**

QIAN MEN

Qianmen Quanjude Roast Duck · Dong Xinglong Jie

Dazhalan Xi Jie · Beijing Silk

Zhushikou Dong-Dajie

Zhushikou Xi Dajie

Tiantan Lu

Qinian Dian

Temple of Heaven Park

Huan Qiu

Longtan

Pearl Market

Longtan Park

Yong-Ding-Men Dong-Bin He Lu

Yong-Ding-Men Xi-Bin He Lu

Second Ring Road

Nan-San-Huan Zhong Lu

Dongzucheng Lu

DONG ZHI MEN

Lama Temple · Beixiao jie

Jiaodaokou · Dong-Dajie

Dong Zhi Men Nei Dajie

DONG ZHI MEN

Dong Zhi Men Wai Dajie

Xinyuan nan Lu

Ping'an Dadao · Dong Si Shi Tiao

DONG SI SHI TIAO

DONG SI

Chaoyang Men Bei Xiaojie

Gongren Tiyuchang Bei Lu

Workers' Stadium

Chaoyang Men Nei Dajie · **CHAOYANG MEN**

Chaoyang Men Wai Dajie

DONG CHENG · **CHAO YANG**

Ritan Park

Xizongbu Hutong · Nan Xiaojie

Ancient Observatory

St. Regis Hotel · Friendship Store

Guanghua Lu

King Deer Cashmere

Jianguo Men Nei Dajie · **JIANGUO MEN** · Jianguo Men Wai Dajie

DONG DAN · **WANGFUJING** · **YONGANLI** · **GUOMAO**

Silk Alley

Oriental Plaza

BEIJING ZHAN

Beijing Railway Station

Beijing Zhan

Guang'an Dajie · Guangqu Men Nei Dajie · Guangqu Men Wai Dajie

Third Ring Road

DONG CHENG

Tiyuguan Lu · Guangming Lu

Jinsong Lu

Longtan Lu

Beijing Curio City

Panjiayuan Lu · Jinsong Zhong Jie

Zuo'an Men Xi Bin He Lu · Zuo'an Lu

Nan-San-Huan Dong Lu

Beijing-Tianjin Expressway

symbol for the subway is a little square inside an incomplete circle, sort of like the letter G.

SLEEPING IN BEIJING

Because Beijing is a city of neighborhoods and traffic is so terrible, where you stay very much defines your trip. Luxury is also important if you are used to Western-style hotels and want the electronics to function. Several hotels have two (or more) branches, so be careful when you choose.

GRAND HOTEL BEIJING
33 Dongchangan Jie (Metro: Wangfujing).

The Grand Hotel Beijing is one of the city's top luxury hotels and the who's-who list of celebs who have stayed here is staggering. My Chinese wedding bed alone was reason enough to book here, but the hotel is also the only one decorated in truly Chinese historical style with antiques and flourishes.

The location is also heaven, overlooking the Forbidden City and at the base of the main shopping street, virtually across the street from the Oriental Plaza mall. The hotel has several restaurants, a shopping mall, a spa and medical treatment (p. 308), and the best breakfast buffet in town.

You can do well with a promotional deal. Otherwise, the average rate is $300 per night. U.S. reservations through Leading Hotels of the World © 800/223-6800. Local: Grand Hotel Beijing © 8610/6513-7788; Beijing Hotel © 8610/6513-7766. www.lhw.com.

GRAND HYATT
Oriental Plaza, Dong Changan Jie (Metro: Wangfujing).

Everything is grand at this corner of town—the Grand Hyatt is across the street from the Grand Beijing. It's located on top of a mall at the base of Wangfujing and across the way from the Forbidden City. All the modern and sleek touches you

Beijing Metro

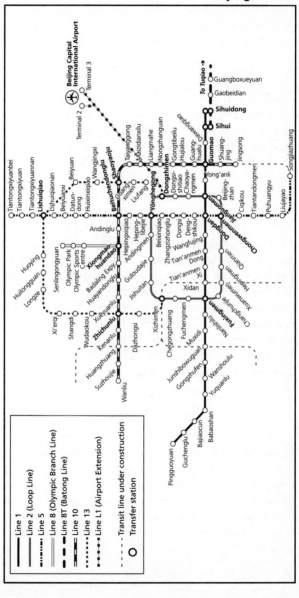

have come to expect are here, including a spa and underground pool. There are two good Chinese restaurants in the hotel. Local © **8610/8518-1234**. www.beijing.grand.hyatt.com.

PENINSULA PALACE HOTEL
8 Goldfish Lane, Wangfujing (Metro: Wangfujing).

From the outside, this hotel doesn't look like much—but it is part of the Peninsula Group from Hong Kong, which knows a lot about running a luxury hotel. Rooms are decorated in Armani-Zen chinoiserie chic. Standard deluxe rooms are traditional, with great bathroom amenities. An executive floor offers extra privileges and a private lounge. The presidential suite made the cover of *Architectural Digest*.

One of the best things about this hotel is the location, which is among the most convenient in Beijing: 1 block from the famed Wangfujing, the pedestrian shopping street; right near Food Street (not that we eat too much street food in China); and you can walk to Tiananmen Square and the Forbidden City (a long walk, but doable). The Peninsula has two excellent restaurants and a multilevel mall of big names.

Prices are uptown but vary with seasons and promotions. U.S. reservations through Leading Hotels of the World © **800/223-6800**. Local © **8610/6512-8899**. www.lhw.com.

DINING IN BEIJING

If one more person tells me the food isn't good in China, I may poke him with my chopsticks. Most luxury hotels have several restaurants, with at least one Regional Chinese restaurant. There are good places to enjoy meals in shopping districts and in some out-of-the-way spots. You may find it frustrating to make reservations yourself, so have your hotel's concierge do it for you.

CHINA CLUB BEIJING
51 Xi Rong Zian Hutong, Xicheng (no nearby Metro).

China Club is the baby of Hong Kong's David Tang, the father of Shanghai Tang, an international style-monger, and the creator of Mao chic. The location is in the middle of nowhere, but the club and restaurant take up a full house, once an imperial palace and lovingly restored. Just to see it all is a trip to the other side of the moon. I thought it was worth doing, but the Red Capital Club experience (see below) is more dramatic. The cost is about $25 per head. © **8610/6605-1188.**

JING
Peninsula Palace Hotel, Goldfish Lane (Metro: Wangfujing).

Just when you are ready to overdose on Chinese food, head over to the Peninsula Palace Hotel, where the fusion restaurant is internationally chic. Fashionable eating and meeting places like this are rare in Beijing, and it is world-class. The restaurant has various open stations and kitchens for all types of cuisine; prices vary with what you order. A treat anyplace, but especially sweet in Beijing, even if you figure it's going to set you back about $50 per head. © **8610/6512-8899.**

LI FAMILY (LI JIA CAI)
11 Yangfang Hutong, Xicheng (no nearby Metro).

If you go to only one restaurant in Beijing, please pick this one— but you might want to reserve well ahead. I have heard it's as difficult to get into as Restaurant Alain Ducasse in Paris. Have your hotel make the reservations for you. On the other hand, with only 3 days' notice not so long ago, I was able to book it. I have eaten here several times, and each time has been consistently good, or better. It's the kind of place that's best enjoyed with a group of 6 to 10 people because there is so much to try.

To start at the beginning: This is the Li family home (honest), and they have room for maybe 40 diners; dinner is served in two different salons or outdoors, weather permitting. You pick the menu not by what you want to eat, but by how much money you want to spend per person. The excellent food just keeps coming. There is no table linen (just oilcloth), and the toilet is the stand-up kind. There is a Western wine list.

Dr. Li, who speaks English, makes the rounds and tells you his life history, which is interesting the first time (but you can expect to hear it every time you visit). He is a mathematics and physics professor who taught in the United States.

You may want to have your taxi driver wait for you because getting a ride back to the hotel may be iffy. For that matter, finding the place at all is a crapshoot—it's in the Houtong and, especially in the dark, difficult to spot. I took four of us to dinner for about $200. © 8610/6618-0107. *Note:* The restaurant doesn't accept credit cards.

QIANMEN QUANJUDE ROAST DUCK
32 Qianmen St. (Metro: Tian'an Men Dong).

This famous eatery is on the far side of Tiananmen Square and across the street from one of my favorite "real people" shopping districts—the stalls across the street from the restaurant are open into the night. You enter the Duck Restaurant through the courtyard, which resembles a driveway. This is a first-come, first-served place, perfect on arrival day if you have jet lag. We ate dinner at 6pm and were surprised to find the place jammed. Most diners were Chinese, but this is a major tourist destination, and several members of the waitstaff spoke English and could help us order. Why a duck? How about all this fun at only $10 per head?

RED CAPITAL CLUB
66 Dongsi Jiutiao, Dongcheng (no nearby Metro).

I took Aaron and Jenny here, and we still haven't stopped laughing. It's a theatrical experience that you will talk about for years. This is a rather touristy spot, but so stylish and gorgeous to look at.

The restaurant is in a private home, which is restored to old Shanghai-communist brotherhood style; there is also an adjoining guesthouse. The menu is a parody of old communist tricks; the style is very David Tang, and I was shocked that he does not actually own this restaurant. Three of us ate here for $100, but we were careful on alcoholic drinks and wine and skipped dessert. © **8610/6402-7150.**

SHOPPING BEIJING

There's no question that Beijing's shopping scene is funkier than Shanghai's. There's a marvelous congregation of fancy stores and big-name boutiques, but prices on designer goods are 20% higher than elsewhere.

Beijing to me means pearls, souvenirs, antiques, and fakes (I don't buy them, I just like to look). This is also DVD heaven for legal discs at good prices. Forget the illegal ones you buy on the street—none of mine were as advertised.

Money Matters

ATMs are easy to find. Note that RMB are being artificially held at around 7.4 to the US dollar but, because the currency is so strong, someday soon you will see 8Y to $1.

Shopping Hours

Stores are open daily, usually from 9:30am until 8pm, but many malls stay open until 10pm, as do stores on the pedestrian street, Wangfujing. Note that office workers having both Saturday and Sunday off is a rather recent phenomenon; as a result, they often spend their leisure time shopping. You might want to plan your ventures accordingly.

Shipping

It costs between $300 and $500 to send a 20-pound package to the United States by FedEx. I suggest you do some research before you leave the United States, then be prepared to take care of the phone calls yourself once in China. There are a handful of FedEx offices in Beijing, but I'd call © **8610/6466-5566** before jumping in a taxi.

For more serious freight, there's a shipping desk that specializes in containers at **Beijing Curio City** (p. 299).

Hotel Gift Shops

Several hotels are attached to small or even medium-size malls; the Peninsula Palace Hotel has a lock on the luxury big names. The China World Hotel's mall (China World Shopping Centre) is more like a mall, and it's attached by some tunnels to the Kerry Centre, another mall (with its own hotel). The Kempinski Hotel is also attached to a mall.

All the big Western-style hotels have some sort of gift shops. Prices in hotel gift shops are always higher than on the street. Usually hotel gift-shop merchandise is classier than what you find on the street and, therefore, worth the extra price. Many hotels have antiques shops in their lobbies.

Museum Shopping

Beijing is one giant museum and has plenty of shopping inside museums, although nothing as sensational as the museum gift shops in Shanghai. On the other hand, there's nothing like a little shopping at Mao's Mausoleum Museum.

Tour & Guided Shopping

All motorcoach tours will make shopping stops whether you want them or not. Yes, of course, the guides get kickbacks. Even if you take a taxi or a private driver, expect kickbacks to be involved, especially when drivers or guides accompany you and translate.

Most hotels offer their own private tours, so you need not travel by motorcoach; hotel excursions are often in a Mercedes-Benz with an English-speaking driver and may even include a picnic lunch. Prices can be as high as $150 for a single traveler or $90 each for two people together in a private car. Keep in mind that you can invariably do these "tours" on your own with a taxi and save a lot of money.

Communist Souvenirs

I admit that the term "communist shopping" is an oxymoron. I guess what I mean is shopping for communist souvenirs—of which there is much to behold. My very first trophy was a ceramic figurine about 14 inches tall. I paid about $35 for her and treasured her, certain she was a genuine piece of art. Years later, I discovered that there is a huge business in communist souvenirs, and these little babies are popped out of the mold and onto the streets by the thousands.

A big item seems to be the Mao cigarette lighter, many of which are musical. I bought about a dozen worker's posters—one real and the rest reproductions. I began my collection in Shanghai but found a better selection (and better prices) in Beijing.

One of my best gift items—which I stocked up on as best I could—was Mao alarm clocks and even Mao desk clocks. They are rather big and heavy, so not ideal for packing and schlepping. The alarm clocks have everything from Illushin airplanes on the second hand to workers who beat their fists in time to the tick-tock.

Communist souvenirs are getting harder and harder to find; you can generally expect them to be newly made, fake, or very expensive.

BEIJING NEIGHBORHOODS

···

Wangfujing

This is the main drag in Beijing. It is a pedestrian-only street that spans the blocks between the Beijing Hotel and the Peninsula Palace Hotel. The selling space is 1.5 million square meters (16.2 million sq. ft.), which is larger than any megamall in the United States. I think that might possibly be the good news and the bad news all crammed into one big wonton.

It is crowded any time of the year and is sure to be packed during the Olympics. Nonetheless, you can stroll, take photos of the brass-cast characters, see the flowers, and marvel that this is the real thing.

A food and street market takes up one portion of the main street—it is adorable and terrifying at the same time. It's cute to look at and easy to shop but very, very touristy—very American-Disney-does-Chinatown, and very much in keeping with the new fanfare of getting ready for the Olympics. It was filled with Chinese tourists when I was there last; they didn't seem to be at all offended by the boiling down of their culture, but I, personally, am desperate to keep a little authenticity somewhere.

The biggest addition is the Western-style Oriental Plaza Mall, which is at the end of the street and includes the Grand Hyatt hotel. In the middle of the street—lined up on the walking blocks—are the big Chinese department stores, fast-food places like McDonald's, some local pharmacies (Chinese medicine–type stores), and even a pharmacy supermarket. There are also some discount stores, a silk shop, a few arts-and-crafts stores, banks, Popeye's Fried Chicken, and so on. Even though it's clean and modern, it does not feel at all like Shanghai—this is the new Beijing.

There is a lot of action in the evening during good weather. One of the reasons is that this is truly a one-stop location—you can buy tea (**Tianfu Tea Shop**), get a **Big Mac** (order by looking and pointing at the pictograms), have dessert at **Haagen-Dazs**, have your photos developed or digitalized, go to gourmet food stores or the supermarket under the **Oriental Plaza Mall**. . . . You can even replenish your supply of meds, have your watch cleaned, get postcards and books, and shop the local version of the 99-cent store. Should you run low on funds, not to worry—there's scads of ATMs and banks right on Wangfujing as well.

Liulichang

I call this "Lily Street" because I can't pronounce the name in Chinese. A fun part of the shopping scene has been cleaned

Wangfujing

Church
Post Office
Pedestrians only

JINGSHAN PARK

China Art Gallery

Wusi Dajie
Dongsi Xidajie
Chaoyangmen Neidajie

Cuihua Hutong

Dongsi Mosque

Dongchang Hutong

Capital Theatre

Lishi Hutong

Qihelou Jie

Daboge Hutong

Holiday Inn Crowne Plaza

FORBIDDEN CITY

Palace Moat

Dengshikou Xijie
Dengshikou Dajie

Baishu Hutong

St. Joseph's Church

Ganyu Hutong

Ganmian Hutong

Bank of China

Xitangzi Hutong

Donghuamen Dajie
Dong anmen Dajie
Jinyu Hutong

Meridian Gate

Chinese Children's Theatre

Calchang Hutong

Jixiang Theatre

Daruanfu Hutong

Waijiaobu Jie
Xizongbu Hutong

Working People's Cultural Palace

Datianshuijing Hutong

Taxi Station

Tiananmen Gate

Xiagongfu Jie

Qingyi Theatre

Dongchang'an Jie

TIANANMEN SQUARE

Museum of Chinese Revolution & History

Chairman Mao Memorial Hall

Zhengyangmen

Nanluogu Xiang

Dongjiaomin Xiang

Area of detail

Beijing

Beijing Medical Department Store 4
Foreign Language Bookstore 1
Grand Hotel Beijing 7
Hutong markets 3
Oriental Plaza 8
Peninsula Palace Hotel 2
Sun Dong An 6
Wangfujing Department Store 5

up and faked up, and is not nearly as inviting or rewarding as it once was. Give me the Pearl Market! I am sick over this insult. How can you trust a squeaky clean antiques shop?

If you decide to visit anyway, note there are two parts to this street, and they do not readily connect visually. On one end, it's more like a series of indoor markets selling fun junk; the other is lined with high-end stores that mostly sell the real thing, and I don't mean Coca-Cola. There are also some book stores and art-supply stores here.

Don't get here too early. I stopped by at 9:30 one morning and stores were just barely opening.

Qianmen/Tiananmen

If these sound suspiciously alike to you, it's because they are basically the same; the Qianmen shopping district is a spoke off Tiananmen Square.

Many of the stores are hundreds of years old; it is one of the oldest shopping districts in town. A little bit funky and junky, it is enormous fun, especially at night. there is a main drag of stalls that are open late at night. A perfect evening consists of shopping around here, having a nice dinner at the Duck Restaurant, and then taking a pedicab ride to Tiananmen Square.

As for Tiananmen Square itself, many vendors wander around the vast plaza, selling things like snacks, postcards, or kites. Inside the nearby museums (and mausoleum), you'll find souvenirs for sale. Tanks for the memories.

Forbidden City

The royal residence part of the old Imperial City, the Forbidden City is a now living museum, with several opportunities to shop. They begin immediately as you enter the front gate and pay your entrance fee. The best thing I saw to buy here— and never saw anywhere else in Beijing or in China—was a silk scarf with a map of the Forbidden City printed on it for about $25. Aaron and Jenny found several vendors within the

city walls and were horrified that they were plying various scams to entice people to buy.

Sanlitan

Most of the old shopping portion of this area was razed, but the new indoor-style market, which is almost like a supermarket, is really a ton of fun—especially if you like fake designer merchandise. It's named **Ya Xiu,** which often appears on hotels' taxi checklist. (In English, you'd pronounce it "Ya Show," which is how it is often written in guide books.) Note that the fakes

Aaron's Turn: Bad News Bears of Badaling

The Badaling part of the Great Wall is more of a tourist trap than anything. You will find the typical vendors here, but the sum total of stores and vendors seems multiplied by 12 and then squared off. It's not even that there are so many of them, but that they are even more persistent (if that is possible) than the ones in town. One vendor actually chased us a good 45m (148 ft.).

However, if you are indeed coming here to shop (aside from sightseeing), don't be discouraged by my report. We found a hidden gem, disguised as a mere coffee shop and named not so aptly as the Badaling Hotel Coffee Shop. You can enjoy the local excuse for cappuccino and shop the humongous selection of goods rivaling the Friendship Store. The shop sells everything from 3m-tall (9¾-ft.) sculptures to pashmina, jade, rugs, antiques, and arts and crafts. And the coffee stand really is amazing.

If you can help it, don't take the tour of the bear park.

are hidden per the new anti-fraud measures. See p. 306 for more on the market.

The little lanes that make up the bar district and have a few cute boutiques are currently being bulldozed. That's progress for you.

Temple of Heaven

Okay, so it's a cultural site to you. To me, it's a shopping neighborhood—and talk about heaven! This is where you'll find the **Pearl Market** (Hong Qiao) and its next-door neighbor, the **Toy Market.** But don't tell your taxi driver "Temple of Heaven." Point him right to Hong Qiao, which appears on every hotel taxi checklist.

Panjiayuan

This district of Beijing plays host to the Saturday and Sunday **Panjiayuan Antique and Curio Market** (read: flea market), which has become synonymous with the name of the destination. Expats often call it the "Dirt Market" because it used to have a dirt yard. (Alas, past tense—this is another place that has been seriously spiffed up.) Nearby (around the corner) is the **Beijing Eye Mart** (Ming Jin Yuan) and then **Beijing Curio City** and other furniture warehouses. Arrive in a taxi and return in a truck.

Great Wall (Badaling)

The most commercial parts of the Wall (Badaling being *the* most commercial and closest to Beijing) have tons of shopping, in terms of souvenirs stalls, and even free-standing antiques shops.

Summer Palace

There isn't a lot of shopping at the Summer Palace (at least, not a lot of good shopping)—but there are certainly more retail opportunities than I had expected. The most important thing you will buy—and it pays to get it from the vendors out front—is a map in English and Chinese. You might also want to splurge for a private guide—there are several (also out front) who will be hawking their services.

BEIJING RESOURCES A TO Z

....

A note about addresses: Although addresses are often listed below, most of the destinations in this section are on the standard preprinted hotel taxi checklists, already written out for you in English and Chinese, which is far more useful than my listings. I've been to every venue on every major hotel checklist; if said venue is not mentioned in this section, there is a reason.

Antiques

Also see "Flea Markets" and "Markets," below.

You may not know it, but you came to Beijing to buy antiques or so-called antiques. This is tchotchke heaven. You will find everything from fake to real, valuable to worthless, and much that looks great and therefore means something to you, regardless of its true value.

Although there are some nice furniture stores here (p. 301), remember to buy furniture in Shanghai if you can because the air there is less dry and furniture is less likely to crack or suffer winter damage.

If you are in town over the weekend and like flea markets, get to the Panjiayuan Antique and Curio Market. Do remember that a lot of the "antiques" were made last week.

A few favorite specific sources:

GREAT WALL ANTIQUE STORE
Great Wall, Badaling (no nearby Metro).

This is in the area I call the Great Mall of China. It is the big antiques store that looks real and does indeed have genuine antiques with wax seals, showing they can be exported. The store holds many rooms of antiques, from many periods and in a multitude of formats. I bought a small rug for about $100 after much bargaining. When I say small, I mean small—less than a square meter (maybe half that), but very nice. My dog sleeps on it.

HOHOHANG ANTIQUE FURNITURE
43 Huawei Bei Li, Jinsongqiaonan Zhaojiachaowaishichang (no nearby Metro).

I wish I were clever enough to find a resource like this on my own, but the truth is it came as a recommendation from the folks at the Peninsula Palace Hotel. This establishment sells furniture only, much of it restored; it has a huge building and warehouse. Actually, there's a showroom and a warehouse—one is out toward the airport, and the other is near the Panjiayuan Antique and Curio Market (p. 300).

Art

COMMUNE BY THE GREAT WALL
Shuigan exit, Badaling (no nearby Metro).

This is an architecture exhibit and should not be confused with the listing below. There is a hotel as well; you can rent the architectural property. As noted by the name and address, this is not in downtown Beijing. www.designhotels.com.

SPACE 798
Dashanzi Art District (no nearby Metro).

If you are in Beijing for only a few days, you will be tempted to write off this destination because it's far away and traffic is bad, because you aren't interested in buying art, or because you want the old China, not the new. Silly *yu*! This is one of the most fabulous places in the world and worth a visit by anyone who likes to see what's hot and trendy.

The space is a former factory, now converted into the SoHo of Beijing, with cafes, artists' workshops, galleries, photographic studios, and a few fashion boutiques.

Take a taxi; have the driver wait. Allow an hour each way in drive time from the Peninsula Palace Hotel (due to traffic, not distance). *Note:* The name in English is sometimes written as Factory 798, so don't be fooled. © **8610/6437-6248.** www.798space.com.

UNIVERSAL STUDIOS
A-8 Chachang Di, Chao Yang District (Metro: no nearby metro).

The name is a pun, a wink, a joke—this isn't a theme park but an art gallery created in an old fish-storage warehouse. © **8610/6432-2620.** www.universalstudios.org.cn.

Arts & Crafts

A few stores on Wangfujing sell arts and crafts to tourists; mostly, I hated them—way, way too touristy. All markets have some crafts; you will probably find what you want at the **Hong Qiao Market** (Pearl Market). I'm not crazy about the selection at **Ya Xiu** market, but you'll be there anyway for some serious shopping, so take a look. **Beijing Curio City** (p. 299) is an excellent source for arts and crafts, as is the **Panjiayuan Antique and Curio Market** (p. 300), possibly the best flea market in the world.

There is a small selection of arts and crafts at the duty-free store in the Beijing airport; almost all hotel gift shops also sell arts and crafts at elevated prices.

Books

FOREIGN LANGUAGE BOOKSTORE
219 Wangfujing (Metro: Wangfujing).

This wonderful store is toward the Peninsula Palace Hotel end of Wangfujing (right across from McDonald's). The Foreign Language Bookstore also sells videos, computer programs, and so on. On the street level are a large selection of fabulous postcards (the artsy kind), many slides of tourist and artist sites and sights, books in foreign languages, textbooks, medical books, newspapers, and kids' books. My favorites are the language books for children—I think they make good gifts.

Cashmere & Pashmina

KING DEER CASHMERE
9 Jianguomenwai Dajie (Metro: Dong Dan).

This tourist store, which sells all kinds of souvenirs and stuff, is a block from Silk Alley and a block from China World Hotel, so it's not inconvenient. It is very, very touristy and tour group–oriented.

SILK ALLEY
Jianguomenwai Dajie (Metro: Dong Dan).

This is not an alley but an enclosed mall filled with stalls that sell everything. Many stores and stalls in Silk Alley sell pashmina and cashmere, some seasonally, others year-round. Just be careful you know what you're getting with anything you buy in Silk Alley. I prefer Ya Show (Ya Xui Market) for similar merchandise—this is often a zoo.

Department Stores

BEIJING MEDICAL DEPARTMENT STORE
153 Wangfujing Dajie (Metro: Wangfujing).

I am not Dr. Kalter's daughter for nothing—show me a place where I can buy prescriptions, play with the over-the-counter drugs, practice Chinese medicine, have my blood pressure taken (free), and touch prosthetic devices, and I am a happy camper. Two blocks from the Peninsula Palace Hotel.

WANGFUJING DEPARTMENT STORE
255 Wangfujing (Metro: Wangfujing).

Happy days are here again: a true 1950s-style department store that's been renovated as such. I love it, if only because it makes me laugh. I also use it as my local one-stop shopping source when I'm staying at the Peninsula Palace Hotel—I've bought luggage and all sorts of things here. Glam it is not, but it's not Shanghai Number One, either—they do try harder. The fountains out front are a hoot.

YA XUI MARKET
58 Gong Ti Beilu, Sanlitan (no nearby Metro).

This is also known as Ya Show, which is how it is pronounced. I have classified this as a department store, but you might want to call it an indoor market. It's clean and bright, and everything (even the cafe) is marked in English. Each floor offers a

Jenny's Turn: Are You Faking It?

Fake handbags in Beijing are as abundant as bicycles. Around every bend there's another false Fendi; behind every door, a knockoff Dior. You become obsessed with finding the best bag at the best price because different markets seem to have different merchandise and differing quality. Where did I see that Dior saddlebag? Can we get back there? It was almost as good as the one at Dior in the Palace Hotel, wasn't it?

We did have a good time at **Ya Xui**, but we were getting tired by all the haggling, and all the fakes began to look alike. Aaron found a stall that sold Triple-A (the best grade of fake) merchandise, and we got purse-size notebooks with calculators inside for about $15. They do make great gifts. The sentiment is real even if the merchandise is not.

different kind of product, so you can truly buy everything here—from fake designer goods to luggage, to arts and crafts, to fabulous flower-stenciled enamel Chinese thermos bottles for $3 each.

The basement sells handbags and shoes, the ground floor has mostly clothes, and up the escalators there's just more and more merchandise. Yes, of course, you can bargain.

You might want to call this a cleaned-up version of Silk Alley. *Note:* There are several ATMs at the entrance.

Designer Boutiques

Many international designers now have stores in Beijing. The most exclusive names are located in a 3 level shopping arcade in the **Peninsula Palace Hotel,** but there are also some in the Hyatt. Expect prices to be 20% higher than in Hong Kong, the United States, and Europe. The reason no one cares is A) you can often get a Birkin without waiting B) when you're rich and Chinese, money is meaningless.

Down

Why eat Peking duck? Simple—so there are plenty of duck feathers to go into down coats and down products, which are laughably inexpensive all over China. Although they are bulky, the comforters, pillows, and coats cost a small fraction of what you'd pay in the U.S. Any department store, including the Friendship Store, will have a selection. I actually found down pillows and comforters in a grocery store. Twin-size comforters cost about $30 each; coats and pillows are less.

Fakes

I cannot condone fake merchandise, but I can tell you that it's pretty easy to find in Beijing. The best places for a wide selection of fake anything are the **Ya Xiu Market** in Sanlitan and **Hong Qiao Market.** At Hong Qiao (the Pearl Market), watches are on the ground floor, and leather goods are upstairs before you get to the antiques and crafts. Ya Xiu is a virtual department store of quasi-brands and others; see p. 306.

With pirated DVDs of supposedly the latest movies, expect great-looking sealed packages with a substitute DVD inside, often porno or a blank.

Flea Markets

BEIJING CURIO CITY
Dongsanhuan Nanlu (no nearby Metro).

Be warned: the "lobby floor" is really tacky and frightened me. Also, the place is very touristy—prices are high, and many vendors speak English. But once you get into the recesses of the ground floor, or up on the other levels, it isn't bad at all, although there are a million better places to shop in Beijing. That said, it's a good one-stop shopping place if it's the best you can do or if you hate the real China. There is a shipping desk in the lobby—naturally, it was closed each time I visited.

PANJIAYUAN ANTIQUE AND CURIO MARKET/DIRT MARKET
Huaweiqiaxi Nan Dajie (no nearby Metro).

Many guidebooks report that this is a "Sunday only" affair, but it takes place on both Saturday and Sunday. From 8:30 to 9:55am, it's a pleasure. Then, at approximately 10am, the market is suddenly mobbed.

This market has been Disneyfied, but the layout remains the same; the vendors on the left (as you face into the market) with their wares on the ground are still the least expensive and most likely to have fun merchandise.

Bargaining is expected. Some of the stuff is fake (really!). Few dealers want American dollars, and they don't take credit cards, so have yuan on you. Prices range from good to better, to you've-got-to-be-kidding lows. I bought two porte-mirrors (a matched set) for $30. How could I leave them behind?

You will have the time of your life. Bargain hard and carry a tote bag or backpack for small items. Dress down; bring small bills; consider having a porter to carry your buys.

This market is 14km (8¾ miles) from the city center; take a taxi south. It cost me about 60 yuan ($7.50) to get there.

Foodstuffs

CARREFOUR CHUANG YI JIA
International Exhibition Center, 6 Bei San Huan Dong Lu (no nearby Metro).

One of the branches of the French hypermarché, this enormous modern supermarket is a destination for those in the neighborhood. There's another Carrefour in the Haidian district.

CHINA WORLD SUPERMARKET/CRC
Basement, China World Hotel (Metro: Jianguomen).

It's fun. It sells legal DVDs for a few bucks and Sugar Smacks in Chinese packaging. It's a rather Western-style grocery store where you can buy snacks for your hotel room, picnics at the

Great Wall, the plane home, or the kids. Take home packages of international brands with Chinese labels on them.

ORIENTAL PLAZA CRC
Oriental Plaza mall (Metro: Wangfujing).

This large Western-style supermarket is so much fun you won't mind the Muzak playing "Happy Birthday" on a loop. You will find local products as well as major international brands with Chinese packaging. There's a takeout department where you can get a picnic for the Great Wall (or anywhere).

WANGFUJING FOOD PLAZA
Wangfujing (Metro: Wangfujing).

Harrods Food Hall meets the new China; many of the gorgeous examples of produce are engineered and have no taste. Other than that, it's great fun to look. I bought many items just for their wrappings; I have no idea what's inside, nor do I care.

YAOHAN SUPERMARKET
Sci-Tech Plaza, 22 Jianguomenwai Dajie (Metro: Fuxing Men).

This place is not worth the schlep unless you're already in the area—then you will find it great fun. This is a famous Japanese market, quite established in China.

Furniture

GAO BEI DIAN CLASSICAL FURNITURE MARKET
Jingtong Expwy., opposite the Chinese Sandalwood Museum, Gaobeidian (no nearby Metro).

New market—complete with Disney torii gate to welcome you. Some stores sell small decorative items.

Aaron's Turn: Gadgets & Watches

You'll encounter quite a few bizarre and unique electronic devices in both Beijing and Shanghai. The greatest selection is in markets, and in Beijing the best choice is at **Hong Qiao** (the Pearl Market). Mostly you'll see watches—the best pay homage to Chairman Mao, the local equivalent of Elvis. At Hong Qiao, the watches are sold from cases and possibly have a longer battery life. They cost $2 to $5.

GUANG HAN TANG
Beijing Classical Furniture Co. Ltd.; showroom in the lobby of the Kempinski Hotel (no nearby Metro).

This is one of the loveliest, most elegant shops in town. Its stock has been edited to Western taste, and the prices probably have been, too.

Furs

Winter in Beijing wouldn't be nearly as much fun if it weren't for the fur business. Furs are inexpensive by U.S. and European standards, and probably not well-made.

But wait. The furs I saw in the fur boutique of the Friendship Store were so chic you could weep. The prices were competitive with New York prices, and I wanted them all.

Malls

Malls are relatively new to Beijing; most arrived in the late 1990s. They are, as everywhere else in the world, a big hangout for teens and tweens on weekends. Several new malls are being built as we go to press; expect more and more as we get closer to 2008 and the Olympics. The current thinking is that traffic is so bad in Beijing that people don't want to travel out of their district or away from their hotels, so most of the new malls are attached to big-name hotels.

CHINA WORLD SHOPPING CENTRE
China World Hotel (Metro: Jianguomen).

Half the brand-name stores in Beijing are in this mall (the other half are in the Peninsula Palace Hotel). There's also a supermarket, a bank, and courier offices, as well as the shops on the hotel lobby level (which is not actually part of the mall, but while you're there—it shouldn't be a loss). It's also easy to get here on the Metro.

FULL LINK PLAZA
18 Chaoyangmenwai Dajie (no nearby Metro).

Academically, this is one of the more interesting malls, but you might not want to take a taxi all the way out here just to see it. The mall has everything from good supermarkets to Gucci and a few other Western designer firms.

KERRY CENTRE MALL
1 Guanghua Rd., Chaoyang District (Metro: China World Complex).

This mall is under and adjacent to the Kerry Centre Hotel, which is right behind the China World complex. The mall has many designer and upmarket shops as well as a few noteworthy local designers. Check out the store run by Caroline Dellen (units 121 and 122B), who dresses a lot of local celebs in her silk and hip Chinese styles. ✆ 8610/8529-9425.

LG BEIJING MALL
Yong An Li (Metro: Dong Dan).

Part of the LG Tower, this mall is right on Chang An Avenue, more or less across the wide boulevard from Silk Alley.

ORIENTAL PLAZA
No. 1 East Chang An Ave., Wangfujing (Metro: Wangfujing).

The fanciest new mall in town, attached to the Grand Hyatt Hotel, is very Western. Sony has an Exploratorium museum here that Aaron and Jenny couldn't stop raving about. I liked the supermarket. For some reason, the mall is built sort of like a snail, which is to say that the designer shops facing outward on the streets do not open into the mall itself. These designer shops are as fancy as they come, but there are no bargains. I popped in to **Tse Cashmere,** thinking that because it's a Chinese-based firm, there might be a price break. Ha. Sweaters were $500.

PENINSULA PALACE HOTEL
8 Goldfish Lane, Wangfujing (Metro: Wangfujing).

This isn't really a mall, but it functions sort of like one. It's like the Galleria in Houston: small and select, with only designer stores on three levels of marble floors. Little about it is Chinese, except that the prices are sky-high. If you have no interest in expensive designer items, go anyway for a quick look because the locals who shop in these stores are so gorgeous that they're worthy of a good long stare.

SUN DONG AN
138 Wangfujing (Metro: Wangfujing).

I like this mall for several reasons—it's in a great location, and it's a local mall, not a tourist mall. There's McDonald's, a Starbucks, lots of crafts stores and CD stores and real-people stores, a grocery store, and a great local scene. The shopping isn't as good as the whole idea of the shopping.

Markets

HONG QIAO (THE PEARL MARKET)
Across from the Temple of Heaven (no nearby Metro).

If you can only shop one place in Beijing, this is it. The so-called market itself is in a modern demi-high-rise with about four floors of merchandise and an additional two floors of fancier jewelry showrooms. The antiques portion has been totally redone so it's very small and cleaned up—stick to the jewelry instead.

There is nothing Chinese or even attractive about the building as you walk into a room filled with small electronics. Past that is a room with counters of dealers who sell watches. Many of the watch dealers have fakes, but you must ask for them. Some of these dealers also sell musical Mao lighters, which you cannot take on the airplane.

Upstairs feels sort of like a cheap department store, but there's luggage if you need some. There's also—at the other end— sweaters, some clothes, and handbags; again, copies are out but also hidden. The good stuff is put away. Then you get to the pearl floor, which must have at least 100 dealers selling all sorts of pearls and semiprecious stones. The "pearls" that I liked (for style and price) were not from oysters, but were made of crushed shells.

At one end of the pearl portion on this top floor, a stairway goes up to two more floors. Ask for the fourth floor or for **Sharon's Stone** (www.sharonpearl.com), a good place for everyday needs. **Fanghua** (www.fanghua.com) is the fancy showroom that takes up half the floor.

Tip: Take a pass on the fish market in the basement.

MING JIN YUAN
Chao Yang District East, Third Ring Road, Huawei Beili 43 (no nearby Metro).

Located around the corner from the famed Dirt Market, this market is filled with 100 or more shops selling designer and no-name frames. Most will make up your Rx in an hour although complicated prescriptions may take several days. My Christian Dior non-scrip sunglasses said Dior in proper logo script when I bought them and soon said Do, although the salesman promised me they were real. Go wild. Buy a lot in the same shop and bargain like mad.

TOY MARKET
Hong Qiao (no nearby Metro).

This building is almost alongside the Pearl Market. It's through an alley and offers floors and floors of fake toys made in the style of the big brands, such as wannabe Legos and so on. When you finish laughing, you will have a ball.

YA XIU MARKET
58 Gong Ti Beilu, Sanlitan (no nearby Metro).

See "Department Stores" (p. 297).

Silk & Textiles

BEIJING SILK
Qianmen Dajie (Metro: Tian'an Men Dong).

This is one of my favorite stores in China. I urge you to poke in, even if you don't want to buy anything—it's scenic and atmospheric, and is smack in the middle of the old-fashioned shopping district of Qianmen (right off Tiananmen Sq. and across the street from the Duck Restaurant).

Fabric is sold off the bolt in two downstairs salons; clothes are sold upstairs. Forget the clothes (although I did see some factory overruns) and concentrate on the velvets, brocades, and gorgeous silks for about $12 a yard, many in unusual fashion colors that you'd expect to find from someone like Giorgio Armani, not Chairman Mao.

SILK & COTTON COMPANY
Wangfujing (Metro: Wangfujing).

This store is modern and not at all funky—it's right on Wangfujing and easy to shop for yard goods or finished scarves and a few clothing items. I bought silk polo shirts (for men) with knit collars for $25 each in soft gray-blue shades that my son went wild for—very Euro chic (and hand-washable). On my last trip, I found an embroidered denim Mao-style jacket for $40. The silks are about $10 to $12 per meter.

YUAN LONG
15 Yongdingmenwai (no nearby Metro).

Touristy—and how. But that doesn't mean it doesn't have some things of interest. The parking lot is filled with taxis and tour buses, and guides are licking their fingers, waiting for their kickbacks. It's way off on the edge of downtown in the southern part of the city, not that far from the southern gate of the Temple of Heaven, but too far to be worth considering unless you come here in a tour bus, which is a possibility.

The store sells a little of everything (while you're trapped) and has an excellent Chinese costume department—all reproductions and very, very expensive ($500). Other than that, it is not a good store and the system is disgusting. If you are taken here, expect to be taken.

ZHANG TEXTILE
China World Shopping Centre (Metro: Jianguomen).

If you adore Chinese textiles and garments, you will go nuts in this store, which is one of the largest galleries in the world specializing in Chinese antique garments. There's some touristy stuff, but the collection of textile hats and helmets alone is enough to make you weep with joy. Because of China's ethnic diversity, there is a wide range of styles. Also here are framed fragments as well as full garments, mandarin rank badges, and that old standby, slippers for bound feet.

Ski Gear

This is a winter shopping occupation, but because of the easy availability of down and the nearby ski resorts, ski clothing—and some equipment—is sold everywhere. There were mobs of *gwailos* (foreigners) buying out a shop in Ya Xiu market that sold **North Face**.

Spas & Treatments

All of the fancy hotels have spa services, and usually you do not have to be a hotel guest to try them. A few hotels also have traditional Chinese medicine treatments.

I had a Chinese medicine massage at the **Grand Hotel Beijing** to help cure me of jet lag. A doctor in a white lab coat performed the treatment; I remained fully dressed as I lay on the table in a clinic created from two hotel rooms. I was covered with a sheet—and sometimes a towel—to give the doctor the traction he needed to move over a clothed body without using oils. The massage cost 300 yuan (about $36); I did not tip.

I ordered the same treatment at the **Peninsula Palace Hotel.** This time I was told I could have the treatment in my room and was asked if I preferred a female masseuse, which I did. She arrived in my room with a table, and I was asked to undress. This, too, was an excellent treatment. It cost the same 300 yuan, and I tipped her $10 American.

Tianjin

Consider a day trip to the former pearl-fishing town of Tianjin, just 2 hours from Beijing. After all, it's not every day you get to see a China Beach. **Mingzhu Fishing Village** is where the pearls are. **Yanghou**—in the Tang Gu part of town—serves as the foreign-goods marketplace, souvenir-hunter's market, and tchotchke place. **Ancient Culture Street,** in the Nanki district, is the leading tourist destination for shoppers and gawkers. It's one big TT, but a lot of fun, the best place for arts and crafts shopping, and has some serious shops for antiques and indigenous crafts. Be sure to explore the side streets that jut off the main road.

INDEX

See also Accommodations and Restaurant indexes, below.

Explore over 3,500 destinations.

TOKYO — 7766 miles
LONDON — 3818 miles
— 4682 miles
TORONTO
— 5087 miles
SYDNEY — 4947 miles
NEW YORK
— 2556 miles
LOS ANGELES
HONG KONG
5638 miles

Frommers.com makes it easy.

Find a destination. ✓ Book a trip. ✓ Get hot travel deals.
Buy a guidebook. ✓ Enter to win vacations. ✓ Listen to podcasts.
Check out the latest travel news. ✓ Share trip photos and memories.
And much more.

FROMMER'S® COMPLETE TRAVEL GUIDES

Alaska
Amalfi Coast
American Southwest
Amsterdam
Argentina
Arizona
Atlanta
Australia
Austria
Bahamas
Barcelona
Beijing
Belgium, Holland & Luxembourg
Belize
Bermuda
Boston
Brazil
British Columbia & the Canadian
  Rockies
Brussels & Bruges
Budapest & the Best of Hungary
Buenos Aires
Calgary
California
Canada
Cancún, Cozumel & the Yucatán
Cape Cod, Nantucket & Martha's
  Vineyard
Caribbean
Caribbean Ports of Call
Carolinas & Georgia
Chicago
Chile & Easter Island
China
Colorado
Costa Rica
Croatia
Cuba
Denmark
Denver, Boulder & Colorado Springs
Eastern Europe
Ecuador & the Galapagos Islands
Edinburgh & Glasgow
England
Europe
Europe by Rail

Florence, Tuscany & Umbria
Florida
France
Germany
Greece
Greek Islands
Guatemala
Hawaii
Hong Kong
Honolulu, Waikiki & Oahu
India
Ireland
Israel
Italy
Jamaica
Japan
Kauai
Las Vegas
London
Los Angeles
Los Cabos & Baja
Madrid
Maine Coast
Maryland & Delaware
Maui
Mexico
Montana & Wyoming
Montréal & Québec City
Morocco
Moscow & St. Petersburg
Munich & the Bavarian Alps
Nashville & Memphis
New England
Newfoundland & Labrador
New Mexico
New Orleans
New York City
New York State
New Zealand
Northern Italy
Norway
Nova Scotia, New Brunswick &
  Prince Edward Island
Oregon
Paris
Peru

Philadelphia & the Amish Country
Portugal
Prague & the Best of the Czech
  Republic
Provence & the Riviera
Puerto Rico
Rome
San Antonio & Austin
San Diego
San Francisco
Santa Fe, Taos & Albuquerque
Scandinavia
Scotland
Seattle
Seville, Granada & the Best of
  Andalusia
Shanghai
Sicily
Singapore & Malaysia
South Africa
South America
South Florida
South Korea
South Pacific
Southeast Asia
Spain
Sweden
Switzerland
Tahiti & French Polynesia
Texas
Thailand
Tokyo
Toronto
Turkey
USA
Utah
Vancouver & Victoria
Vermont, New Hampshire & Maine
Vienna & the Danube Valley
Vietnam
Virgin Islands
Virginia
Walt Disney World® & Orlando
Washington, D.C.
Washington State

FROMMER'S® DAY BY DAY GUIDES

Amsterdam
Barcelona
Beijing
Boston
Cancun & the Yucatan
Chicago
Florence & Tuscany

Hong Kong
Honolulu & Oahu
London
Maui
Montréal
Napa & Sonoma
New York City

Paris
Provence & the Riviera
Rome
San Francisco
Venice
Washington D.C.

PAULINE FROMMER'S GUIDES: SEE MORE. SPEND LESS.

Alaska
Hawaii
Italy

Las Vegas
London
New York City

Paris
Walt Disney World®
Washington D.C.

FROMMER'S® PORTABLE GUIDES

Acapulco, Ixtapa & Zihuatanejo	Florence	Rio de Janeiro
Amsterdam	Las Vegas	San Diego
Aruba, Bonaire & Curacao	Las Vegas for Non-Gamblers	San Francisco
Australia's Great Barrier Reef	London	Savannah
Bahamas	Maui	St. Martin, Sint Maarten, Anguila &
Big Island of Hawaii	Nantucket & Martha's Vineyard	St. Bart's
Boston	New Orleans	Turks & Caicos
California Wine Country	New York City	Vancouver
Cancún	Paris	Venice
Cayman Islands	Portland	Virgin Islands
Charleston	Puerto Rico	Washington, D.C.
Chicago	Puerto Vallarta, Manzanillo &	Whistler
Dominican Republic	Guadalajara	

FROMMER'S® CRUISE GUIDES

Alaska Cruises & Ports of Call	Cruises & Ports of Call	European Cruises & Ports of Call

FROMMER'S® NATIONAL PARK GUIDES

Algonquin Provincial Park	National Parks of the American West	Yosemite and Sequoia & Kings
Banff & Jasper	Rocky Mountain	Canyon
Grand Canyon	Yellowstone & Grand Teton	Zion & Bryce Canyon

FROMMER'S® WITH KIDS GUIDES

Chicago	National Parks	Toronto
Hawaii	New York City	Walt Disney World® & Orlando
Las Vegas	San Francisco	Washington, D.C.
London		

FROMMER'S® PHRASEFINDER DICTIONARY GUIDES

Chinese	German	Japanese
French	Italian	Spanish

SUZY GERSHMAN'S BORN TO SHOP GUIDES

France	London	San Francisco
Hong Kong, Shanghai & Beijing	New York	Where to Buy the Best of Everything.
Italy	Paris	

FROMMER'S® BEST-LOVED DRIVING TOURS

Britain	Ireland	Scotland
California	Italy	Spain
France	New England	Tuscany & Umbria
Germany	Northern Italy	

THE UNOFFICIAL GUIDES®

Adventure Travel in Alaska	Ireland	San Francisco
Beyond Disney	Las Vegas	South Florida including Miami &
California with Kids	London	the Keys
Central Italy	Maui	Walt Disney World®
Chicago	Mexico's Best Beach Resorts	Walt Disney World® for
Cruises	Mini Mickey	Grown-ups
Disneyland®	New Orleans	Walt Disney World® with Kids
England	New York City	Washington, D.C.
Hawaii	Paris	

SPECIAL-INTEREST TITLES

Athens Past & Present	Frommer's Exploring America by RV
Best Places to Raise Your Family	Frommer's NYC Free & Dirt Cheap
Cities Ranked & Rated	Frommer's Road Atlas Europe
500 Places to Take Your Kids Before They Grow Up	Frommer's Road Atlas Ireland
Frommer's Best Day Trips from London	Retirement Places Rated
Frommer's Best RV & Tent Campgrounds in the U.S.A.	